Rol

Feb 21

INFORMATION MODELING

PRENTICE-HALL
OBJECT-ORIENTED
SERIES

B. MEYER
Eiffel: The Language
Object-Oriented Software Construction

D. MANDRIOLI AND B. MEYER (EDS)
Advances in Object-Oriented Software Engineering

J.-M. NERSON AND B. MEYER
Object-Oriented Applications

D. COLEMAN ET AL.
Object-Oriented Development: The Fusion Method

B. HENDERSON-SELLERS
A Book of Object-Oriented Knowledge

H. KILOV AND J. ROSS
Information Modeling: An Object-Oriented Approach

M. LORENZ
Object-Oriented Software Development: A Practical Guide

P. J. ROBINSON
Hierarchical Object-Oriented Design

INFORMATION MODELING
An Object-Oriented Approach

Haim Kilov
James Ross

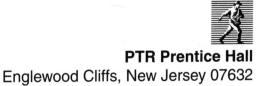

PTR Prentice Hall
Englewood Cliffs, New Jersey 07632

Library of Congress Cataloging-in-Publication Data
Kilov, Haim.

     Information modeling : an object-oriented approach / Haim Kilov and James Ross
         p. cm.
     Includes bibliographical references.
     ISBN 0-13-083033-X
     1. Data base design   2. Object-oriented data bases.   3. System analysis.
     I. Ross, James. 1951- . II. Title.
QA76.9.D3K53 1993   93-34253
658.4'038'011—dc20   CIP

Editorial/Production Supervision: Lisa Iarkowski
Acquisitions Editor: Paul Becker
Buyer: Alexis Heydt
Cover Art: The Imagebank
Cover Illustrator: Stanislaw Fernandes

 © 1994 PTR Prentice Hall
Prentice-Hall, Inc.
A Paramount Communications Company
Englewood Cliffs, NJ 07632

LIMITS OF LIABILITY AND DISCLAIMER OF WARRANTY
The authors and publisher of this book have used their best efforts in preparing this book. The
publication of this book does not imply the authors' (or their employers') or publisher's approval of, or
agreement with, the contents. The authors (including their employers) and publisher make no warranty
of any kind, express or implied, with regard to the contents of the book. The authors (including their
employers) and publisher shall not be liable in any event for incidental or consequential damages to
persons or property in connection with products liability, negligence or otherwise, from any use or operation of any methods, products, instructions, or ideas contained in this book.

The publisher offers discounts on this book when ordered in bulk quantities. For more information,
contact: Corporate Sales Department, PTR Prentice Hall, 113 Sylvan Avenue,
Englewood Cliffs, NJ 07632. Phone: 201-592-2863. FAX: 201-592-2249.

The authors, Haim Kilov and James Ross, are affiliated with Bellcore. Their email addresses are
Haim Kilov haim@cc.bellcore.com
James Ross jmr3@cc.bellcore.com

Eiffel is a trademark of NICE (Non-Profit International Consortium for Eiffel)
CICS is a trademark of IBM

Printed in the United States of America
10 9 8 7 6 5 4 3 2 1

ISBN 0-13-083033-X

Prentice-Hall International (UK) Limited, *London*
Prentice-Hall of Australia Pty. Limited, *Sydney*
Prentice-Hall of Canada, Inc., *Toronto*
Prentice-Hall Hispanoamericana S.A., *Mexico*
Prentice-Hall of India Private Limited, *New Delhi*
Prentice-Hall of Japan, Inc., *Tokyo*
Simon & Schuster Asia Pte. Ltd., *Singapore*
Editora Prentice-Hall do Brasil, Ltda., *Rio de Janeiro*

Contents

Preface

Young though it may be, our field is already subdivided into compartments with too few communications. What do you mean by "our field," one can hear the reader say: why don't you name it? But that's already part of the problem. If you say "computer science," you alienate those who consider themselves software soldiers from the trenches, and distrust theory for theory's sake. Say "data processing," and many will think that you are only talking about COBOL programming. "Software engineering" is less divisive, but still restrictive: isn't there more to what we do than engineering and, when we try, do we succeed at being engineers? "Software science" is attractive, and I confess it would have my preference, although the term was abusively pre-empted years ago by one particular theory. Perhaps we should, after all, be talking just about "software." As usual, these language uncertainties reflect deeper divisions: scientific computation versus systems programming and commercial development; analysis versus formal specification; in universities, information systems versus computer science; software design versus coding. Balkanization is everywhere.

It is one of the great merits of Haim Kilov and James Ross that they are able to speak several of the languages of the software world, and to establish bridges between subcultures that ordinarily might not talk to each other—less in general out of actual dislike than for the more mundane reason that they do not know about each other. The topic of information modeling is an ideal target for such a unifying effort, as it has largely remained separate from other areas whose developments have often tackled concepts and techniques very close to it. For example there has been relatively little cross-fertilization so far between the work on analysis methods, object-oriented or not, and the work on formal specification, object-oriented or not. Kilov and Ross make the connection, for the benefit of both sides.

Another area where their contribution will be welcome is the application of software concepts to modeling. Many programmers have at one time or another had the temptation to apply concepts of their trade to topics outside of it, so powerful are the metaphors and techniques of programming (when applied thoughtfully and systematically) for describing things and events of almost arbitrary nature. It was one or the flashes of genius of the creators of Simula, the first object-oriented language, to go beyond this intuition and to posit that programming is modeling. As with any other equation, this one should be read both ways. To program is to build a model of some system; however, it is also true that to model is to program, and that the techniques and tools of software development provide tremendous help for modeling various systems, in particular the systems which lie at the core of this book's investigation: enterprises.

The idea of treating programming techniques as a catalyst for analysis will be received with surprise in some quarters, since there is a well-established feeling, in the very community to which this book is addressed, that programming (or "coding" as it is sometimes called) is lowly, whereas analysis is high-level. Kilov and Ross do an excellent job of dispelling this myth. Their book will be precious to anyone who thinks that understanding and modeling the way organizations function is an essential goal, which requires the use of systematic techniques and tools, be they called tables or hierarchies, specification or analysis, proofs or business rules, Simula or Eiffel, Object-Z or SQL, relations, or contracts.

Bertrand Meyer

Introduction

"It is the sole purpose of the specification to act as an interface between the system's users and the system's builders. The task of 'making a thing satisfying our needs' as a single responsibility is split into two parts: 'stating the properties of a thing, by virtue of which it would satisfy our needs' and 'making a thing guaranteed to have the stated properties'. Business data processing systems are sufficiently complicated to require such a separation of concerns, and the suggestion that in that part of the computing world 'scientific thought is a nonapplicable luxury' puts the cart before the horse. The mess they are in has been caused by too much unscientific thought."
[Dijkstra 82]

This book is about making analysis as disciplined as programming. We show how the analyst may use the same concepts of "good thinking" as the programmer—abstraction, precise understanding of behavior, and reuse—to end up with a specification that is understandable and formal. The book is not about drawing pictures; it is about formal specification of behavior, at the right level of abstraction, as an approach to system analysis.

Some important concepts presented in the book are well known within the area of programming [Dijkstra 72, Dijkstra 76, Meyer 88], but less well known and somewhat novel within the areas of information modeling and, more broadly, system analysis and design. The need for clear and precise understanding of the system to be modeled—and of its formal specification—has been understood in these areas only recently [Wirfs-Brock 90, OODBTG 91, ODP 2].

Our approach is disciplined because it is based on the explicit acknowledgment of the need to understand and provides generic reusable concepts that help the client, the modeler, and the developer in doing so. These concepts are independent of a particular application, implementation, methodology ("technique"), or tool, and therefore permit, and in fact encourage, communication between these. The concepts are presented in a precise and explicit (i.e., formal) manner—the only manner that guarantees understanding.

Of course, there exists no algorithm for information modeling, as there exists no algorithm for "traditional" programming. However, a disciplined approach to information modeling will help, as a disciplined approach to programming does [Dijkstra 76].

Precise and explicit specifications are necessary to understand a "system," for example, an enterprise. Naturally, for a sufficiently complex system a complete specification is impossible due to limits in our intellectual abilities, so irrelevant details need to be suppressed. Suppression of irrelevant details is called **abstraction**. Understanding system behavior means providing an unambiguous (i.e., precise and explicit) specification of this behavior. This specification should be separated from its implementation, and the declarative approach (i.e., defining what should be true before and after an operation, rather than how it should be implemented), well known in programming methodology [Dijkstra 76], is appropriate at the analysis level as well. Intellectual economy (reuse rather than reinvention) is possible only if the construct to be reused is understood, that is, if its specification exists and is precise and explicit.

We can apply these ideas to a FORTRAN integer, a FORTRAN "scientific subroutine library" (with a good specification based on numerical analysis), a Smalltalk class library, and a library of object-oriented analysis constructs like composition, containment, or dependency.

A graphical representation is not necessary for understanding and using the concepts and approach presented in the book. Although a graphical representation is suggested, it is by no means endorsed as the only correct one to be used for those who use pictures; any graphical representation that has sufficient expressive power to represent the concepts discussed here is acceptable. Similarly, for those who do not emphasize pictures—and there are many of us—any linear representation language that has appropriate expressive power (and structuring facilities) is acceptable.

The book in general, and the contents of the generic association library for analysis in particular, are methodology- and tool-neutral. We are not proposing a new methodology; nor are we promoting a new and better tool. We will show a few guidelines for refinement of an information model using an implementation-specific library, but this is not the emphasis of our book. There exist quite a few excellent books on these issues; we will not repeat them.

The approach presented in this book has been successfully used for several years and has drastically improved understanding of many complex models in the telecommunications area. The book is a result of theoretical deliberations and the actual application of ideas encountered in literature and discussed with many colleagues. The essence of some of these ideas is presented in the references. The book takes into account numerous comments received from reviewers (including Bellcore subject matter experts and information modelers) and, most important, the experience of information modeling for many application areas performed within Bellcore.

The book shows, in particular, why and how "object modeling" and "entity-relationship (ER) modeling" should be harmonized rather than considered separately, with only a sketchy relationship between the two. More generally, it shows how to bridge the still existing gap between "data modeling" and "process modeling," which may result in complex and inconsistent models with semantics hidden in application code. We show how to solve these problems by using understandable specifications that serve as contracts between the client and the developer.

We do not invent and present another (or the "best") method of information modeling; nor are we trying to state that we know it all. On the contrary, the existing rich experience of programmers and modelers will be understood, reused, and formalized. Many readers will find familiar concepts from such areas as object information management, extended ER modeling, and programming methodology. An information modeler who had been using concepts from ER modeling will encounter here these same concepts in a more precise, abstract, and understandable form, so there will be no need to "unlearn." Questions such as *Is this a relationship or a composition? I don't see the difference between the two"* will be less likely because both (symmetric) relationships and compositions have been precisely defined. Moreover, the modeler will not need to use implementation terms like "foreign keys," "normal forms," and so on, frightening to the subject matter experts: modeling concepts can be perfectly understood in an abstract (i.e., implementation-independent) manner.

Our approach to information modeling is in accordance with national and international standardization documents. It has significantly influenced, has been influenced by, and corresponds to the Reference Model for Object Data Management created by the American National Standards Institute (ANSI) Object-Oriented Database Task Group [OODBTG 91], and the General Relationship Model for Management Information Services created by the International Standards Organization [GRM 93]. It is also in harmony with the specification of semantics within the important international standards family of the Basic Reference Model for Open Distributed Processing [ODP 2, ODP 4, ODP F] as well as with the Modeling Principles for Managed Objects produced by Open Systems Interconnection/Network Management (OSI/NM) Forum [OSI/NM Forum 91]. Moreover, this approach is in complete agreement with the mission of the recently created ANSI standards committee X3H7 on Object Information Management. More details about the standardization activities in these areas are presented in Chapter 7.

The information modeling concepts are represented in the book by precise declarative specifications of behavior using invariants and pre- and postconditions for operations. The approach to discrete mathematics[1] in general, and to predicate calculus in particular, taken here is the approach of a user. The underlying concepts are simple and quite clear; assertions are used as a tool for better understanding rather than for their own sake[2]. The presentation here is not intended to be complete and will not include a rigorous formalization of semantics. (After all, [Dijkstra 76] proposed a disciplined approach to programming without proving its soundness and completeness—(some of) these proofs came later. We in information modeling are not at this stage yet; nor are we even at the stage equivalent to [Dijkstra 76]; but we are getting there.) The goal here is to show how an abstract and precise specification of an information model leads to much better understanding of the subject matter(s) among both users and developers. Assertions are perfect tools for this; therefore, we will be using them.

The approach to object behavior we are using here is close to the "framework" one [Johnson 91], that is, to "designs of sets of objects that collaborate to carry out a set of responsibilities." The generic concepts we are describing represent abstract object types with shared behavior (we specify it declaratively). The behavioral dependencies that are usually "spread across many class definitions" [Helm 90] are put together and made explicit in our approach. The generic association library presented here is application-independent because it is based on behavior common to all applications—primitive Create-Read-Update-Delete (CRUD) behavior of associated objects. An application instantiates appropriate elements of this library. Need-

---

[1]Mathematics: the art and science of effective reasoning [Dijkstra 86].

[2]It is analogous to the (rather well-known in that area) approach of a physicist to calculus [Zeldovich 82]: no existence proofs for their own sake, no foundational formalisms, and so on. Some readers may consider this approach to be not sufficiently rigorous; although such rigor is possible [ter Hofstede 91], it is certainly not the goal here. Unfortunately, all too often very deep and abstract foundational concepts have been used to explain intuitively clear things—in the same manner as the "ε-δ technique" has been used for explaining derivatives and integrals in calculus. The results in both cases were disastrous: for too many people these simple concepts were daring and caused feelings close to mystical trepidation [Zeldovich 82].

less to say, the library is extensible, and the same approach may be used for the creation of application-specific libraries as well.

Path Forward

The book describes information modeling in the same way as a programming text describes programming. The book starts with the "why" (i.e., the concepts) of information modeling. Then it continues with the "what" and "how." The "what" presents the contents of a generic association library for analysis. The "how" presents the guidelines for creating information models based on the "why" and using the "what." In particular, the "how" shows a possible way from the early stages of understanding, when imprecision is tolerated (and may be necessary), to its later stages, where precision is essential.

Chapter 1 explains why specifications are important and compares how they are used in diverse areas of human endeavor. In particular, it distinguishes between traditional and software engineering—including analysis—and stresses the importance of (discrete) mathematics to succeed in the latter.

Chapter 2 shows why abstraction and precision are essential for understanding and specifying a system, and for both analysis (information modeling) and programming. It shows why information modeling is equivalent to building and reusing precisely defined class libraries of interrelated objects, and why these libraries should refer only to the business rules of the enterprise. It shows how business rules may be defined using contracts.

Chapter 3 provides an approach for specifying contracts that define business rules in a precise and explicit manner; it also discusses important concepts like the interplay of different contracts (inevitable because things in information modeling are interrelated). Contracts for primitive CRUD operations may be used to find generic information modeling building blocks common to all applications.

These generic information modeling building blocks are based on the general concept of an association discussed in Chapter 4. It is shown that the properties of an association and its components can be completely specified by declaratively defined behavior. Each particular building block is a subtype of this general association.

A library of these generic building blocks (associations) is presented in Chapter 5. Their definitions are based on behavioral concepts common to all applications, that is, on the invariants for and primitive CRUD operations applied to interrelated objects. Some of these associations are well known from ER modeling (e.g., relationship associations, dependencies, and subtyping associations), and others are less well known (e.g., reference associations); all of them are precisely and explicitly defined using invariants. This association library precisely specifies the generic semantic integrity constraints for information models in an application-independent and implementation-independent manner. These semantic integrity constraints help one to understand the modeled information and allow modelers to reuse concepts from a prespecified generic library whenever possible.

Chapter 6 shows you how. It presents a very detailed example of information modeling. It describes the considerations underlying the choice of particular associations from the library when an information model of an application area is created. It shows how to extract information from subject matter experts in order to help both the modelers and the subject matter experts understand the problem and properly manage complexity. It also shows certain reusable patterns of an information modeler's reasoning.

Finally, Chapter 7 describes how national and international standardization activities related to object information management influence and are influenced by information modeling concepts described in this book.

Appendix A presents a partial formal specification (in Object Z) of two simple generic associations. These specifications include many comments, so that a reader who does not know Object Z will not encounter insurmountable difficulties.

Appendix B describes how an association defined using business rules may be refined into an implementation using a (relational) DBMS. A library of refinements can be used for this purpose: the developer will, depending on implementation considerations, pick and choose one of several appropriate components of this library to refine an association defined by an information modeler together with a subject matter expert.

Appendix C describes some experiences in application modeling and, especially, in combining different applications into a enterprise-wide information model.

Appendix D presents contract specifications for defining some primitive CRUD operations applicable to the elements of the generic association library described in Chapters 4 and 5.

Acknowledgments

The conceptual inputs to this book have been provided by works of E.W. Dijkstra, William Kent, Bertrand Meyer, J.M. Spivey, and others. Many thanks for interesting and helpful discussions (and sometimes heated debates) that helped to formulate the concepts and guidelines presented here go to Erin Blair, Richard Chenglo, Robert Davis, Mike Fargano, Harry Goldberg, Paul Hawes, Steve Hoberman, Bruce Horowitz, Marvin Israel, Luke Kane, Peter Koppstein, Tony Kwong, Kam Lam, Kirk Laurence, Agnes Lee, Dennis Lee, Joyce Leslie, Dave Luber, Paul Matthews, Bertrand Meyer, Marvita Oliver, Lisa Phifer, Laura Redmann, Madhu Singh, Hassan Srinidhi, and Gomer Thomas. Most of these colleagues have used these concepts and guidelines in their work as information modelers (especially members of the Bellcore Data Architecture group) and subject matter experts. Special thanks go to Al Aho, Bertrand Meyer and Laura Redmann for their reviews of the manuscript. Thanks also go to the members of the ANSI standardization bodies—colleagues from the Object-Oriented Database Task Group, Database System Study Group, Object Information Management Technical Committee (X3H7), and Open Distributed Processing Technical Committee (X3T3)—for useful discussions and feedback on some of the ideas presented here. Naturally, this book does not necessarily represent the viewpoint of these standardization bodies. Some portions of Chapters 2 and 5 and of Appendix D are substantially revised versions of their early forerunners, Bellcore reports [Framework 92] and [Materials 92]. Special thanks go to Bertrand Meyer for encouraging us when the book was in its very early development stages. Paul Becker from Prentice Hall provided tremendous help in processing the manuscript. The help of Lisa Iarkowski from Prentice Hall in bringing the manuscript to production is greatly appreciated. In addition, the authors would like to thank the following copyright holders for the permission to reprint copyright material: Cutter Information Corporation, publisher of *American Programmer*, for the quote on page 1; Prentice-Hall for the quotes on pages 15, 24, 53, 78, 166, and 183; SIGS Publications for the quote on page 21; and Springer Verlag for the quotes on pages xv, 3, 7, 16, 22, 75, 101, 137, and 155. We would also like to thank the authors of the copyrighted material just mentioned: E.W. Dijkstra, David Gries, C.A.R. Hoare, Micheál Mac an Airchinnigh, Bertrand Meyer, Carroll Morgan, Robert Shelton, Susan Stepney, A.J.M. van Gasteren, and Heinz Zemanek. Finally, we want to thank Bellcore for all kinds of help, support, and encouragement for this work.

Joseph Morabito contributed to the text of Chapters 4 and 5 and Appendix D, and Naidu Guttapalle contributed to the text of Chapter 5 and Appendix D.

The authors would greatly appreciate all feedback.

Specifications

1

"The programming challenge is a large-scale exercise in applied abstraction and thus requires the abilities of the formal mathematician blended with the attitude of the competent engineer." [Dijkstra 93]

> *Development manager to staff: "You people start coding; I'll go and find out what the requirements are." (Folklore).*

This piece of folklore is a standard joke—of course we all know that you cannot start to solve a problem before the problem is known. You need a specification of the problem. In traditional engineering this has been acknowledged and addressed. The engineer writes a specification—an engineering drawing, for example—and is personally responsible for its correctness. A good engineer can convince the customer that the specification is correct, and the engineering designs produced by the good traditional engineer are understandable to the builder—they are precise, and they are not supposed to be misinterpreted. Of course, the builder is responsible for following the engineering design and does not produce a new one.

In software engineering, specifications are often vague, inadequate, or misleading, and therefore customers and implementors often ignore them. A requirements document is usually delivered in an attempt to communicate the understanding of the business problem. However, it often provides an uneven level of detail: things are either overspecified or underspecified. (As Peter Coad has observed, the seeming attitude of some analysts is, "We just write specs here, we don't read them.") The information requirements may provide details not required for understanding the business: the requirements

1

may be specified in terms of implementation (foreign keys, screen formats, field lengths, and field names), or the information requirements may be presented only through prototypes and examples. This approach is too vague and may require human decision makers to be part of the run-time system.

In software engineering, requirements documents are usually prepared for expert consumption, and things that are evident to subject matter experts (SMEs) may not be explicitly stated: the reader is supposed to have knowledge of the subject matter to understand them. The implementors, nevertheless, are forced to be explicit, complete, and precise: their programs cannot rely on implicit understanding or knowledge. As a result, the implementors often have to provide—and even invent—the missing knowledge, explicitly include it in their program, and use the program as a specification. These descriptions may or may not correctly define the business problem, depending on the subject matter expertise of the implementor. The situation becomes clear too late: at the earlier stages, neither the specifiers nor the implementors may be aware of the problem. In the end, the complete and precise system specification often exists only in the collective heads of programmers and therefore can be deduced only from application code.

On the other hand, the customers also have problems: vague and slippery descriptions—almost inevitable when a natural language is used—interspersed with implementation jargon are often incomprehensible, incomplete, or incorrect, without the customers being able to rectify the situation or even understand that it has to be rectified. The situation often becomes only worse if customers and implementors try to rely on various silver bullets rather than on disciplined programming concepts.

If software engineering were like traditional engineering, the software engineer (analyst) would be responsible for writing a correct specification, understandable by the customer and the traditional programmer (builder); and the traditional programmer would be responsible for following the specification rather than producing another one in the application code.

So the analyst—for whom we may reserve the term "requirements engineer"—needs to be responsible for developing precise specifications of the problem to be solved. The analyst must understand and make explicit the business knowledge of SMEs, satisfy the SMEs that this understanding is correct, and communicate this understanding to implementors. All this requires the attitude of a competent engineer.

However, the profession of a software engineer requires more than the attitude of a competent traditional engineer: analogies between programming and traditional engineering go only so far. A good programmer must be not solely an engineer, but also a mathematician—an "abstractor" and inven-

> *"As mathematics is unique in the way in which it combines generality, precision, and trustworthiness, it is not surprising that computing science emerged as a discipline of a distinctly mathematical flavour." [Dijkstra 86-1]*

tor, responsible for creating techniques and concepts as well as solutions using them. We consider here mathematics as "the art and science of effective reasoning" [Dijkstra 82] rather than the study of particular mathematical objects. Just as a mathematician (or a physicist) creates a **library of concepts** reusable in all areas of engineering, a gifted programmer creates a library of concepts reusable in all applications. In traditional engineering, this would usually not be the occupation of the engineer, but of the scientist.

An analyst develops specifications of the correctness and consistency of business information, and this activity belongs to programming. An analyst uses building blocks different from the ones used by a traditional programmer, but the approach is the same. Therefore, as we will show, analysis of business systems requires the discipline of programming, so the analyst must be both a competent engineer and a *skilled mathematician* who knows how to abstract—to cope with the complexities of information management problems—and how to be precise—to cope with the discrete nature of information management problems. Information modeling presented in this book is a disciplined approach to analysis that uses programming concepts to produce a clear specification of the way the business runs, that is, how it manages information.

1.1. Software Engineering

The software engineer deals with very complex artifacts, uses the same general concepts in a wide variety of applications, works with discrete mathematical models, and accommodates constantly changing requirements. As we shall see, the explicit use in software engineering of the programming approach, which explicitly uses abstraction, precision, and reusable libraries, is substantially more essential for success than in traditional engineering.

- *Complexity*: Software analysis and programming deal with much more complex systems than those of other branches of engineering. As an illustration, a single line of code is perhaps eight orders of magnitude smaller than the software system of which it is a part, yet programmers create and maintain both complete software systems and their building blocks, which may be a single line of code. In civil engineering, an atom is perhaps eight orders of magnitude smaller than the structure of which it is a part, yet civil engineers do not create or maintain atoms or even molecules or even material, as such. These are already available. They create and maintain higher-level structures and their building blocks. An atom is not a building block accessible to the builder of a traditional engineering system, who reuses available material; yet a line of code is a building block accessible to—and often built by—the programmer of a 10,000,000-line system [Dijkstra 76]. A traditional engineer specifies using building blocks that are there and well known; the software engineer specifies using primitives or building blocks that he or she may also have created.

• *Generality*: For any software development problem, a good programmer uses the same generic concepts and discipline at different levels. The solution elements are general and therefore simple. The same programmer or the same programming team may design and build both a 10-line and a 10,000,000-line module (the concepts for building a 10-line module are exactly the same as the concepts for building a 10,000,000-line program using this module). In traditional engineering, the solution elements are application-specific and therefore complicated. When solving an engineering problem, the traditional engineer works on closely related levels using these application-specific concepts (e.g., the civil engineer does not ordinarily dive into solid-state physics).

Because the solution elements in programming are general and therefore simple, they apply across application domains. The same programmer or programming team may design and build both a financial application and a telecommunications application. Because the solution elements in traditional engineering are application-specific and therefore complicated, the traditional engineer is specialized, working on closely related levels of abstraction and in a particular area of engineering: concepts used by an automotive engineer are quite different from the concepts used by a civil engineer.

Without an appropriate (i.e., application-specific) library, an automotive engineer would have to deal with low-level (generic) libraries from combustion physics, atmospheric physics, and locksmithing to get the job done. Instead, the automotive engineer works with more appropriate building blocks such as an engine, tire, and door lock. Even when designing a new engine, these concepts are ap-

propriate, and it is the rare advanced prototype automobile that requires going down a level: using general ideas to invent new ways of
solving old problems (e.g., an automatic transmission, an electric engine, a non-pneumatic tire, or a keyless door lock).

- *Precision*: Software development is based on discrete mathematics,
  whereas traditional engineering is, in most cases, based on "continuous" mathematics. A small change in an argument in continuous
  mathematics usually leads to a small change in the result, whereas a
  small change in an argument in discrete mathematics may lead to a
  drastic change in the result. Therefore, a small change in a program
  may produce profound effects; a small change in an engineering design is more predictable.

  Traditional engineering is as precise as it need be, but no more.
  The skill of the competent engineer includes dealing adequately with
  imprecision (so that, e.g., using a slide rule instead of a computing de-
  vice—a calculator—may be the better approach for some calcula-
  tions: the result from the calculator is too precise and may mislead the
  customer or implementor, or even the engineer, into a false sense of
  certainty [Petroski 85]). The level of error tolerance in a traditional
  system is nonzero: a small crack in a house foundation usually does
  not matter.

  Software engineering must be absolutely precise. The skill of the
  competent programmer includes dealing adequately with precision.
  The level of error tolerance in software development is zero: changing
  one bit in a program may lead to disaster. By the same token, a small
  change in the specification of a software system may lead to drastic
  changes in its implementation. Even for numbers, if you want to represent the number 1,000,000 in a computer, you cannot be one bit off
  in the 64 bits it may take to represent it. Programming folklore is full
  of examples when changing one character in a program text led to sur-
  prising results.

- *Understandability*: In traditional engineering, a problem is usually
  understood reasonably well. The components for its solution may and
  often do change. In software engineering, a problem is often not well
  understood, although the (elementary and generic) components for its
  solution are stable and problem-independent. (Some well-established
  areas like banking are exceptions because the problem is well understood, and there exist problem-specific solution components.)

  In programming, new information systems are constantly changing and requirements-driven, that is, dependent on what individual consumers want without regard to technology. In traditional engineering, new versions of a car are usually the "same" and technology-driven, that is, dependent on what can be manufactured in existing and evolving plant. Substantially new features (e.g., anti-lock brakes or electric-powered engines) require invention and are rare.

As a result, the programmer is often technology- and application-independent; a software designer can move between application areas and relies on SME knowledge to develop applications. A traditional engineer, on the other hand, is closely tied to a particular application (e.g., automotive design) and knows this application very well.

- *Reuse and invention*: In both software development and traditional engineering, things may be reused. The programmer reuses low-level, generic concepts of programming (e.g., DBMS functions or—on a more basic level—sequence, selection, and iteration). As a rule, the traditional engineer uses high-level, very complex, application-specific concepts (e.g., internal combustion engines and braking systems). An engineer who reuses something from a different application is an inventor. On the other hand, a software developer very often reuses something from a different application because software is generic and applicable everywhere, and therefore has to be an inventor in the course of everyday activity. Needless to say, the number of such software developers is not (yet) too large, and this is one of the reasons for the lack of reuse in today's software.

The libraries created in programming (including analysis) and in traditional engineering are on different levels. Programming, as are physics and mathematics, is a "lower-level" general-purpose provider of generic reusable libraries. In programming, the contents of a generic library can be reused in quite different applications: the same concepts of programming are used for both a telecommunications and a financial application. On the other hand, in traditional engineering, the contents of a civil engineering library cannot be reused in nuclear engineering; nor, in programming, can the contents of a telecommunications library be reused in a system for a financial application.

Traditional engineering does not invent new concepts and capabilities each time a problem is solved. The usual occupation of professional engineers is the invention of a new design based for the most part on existing capabilities and concepts (e.g., a design of a new car). Inventing a radically new, reusable capability (e.g., an anti-lock braking system) is also an occupation of the professional engineer, but most engineers are not occupied with such problems. Engineering also invents abstract concepts (e.g., the idea of a thermodynamic cycle [Ferguson 92]) to analyze technical problems. Here the distinction between the scientist and the engineer is blurred. Again, most engineers are not occupied with such problems.

In traditional engineering, the contents of generic libraries from physics and mathematics can be reused in quite different applications. A civil engineer, however, is not a physicist or mathematician; a civil engineer creates libraries for other civil engineers, but not lower-level libraries for all engineers. On the other hand, a financial application programmer can be a creator of both a generic programming library and a financial application-specific library. For a good application programmer, it is not very unusual to create a new generic library or a new element of an existing generic library, if such a need arises: "the computing scientist is regularly confronted with problems for which the relevant concepts, notations, and theory have not been developed yet" [van Gasteren 90].

Like a traditional engineer, a programmer reuses concepts and capabilities; unlike a traditional engineer, a traditional programmer mostly reuses generic concepts and capabilities. Like engineers, the usual occupation of traditional programmers is the invention of a new design based on existing—but general—concepts and capabilities (e.g., a new program that manages employee information and reuses

> *"The greater concern with methodology is the consequence of the fact that computing science is one of the less knowledge-oriented branches of applied mathematics." [van Gasteren 90]*

relational DBMS table and tuple management procedures). Inventing a new, reusable capability (e.g., a trigger operation in a relational DBMS) is also associated with programming, but most programmers are not occupied with such problems. Programmers also invent new concepts (e.g., the concept of cooperating sequential processes). This activity is usually thought of as computing science. A computing scientist is a gifted programmer.

1.2. *Analysis and Programming*

Analysis is a form of programming. There is no silver bullet for programming, but many programmers have discovered that a disciplined approach to programming (e.g., modular code requiring a precise and abstract specification of a module) leads to correct code. Similarly, there is no silver bullet for analysis, but some analysts are discovering that a disciplined approach to analysis (i.e., creating and using precise and abstract information models to specify business rules) leads to correct and understandable requirements specifications used by both customers and implementors. A disciplined approach to analysis uses the same concepts as disciplined traditional programming.

An analyst should specify business rules in the same way a programmer specifies a module. The specification of business rules should be abstract and precise and should use a library of appropriate specifications (building blocks).

1.2.1. Abstraction

Abstraction should be applied at all levels of information management, just as it has been applied to traditional programming. Abstraction is as necessary to make a specification manageable as it is to make a computer program manageable. Often a specification is too complicated (hundreds and even thousands of pages are not uncommon) and does not lead to a real agreement between the SMEs (customers) and the programming staff. Due to the limited nature of human intellectual abilities, if a specification is too complex it cannot be completely understood nor, therefore, adequately implemented. Not every detail has to be agreed upon—the need for understanding is more important than the need for representing all the details.

When we deal with business problems at an inappropriate level, we overemphasize "program design" and underemphasize "solution design" approaches. A good salesperson knows not to market drills, because people don't care about drills—they care about making holes. As long as analysis uses the low-level programming concepts of information systems, we are missing a major point: customers are not interested in programs; they are interested in solutions to their information management problems. The business runs on rules that define the "real business of the business" [Shelton 92], and these rules should not be made to conform to a computer implementation. Therefore, the specification has to be formulated only in terms of business rules. For example, the implementation may not allow a dependent to have more than one parent because of the way an instance of a dependent is identified using a component key; the business, however, acknowledges multiple parents of a dependent, and therefore the business has to deal with this unnecessary and often annoying restriction imposed by the implementation.

Additionally, even for a manageable specification, the distance between the elementary building block—a single instruction—and the system to be built is too large and cannot be covered with one jump. Programmers are often doing analysis work using the generic concepts of programming (e.g., DBMS procedures, loops, selection, etc.), but they have a disciplined approach and consciously use abstraction and precision (e.g., function calls, abstract data types, and predicate calculus). For analysis, the same disciplined approach is appropriate; but the library of generic programming concepts is at too low a level for analysis. The programmer doing analysis is forced to understand the higher-level business concepts in terms of low-level programming concepts. Something is needed in between; that is, intermediary building blocks.

1.2.2. Precision

In programming, engineering, and everyday life, often we have to know exactly **what** needs to be done, without specifying **how** this may be accomplished ("get from here to there," "buy a house," "open an account," or "add an employee to a project.") A precise, declarative specification of what needs to be done is essential for programming and analysis because in real life we often can rely on common sense and human intervention; and in engineering, we often can rely on "engineering" common sense—the existing body of knowledge. This is not so in programming because a human user should not intervene at runtime.

Program code must be precise; if the specification of the problem to be solved by program code is not precise, the specification probably cannot be used as is because, for example, it is incomplete and assumes that its user already knows quite a few things that are not explicitly specified. Then an intermediary appears who translates the wishes, emotions, and the "well-known facts" of the SME ("discover the customer's needs and intentions" [Dijkstra 82]) into some precise specifications, that is, something understandable to the programmer. Often, this role of intermediary is played by the programmer, and the resulting specifications are based on coding technology, if they are made explicit at all.

To make a specification usable, the analyst must precisely specify business operations, just as the traditional programmer precisely specifies computing operations. In other words, business operations must be specified declaratively by asserting what has to be true before and what will be true after the operation. This specification is known as a contract, which specifies the assertions—the **precondition** and the **postcondition** of an operation. All the operations are executed within some context that describes the "stable state" of the system (i.e., the state that is always there outside of an operation). This is called an **invariant**.

1.2.3. Reuse (and Invention)

In traditional engineering—which is much more specialized and knowledge-oriented than programming and analysis—the creation and reuse of libraries has been happening for a while (decades in nuclear engineering and centuries in civil engineering). Of course, in all these areas new libraries and new library elements are still being invented.

In both traditional engineering and programming, reusable building blocks do not appear out of thin air. Someone has to invent the idea for them (e.g., a relational model of data or communicating sequential processes). Someone has to build the library, that is, to precisely specify elements of the library and perhaps to implement them. Then the library can be reused. In traditional programming, this is relatively common: some application-specific libraries have been available for some time (e.g., Fortran scientific subroutine packages). Many of these concepts are becoming directly available as reusable libraries in object-oriented programming environments such as Smalltalk and Eiffel™. Applying these ideas drawn from programming to analysis leads to libraries of concepts applicable to analysis. Some of these concepts are application-specific (e.g., libraries of telecommunications concepts); some others are generic (e.g., the library of generic associations for information modeling presented in this book).

Sometimes an appropriate library exists for analysis (e.g., in certain financial and scientific applications, simplifying information management in these areas), but they usually cannot be reused outside of their application area without significant changes. There are, in addition, some generic building blocks, such as the concept of relationship in ER modeling, which, though not formally defined, are appropriate for analysis. However, in general, the analyst has few appropriate concepts. There are almost no libraries for understanding a system besides those containing highly generic concepts used in traditional programming, that is, at a level—frame of reference—different from that of analysis.

As a result, engineering each new software system may become as complex as handcrafting a new automobile. Low invention and high reuse is possible only when there are libraries of building blocks available on the appropriate level for analysis.

The traditional programmer understands that different systems use the same ideas and, *if there's time*, the programmer formulates (specifies and programs) them and reuses them. Although a good programmer invents and builds reusable components during programming, (re)using should happen much more often than building.

A good analyst understands that different **enterprises** share the same sets of business rules. Naturally, modeling becomes much easier if existing building blocks can be reused instead of being invented while modeling. Often, such reuse is possible: the enterprise to be modeled is usually not the very first in its application domain, and some existing experience, including domain-specific components, can be (carefully!) reused. Moreover, a gifted analyst understands that different **application domains** share the same sets of business rules. These rules are represented in generic information management constructs: SYMMETRIC RELATIONSHIPS, DEPENDENCIES, COMPOSITIONS, and so on, with their operations, are a few examples. Similarly, in traditional programming different application programs share the same sets of generic programming constructs: stacks, lists, trees, and matrices, with their operations, are a few examples. There exists no substantial difference between these two universes.

1.3. Information Modeling

Our goal in this book is to make analysis—creating specifications—as disciplined as programming.

An analyst is a programmer, and as a programmer, an analyst reuses generic concepts and capabilities. However, existing concepts in analysis are quite limited and not always well defined; therefore, the analyst often does invent or even reinvent concepts and capabilities each time a problem is solved. Programming is complex and requires invention, but not everyone should invent reusable concepts and capabilities! The inventor creates the library of reusable things (including concepts), and the practitioner reuses them. In traditional engineering, with its huge libraries, there exists a clear distinction between a library creator and user. In traditional programming—a relatively mature discipline—the libraries are often substantial, and there often exists a difference between a library creator and a user. In analysis, the libraries are usually small or not precisely specified; it may not be clear to the potential user whether the existing library elements are applicable or have to be (re)invented, so there is often no difference between a library creator and user. Too much effort, therefore, goes into starting from scratch; and any good engineer knows that a precisely specified wheel should not be reinvented.

The analyst must often be both a scientist (inventor) and practitioner. If analysis were as mature and disciplined as programming, the usual occupation of the software engineer would be the invention of a specification based on existing components (e.g., an information model that specifies rules for project management and reuses generic associations). Inventing a generic, reusable component (e.g., the COMPOSITION generic association) would also be the occupation of the software engineer, though most software engineers would not be preoccupied with such problems. Software engineering would also invent new concepts (e.g., the concept of associations between objects); inventing this kind of concept is usually thought of as computing science.

Software engineering is inherently complex—substantially more complex than other engineering disciplines—and it can, and should, use a disciplined approach at all levels of information management, from understanding the business enterprise to coding a program. Such a disciplined approach is indeed used at the low level of software design and construction—it's called programming.

The programming approach to understanding and solving problems is appropriate for developing specifications of business problems as well—it's called information modeling. An information model presents a simplified view of the business enterprise by specifying the available business operations as precisely and explicitly as one specifies an abstract data type for a traditional computer program.

Analysis, like programming, can become disciplined only when it uses concepts that are understood and explicitly formulated. In this book, we apply programming concepts to the field of analysis, while keeping the good ideas from analysis.

"Let's reuse what good programmers do . . ."   The concepts from traditional programming (like assertions) can and should be reused in information modeling. Using declarative specifications of behavior (i.e., specifying invariants and contracts) at the right level of abstraction (i.e., independent of concerns other than business rules) brings a programming discipline to analysis. Additionally, the approach used in traditional programming for creating, updating, and reusing class libraries can and should be reused in analysis.

"Let's keep what good modelers have done . . ."   A lot of valuable knowledge has been accumulated in modeling, and this knowledge can and should be reused under the condition that it is properly understood, that is, (re)formulated in a precise and explicit manner. Characterizing information using objects and their associations is a valuable aspect that has been introduced by some traditional analysis techniques. Information modeling reuses, among others, important concepts from extended ER modeling and defines them in a precise and formal manner. In particular, definitions of generic associations use, when necessary, such elementary concepts—familiar to an ER modeler—as mandatory/optional participation, cardinality, and so on. As you will see later, these concepts are defined precisely and in a unified manner, using object behavior. By using this unified approach, object analysis does not artificially separate and then merge "data modeling" and "process modeling," an activity in which information is too often lost or misrepresented.

"And the result is . . ."   This book presents an approach to analysis that uses the same disciplined concepts as programming to specify the business rules that define behavior of associated objects. This book presents a generic library of associations for analysis (information modeling) and guidelines for using the library. In particular, we show the software engineer how to understand, reuse, and create a library of generic building blocks to specify any application domain, just as traditional programmers understand, reuse, and create libraries of generic building blocks to code any application program.

These ideas are, of course, those used explicitly in object-oriented software development. The object concept in software development specifies a thing in an abstract, precise, and explicit manner, independent of its implementation. These ideas also apply to the understanding and explicit specification of an object and an association. This book will show that objects in specifications follow the same rules as objects in programs.

The Concepts

*"O*ur departure from tradition is this: we banish the distinction between specifications, subspecifications (super-programs?), and programs. To us, they are *all* programs; what we give up is that all programs are directly executable. What we gain is a more uniform approach in which programs play a role at every level. ... At the top of the hierarchy we find abstract programs, not necessarily executable. ... At the bottom of the hierarchy we find executable programs, which we call *code.*" [Morgan 90]

2.1. Making Analysis Disciplined

Some information management activities have traditionally been termed programming, others design, still others planning, **specification**, or modeling. To succeed, they should all use essentially the same underlying concepts [Meyer 89, Morris 90, Morgan 90, BETA 91]—"it is all programming at different abstraction levels." Although the importance of abstraction, precision (including the use of assertions), and reuse have been acknowledged in traditional program construction, in analysis this need has not yet been widely acknowledged, much less implemented.

As in programming, the analyst is faced with an enormously complex task. However, the frame of reference used by analysts is often not really appropriate to the task. Time and again, the **abstraction** level used by the analyst is based directly and improperly on outdated implementation technology. (For instance, manual coding of enumerated data types is considered in some areas to be analysis.[1] The overemphasis on attributes in information modeling is another example. These are ideas drawn from database implementation.)

---

[1] In a recent international standard [ISO/IEC 91-2], the values of attributes are alphabetized and numbered; for example, for *securityAlarmCause* we have *authentication error ::= [securityAlarmCause 1]*,

15

When analysts try to understand the problem at hand—usually by interacting with SMEs—they use the suitable frame of reference. In other words, the analyst often starts with business rules that are naturally at an appropriate abstraction level. However, the specification of these rules is often not

> • *As opposed to "programming," a despicable occupation fit for the toiling masses, design is a noble craft, the only worthy of consideration by the data processing elite.*
> • *This craft is carried out by drawing circles and connecting them with arrows. [Meyer 89]*

precise because of inappropriate specification mechanisms, such as natural language, examples, and pictures. For a SME, such a specification may be sufficient: many facts are well-known ("default" or "evident") to the SME, and therefore they are not included in the specification. However, modelers and information system developers are not SMEs, and they may therefore miss or misunderstand the facts that are not precisely and explicitly included in the specification. (Moreover, because an incomplete and ambiguous specification cannot be fully understood, it cannot be verified.) In the search for precision, the analysts jump to a wrong abstraction level—the level of computer implementation and tools rather than business rules. As a result, some fragments of the specification become precise and usable by the developer, but often not by the SME. Other features of the business rules remain unstated or imprecise.

In other words, **understanding** the business requires both the right level of abstraction and a precise specification.

Good analysts are good thinkers, that is, good programmers [Dijkstra 76-1]. Even when an analyst applies generic thinking concepts that a good traditional programmer also uses (e.g., boolean algebra, predicate calculus, relations, and subtypes), the concepts may be in a frame of reference not appropriate for analysis. Although these concepts are application-independent and reusable for developing a specification, the analyst cannot specify a system of any real complexity using only them: the specification's details will hide the big picture essential for understanding by a human being. The ana-

---

breachOfConfidentiality ::= [securityAlarmCause 2]; cableTamper ::= [securityAlarmCause 3], etc. This is questionable even for implementation; it hinders understanding the system, which is the job of analysis. It achieves only superficial interoperability, and does not consider semantic interoperability at all: what if another *securityAlarmCause* will be needed between causes number 3 and 4?

lyst who describes banking using just elementary programming concepts and elementary objects (e.g., in C) will find it intellectually disastrous, although theoretically it is possible. This elementary programming frame of reference deals with bits, bytes, integers, and operations on them, and the analyst needs a more appropriate frame of reference, with concepts that are not too elementary, to avoid excessive detail. Information modeling provides this more appropriate frame of reference. It reuses abstract data types, and, moreover, explicitly stresses **associations** between things. These abstractions make the amount of detail comprehensible.

To understand a thing, you have to specify it as an object—an abstract data type. In this manner, you will specify the "what"—the externally visible properties of the thing, including the operations in which the thing participates—rather than the "how"—the manner in which these properties may be implemented. You need to specify the thing precisely, and to do that you have to use concepts based on predicate logic.

Understanding an association between objects includes understanding both its components ("isolated" abstract data types) and the properties of the appropriate collection of associated objects. Finally, to understand a particular enterprise you need to understand its business rules (i.e., its objects and their associations) rather than their underlying details. This approach of separating concerns has been known and successfully used in programming for some time [Dijkstra 68].

Understanding the objects and associations of an enterprise does not mean that you have to invent concepts to describe each and every one of them. This job is aided by knowing and **reusing** recurring patterns. Finding these patterns demands enormous invention, and not every analyst should

> *"Is your design so simple that there are obviously no deficiencies, or so complicated that there are no obvious deficiencies?"*
>
> **— Attributed to C.A.R.Hoare**

have to invent: invention is not everyone's job. Fortunately, the approach used in traditional programming may be reused in analysis. Programmers create and use object class libraries all the time (it may not be called a "class library" as in Smalltalk or Eiffel; e.g., an integer together with its permissible operations in Fortran define an object class). This book introduces an approach for creating and using a library of generic reusable concepts—a generic association library—for analysis (information modeling).

Additionally, a well-understood application area with many successful implementations has an application-specific library of reusable objects and associations. Deployment of another application of this kind would require little invention and high reuse, and therefore could be rapid. However, solutions of new and complex problems are never rapid or easy. Nevertheless, as Ronald Shultz has pointed out, there exist attempts to promote cookbook approaches to all problems. These approaches try to decompose software engineering into very simple and very discrete activities and steps. Cookbook software approaches are characterized by "fill-in-the-blank" forms, checklists, and volumes of procedures. Such approaches assume that individuals can quickly learn and execute a simple set of activities [Dijkstra 82]. Foot soldiers are not supposed to know the art of war: they just follow directions. This approach presumes that there is no need to understand what you are doing, as somebody else has done it for you. Therefore, it is relatively easy to automate the deployment of applications of this kind. As a corollary, programmers who have done this job may be replaced by tools, so for them the prophecy about "the death of programming" may materialize.

Development of the simple, well-understood banking application may be rapid because almost no invention is needed—existing concepts and constructs are reused, and no new ones need to be created. In these cases, even primitive tools help a lot because the job to be done is more mechanical than creative (and better tools would help in a very substantial manner). New or nontrivial applications cannot be rapidly developed, and here tools usually don't help much because no tool is a substitute for thinking. On the other hand, the object approach to programming and, more generally, to all stages of information management relies on the intellectual ability and inventiveness of the programmer and analyst. Small groups of highly qualified people are usually orders of magnitude more productive than large groups of less qualified people. (Consultants are often deservedly successful as a result of this property.)

2.2. Understanding

The development of corporate information systems requires understanding the business. Since the goal of an information system is to correctly manage business information rather than to have code written, the business rules have to be understood and communicated to the customers and programmers. The rules of the business are complex, and therefore they must be defined and communicated in a way that promotes understanding. In other words, we have to manage complexity—our intellectual abilities are limited.

A good analyst manages complexity to promote understanding.

The analyst may use two approaches of defining and communicating how to get from here to there. The first is simple: use step-by-step directions (go 1.2 miles, turn right, after 7th light turn left, and so on—very simple and very discrete activities and steps, see above). The second is more complicated: use a map to determine the path. However, **change is inevitable**. In the first case, if one of the lights is broken, you are lost with no way to get there because you are not supposed to understand what you are doing. In the second case, you will lose some time, but you will get there because you are required to understand what you are doing. For the second case, you have to know that a map exists, and you have to know the basics of using a map. This requires some intellectual effort.

A cookbook-like method can be used by any analyst well-versed in banking to develop good requirements for the basic information systems of a new bank in town, presuming there is no substantial difference between banks. This will be a reuse "as is": almost no change to the existing class libraries is needed. To reuse as is, the analyst need not formulate the essential properties of the enterprise. However, analyzing a new banking application (e.g., support for an automated teller machine—ATM) requires thinking: creativity and an in-depth understanding of finances and customer needs is essential. This is exactly what a good analyst is doing!

The job of the analyst is to define and communicate business rules. The singular goal of information modeling is to formulate business rules. Precise definitions of the business rules are necessary, but they are not sufficient. These precise definitions must be understood by a human, that is, they must be intellectually manageable. This need for intellectual manageability has been acknowledged in traditional programming for a long time [Dijkstra 72]. In analysis, this need has often been ignored, with well-known consequences.

A good example of the need for intellectual manageability in complex systems is the tax code: two accountants filing a return for the same person in the same year may come out with two different results. Yet the tax rules are (on the surface) precise; it's just that no one can understand them. These rules include too many irrelevant details. Some of these rules contradict others, or at least permit an interpretation that contradicts the interpretation of others; and some real-life situations are not precisely defined with respect to tax consequences.

These kinds of complex systems have been around for a long time, but we have relied on qualified humans to make them work; humans successfully deal with vagueness (accounting and business were, in the last century, more craft than science, and even the mundane activities of corporations were accomplished using individual experience and knowledge). Computer systems, however, do not deal with vagueness, and we are being forced by bigger and more complex needs to use them.

The need for systems to be understood leads to the need for making analysis a discipline rather than a craft[2] (compare [Dijkstra 82]). This discipline requires thinking. The two key characteristics of this discipline are abstraction and precision.

2.2.1. Abstraction

For a complex system, a complete specification is impossible due to limits in our intellectual abilities [Dijkstra 72]. To provide the precise and explicit specifications necessary to understand the system, irrelevant details need to be suppressed [ODP 2]. Making a system intellectually manageable is called abstraction.

2.2.1.1. Encapsulation

An important aspect of abstraction, well known in object-oriented programming, is encapsulation, which means that information is understood not by knowing its detailed structure, but by knowing what you can do to it (its "behavior").[3] More technically, this means "hiding representation and implementation in order to enforce a clean separation between the external interface of an object and its internal implementation" [OODBTG 91]. In other words, the visible behavior of a system is independent of its implementation.

Encapsulation should be used not only in traditional programming. When specifying business rules—during "planning and analysis"—implementation is irrelevant and should therefore be ignored. For example, a traditional bank existed long before its software implementation. Its behavior (which for analysis corresponds to its business rules) is the same as that of another traditional bank, although one may use a mainframe and a relational DBMS for its information system, the other may use a network of micro-

---

[2]Where things are transferred by osmosis, and not explicitly.

[3]To quote P. Halmos's "Naive Set Theory" [Halmos 60]: "The familiar axiomatic approach to elementary geometry . . . does not offer a definition of points and lines; instead, it describes what it is that one can do with those objects."

computers and a different DBMS, and still another may use a file system or no computer at all.

By **specifying** the business rules independent of its implementation in a computer system, the information model preserves the essential "business of

> *"Only in the last few years have business people experienced the insight of working with analysts who model the real business of the business ... " However, "from the get-go, many of us were taught to conform the business to computer-based models.... We learned that applications controlled the data—so today businesses are spending billions of dollars trying to reassemble into shared structures the very business data that we spent several decades decomposing into separate and disjoint islands." [Shelton 92]*

the business," that is, it does not hide or distort the properties of the enterprise that are of interest to the user. Because **business rules are computer-independent**, specifying them requires a set of technology-independent concepts, such as objects, associations, and behavior, which should be reusable in any system specification. The information modeling approach promoted here provides a reusable set of concepts applicable for modeling any information, independent of its application domain, implementation technology, or analysis methodology.

This approach is implementation-independent because it uses generic information modeling concepts. In particular, these concepts define associations between objects (e.g., see Chapter 5) without using the structural properties (i.e., attributes) of these objects.[4] Explicit associations are implementation-independent, whereas attributes of associated entities may be used as an implementational (e.g., relational) way of representing associations [Kilov 91, Embley 92, GRM 93]. In the latter approach, business rules are often not visible to the client.

2.2.1.2. Information Hiding: The Result of Hiding Irrelevant Details

Encapsulation does not necessarily **enforce** the separation between the external interface and internal implementation: it only facilitates this separation by packaging the implementation within a "conceptual barrier" [Wirfs-

---

[4]However, when finding objects, representative attributes may be of help.

Brock 90]. This barrier may be transparent or opaque[5] (Ed Berard), and therefore, "encapsulated" does not necessarily mean "hidden." The concept of a procedure, well known to any programmer, is a good example of encapsulation: instead of considering the implementation of a certain operation, the procedure client just uses the existing one. The definition of a procedure is implementation-independent. However, this concept alone does not lead to information hiding: the client may not even use the encapsulation facilities, if the underlying data structures are available.

Information hiding means that only operations that preserve information correctness are available to the client. In analysis, it is even more important than in programming because the frames of reference of specification (business rules) and implementation (e.g., a DBMS) are too far apart. A SME does not need to speak the DBMS language, and a programmer does not need to speak the business rule language.

Information hiding is achieved by a disciplined approach (in all areas of information management, e.g., in traditional procedural programming or in analysis). In both programming and analysis, you need to use some language to create a program or a model. Some languages support information hiding (e.g., programming languages with abstract data types, or Object Z); some others do not. Even if the output of programming or analysis, for some rea-

> *"Program into a language and not in it."* *[Gries 81]*

son or other, has to be presented in an inadequate language, a disciplined programmer or analyst will create a program or a model with some notation that is adequate for supporting the disciplined approach. After that, the program or model will be translated into the output notation. For example, a disciplined approach to programming is possible even if your output notation is FORTRAN (compare [Gries 81]) or an assembly language. By the same token, a disciplined approach to analysis is possible even if your output notation is an old-fashioned computer-aided software engineering (CASE) tool. (This tool considers "data" and "processes" separately, requiring the client to think in terms of underlying data structures, i.e., making irrelevant details available to the client. As a result, the client may misuse these details and therefore violate information integrity.)

---

[5]Or partially transparent, like in some "modern" programming languages.

2.2.1.3. Separation of Concerns and the Importance of Correctness

The concerns of correctness should be separated from those of technology. Often the client wants to include in the specification such technological information as response time, commitment of transactions, distribution considerations, and so on. This may be acceptable, but such information should be clearly separated from correctness (semantic) information. Correctness should be stressed as the critical aspect of a specification. In an example cited by G. Weinberg in 1971 [Weinberg 71], an incorrect but fast system was preferred to a correct but slower one: the fast system could process the input quicker than the punch cards were input. In this case, the specification considered correctness and speed on an equal footing, and when a compromise was needed, correctness fell victim. If the information need not be correct, technological criteria need not be meaningful.

As another important aspect of separating concerns, a "typical" specification document consisting of hundreds of entities (or managed object templates [ISO/IEC 91-2]) is too often equivalent to an alphabetized data dictionary; it does not separate concerns, as the users have to read what they do not need.

As still another example, the concerns of user interface should be separated from both the semantics of the application and technology. ("User interface guidelines" for a famous personal computer have been successfully specified in a manner completely independent of the problems solved on this computer. The frameworks for Hypertext—another system driven by user interface considerations—have been successfully specified using formal notations [Lange 90, Halasz 90].)

2.2.2. Precision

The complexity of enterprises makes their precise and explicit specifications the only way to understand them (and if you think you understand the business, but don't have a precise specification, think again!). As mentioned above, understanding requires the suppression of irrelevant details, so that an operational approach (e.g., many pages of C code), although precise and explicit, is inappropriate. However, a declarative approach, well known in system design and programming [Dijkstra 76], is appropriate for analysis as well. The declarative approach uses invariants for specifying a stable system state and pre- and postconditions for specifying operations (see below). This "Aristotelian approach" [BETA 91] imposes on the analyst the mathematical rigor required of the programmer, who ultimately must write precise, formal code suitable for machine execution.

The declarative approach presented here does not need or use terms like "roles," "events," "agents," and so on, which are often defined vaguely (by examples) if at all, and mean different things in different documents. A set of examples is never exhaustive, and is therefore inadequate for defining a concept. Dealing with a set of examples in analysis looks—in the best case— like dealing with a set of test cases in programming. By using examples, you can find an error, but you can never be certain that all errors are found! Moreover, although a test case is clear, an analysis example often presumes existing knowledge that is never made explicit.

The declarative approach to analysis is the only possible one for understanding complex information systems (i.e., for information modeling) and for successfully making these systems computer-based.

System behavior can be specified by a set of contracts applied to collections of objects. A collection of objects is defined by its invariant, that is, by an operation-independent condition that should be TRUE outside of any operation in which objects belonging to this collection participate. Each contract is between a customer of an operation and an implementor of this oper-

> *"Perhaps the most distinctive feature of contracts as they occur in everyday life is that any good contract entails obligations as well as benefits for both parties. This is true of contract between classes, too: The precondition binds clients: it defines the conditions under which the call to the routine is legitimate. The postcondition, in turn, binds the class: it defines the conditions that must be ensured by the routine on return." [Meyer 88].*

ation.[6] Each contract completely and unambiguously defines an operation by precisely specifying customer expectations—the final state of the operation (postcondition)—and implementor's requirements—the initial state of this operation (precondition) [Meyer 88, Meyer 89, Meyer 92, OODBTG 91, Wirfs-Brock 90]. In other words, the contract states that if the customer satisfies the precondition then the implementor will satisfy the postcondition. These considerations apply to all levels of information management, and this book shows how they apply to analysis.

---

[6]A customer is sometimes called a client, and an implementor is sometimes called a server. Either may be a human being or a system.

   This is similar to the way contracts are used in everyday life, except that the lawyers who prepare them do not use the terms pre- and postconditions for these concepts. When buying a house, there exist several levels of specification of an appropriate contract. The simplest and most superficial of them refers to the address of the property, the names of the old and new owners, the price, and the possession date. This contract may be negotiated without any outside help. Note that everything in this contract is formal. However, the next stage is deeper and usually requires the help of a specialist (a lawyer). It produces a document of several pages which enumerates the preconditions for this operation and clearly states the postconditions for it. It is here that title, mortgage, inspection, easement, and other issues are precisely—and, again, formally—stated. There is no need for the customer to state these conditions: a specialist has an existing class library and may instantiate (parameterize) it in accordance with the demands of the client. Only seldom is this class library not sufficient (note that a good specialist—a "lawyer specializing in real estate"—has a library of larger size than an average specialist). If there is a need, these specifications may be refined further, again, in a precise and formal manner. And note also that in this process, most of the specification documents are not written in English: they are written in "legalese"! The customer may get into these documents in as deep or shallow a manner as heor she is interested in and feels comfortable with.
   In our example, for the operation:

   transfer ownership of the house on 22 Elm Street from Mr. Smith to Ms. Jones for $200,000,

   which is executed within the context of the following invariant:

   each house has exactly one owner

   AND

   the market value of the house on 22 Elm Street is $200,000,

   the precondition is:

   the house located on 22 Elm Street is owned by Mr. Smith

   AND

   Ms. Jones has at least $200,000,

   and the postcondition is:

   the house located on 22 Elm Street is owned by Ms. Jones

   AND

Ms. Jones has $200,000 less than before the transfer of ownership

AND

Mr. Smith has $200,000 more than before the transfer of ownership.

The customer relies on the specification to use the operation; the implementor relies on the specification to implement the operation [Morgan 90]. Both parties must understand their obligations and rights as specified in the contract. Defining a specification (which includes both invariants and contracts for operations) means mapping from imprecise requirements existing in a "real-world" environment to precise specifications; this process of formalization cannot be formalized. Note that imprecise information may be needed about justifications for the decisions made, historical and future considerations ("goals"), roadmaps, examples, and so on. This information should be included in the specification (e.g., as comments) because it may be of help, especially to clients but also to implementors. Understanding what to do is the most challenging and difficult activity in creating a system; doing it is (relatively) easy. This applies to all levels of information management: inventing the concept of a relational DBMS, or the Backus-Naur form for specifying the syntax of a computer language, or the concept of semaphores for communicating sequential processes ranks like a scientific discovery (Dijkstra).

2.2.3. Pragmatic Aspects of Specifications

Even if you know how to create abstract, precise, and explicit specifications, you don't live in a fixed world of one system and one specification. You don't want to reinvent concepts (i.e., object (and association) types) for each new specification you write. You don't want others to reinvent object types you have already invented: others can buy and reuse your types for much less than it will take to reinvent them. Also, although you want to reuse existing object types, you don't want to be constrained by them—object type libraries should be extensible. To extend them, you need invention.

2.2.3.1. Reuse

Specifications can and should be reused. Precise (i.e., formal) definition of these constructs makes them accessible to users and implementors alike. Those vertical solutions that are sellable meet this criteria. More vertical solutions would be sellable were they more precisely defined.

Intellectual economy (reuse rather than reinvention) is possible only if the construct to be reused is understood, that is, if **its specification exists and is precise and abstract**. (You cannot reuse a construct described only by examples: it may not be applicable in a context that does not **exactly** correspond to one of these examples.) Abstraction is needed because for a construct to be reusable, it cannot be too complex. Precision is needed because for a construct to be reusable, it should be absolutely clear whether or not the construct satisfies certain properties.

Reusable frameworks are common in traditional programming. For example, the concepts of sequence, selection, and iteration are well defined and commonly reused in programming; the concepts of relations, keys, and domains are well defined and commonly reused in relational database implementation.

Often, entire applications are reused. Each and every time you sit at your terminal and use your favorite word processor, you are reusing. This "reuse-in-the-very-large" [Batory 91] leads to rapid and usually acceptable solutions of well-understood problems: a typical payroll application, a simple relational database, or the creation of a document reuse; respectively, a payroll package, a relational DBMS, and a word processor. Consider also how lawyers reuse real estate contracts. Usually, a lawyer has several "standard" contracts, picks an appropriate one, and fills in the blanks (i.e., inserts actual parameters).

Most problems, however, are not well understood and do not exactly correspond to existing well-known problems. Reuse-in-the-very-large is therefore not a solution to these problems. For example, a typical specification for banking cannot be reused outside of the banking area; it cannot, for example, be used for mutual fund management.

Even when reuse-in-the-very-large is not possible, different applications certainly have areas in common. Information modeling takes advantage of these commonalities by providing precisely specified and reusable sets of generic object behaviors, namely, common behaviors for creating, reading, updating, and deleting business objects in the context of their associations with other objects. These specifications may be reused by all applications. A generic library of reusable specifications is presented in Chapter 5. Application-specific behaviors (e.g., *hire an employee*) may be built upon these generic behaviors (e.g., *create an employee, add an employee to a department, update department's budget,* and so on). (Defining concepts reusable in different business areas is difficult and requires an abstractor [Cunningham 89] to find and formulate the common concepts; and the modeler reuses them.)

2.2.3.2. Extensibility

The object class library used in specifications should not be frozen forever. For instance, if several application domains share a common concept, it could and should be added to the library of generic concepts for later reuse. In a simpler case, new application-specific concepts are often added to particular application domains (e.g., the concept of a variable-rate mortgage was added to the domain of banking relatively recently; the concept of Caller ID was added to the domain of telecommunications only recently.) In a more complicated case, a new concept spans application boundaries because it may be reused by many of them (e.g., hypertext or notification). Extensibility is very common in traditional programming; for example, a new subroutine can be added to the FORTRAN scientific subroutine library.

2.2.3.3. Invention

The above may suggest that specifying is easy: just reuse available concepts. This is very far from being true. Understanding concepts useful for analysis is necessary, but not sufficient: just as understanding programming constructs does not automatically lead to good programming, understanding modeling constructs does not automatically lead to good modeling. Even in "simple" cases, problem solving often demands a nontrivial amount of thinking, even ingenuity, as shown in good programming texts [Dijkstra 76, Gries 81]. No complex programming constructs are used there, not even procedures, and the programs are at most twenty lines long (although they are often highly nontrivial)!

2.3. Understanding in Information Modeling: Concepts and Contracts

This section shows how the key characteristics of understanding described in the previous section apply to information modeling through the use of contracts. It shows how an information model can be decomposed into layers (frames of reference) for intellectual manageability, and how properties of business information can be specified by means of contracts in the appropriate context.

2.3.1. Contracts and Layers

Successful information modelers understand that they are programmers at a different abstraction level. Programming uses, and information modeling should use, contracts as the most important concept. In programming terms, a contract may be visualized as a procedure call protected by constraints, that is, surrounded by a precondition, a postcondition, and existing within an environment (context) characterized by an invariant. In other words, **a contract for an operation should state what condition should be true as a result of the operation (postcondition) and what condition should be true before this operation is permitted to start (precondition). The contract's context is specified by invariants, that is, statements specifying what must always be true of business information outside of any operation.** In other words, the postcondition for an operation specifies the final state of the operation, and the precondition—the permissible initial state for the operation to reach this final state.

The most important difference between a typical contract considered from a programming language viewpoint[7] [Meyer 88] and a contract considered from an information management viewpoint is the explicit acknowledgment of interclass relationships. These relationships are defined by their assertions (invariants and pre- and postconditions for operations), which refer to visible properties of a collection of several related classes[8] (see Section 2.4.2). An operation for which the contract is specified usually spans (is shared by) several classes; that is, the pre- and postconditions for the operation refer to properties of all these classes. For example, the contract for opening a bank account refers to the properties of a customer, an account, and a transaction: it refers to customer information, creates an account, and also creates the first transaction for this account—*open*. An invariant usually refers to visible properties of object instances belonging to different classes; for example, *the existence of a transaction implies the existence of a corresponding bank account, which in turn implies the existence of a customer.*

Associations between subsystems ("COMPOSITIONS," see Chapter 5) may be specified in exactly the same way as associations between entities—by using pre- and postconditions and invariants. This approach is in agreement with the position taken by the recent ISO Open Distributed Processing draft standard: "The whole of a system may be an entity and may be modeled by an object" [ODP 2].

Let's recall a very important observation made by Dijkstra in 1968: "It is apparently essential for each level to make a clear separation between 'what

---

[7]Usually based on the concept of isolated abstract data types.

[8]To be more precise, a "type" defines a protocol shared by a group of objects called instances of the type, whereas a "class" defines an implementation shared by a group of objects [OODBTG 91]. Related, but different, definitions are provided by [ODP 2] (a type is a predicate, and a class is a set of objects satisfying a type). However, in many cases we will use these terms interchangeably, as in [OODBTG 91].

it does' and 'how it works'" [Dijkstra 82]. Once the "what" at a particular abstraction level is specified, it may be implemented; "how" it is implemented depends on the capabilities of the next available level. Implementing means specifying the "how" in terms of the next (available) level. A specification can be refined into a more detailed specification. Objects, their associations, and operations on them at higher levels are refined into objects, their associations, and operations on them at lower levels. At the lowest level, the specification is executable by a computer and is traditionally called a computer program. However, the rules for constructing specifications at all levels of refinement are the same. At each level, a specification is constructed using building blocks appropriate for that level which are glued together by the glue appropriate for that level. The specifier prefers to reuse rather than invent these building blocks.

The specification of the operation *transfer employee* may be refined by writing a specification that includes, among others, the operation *create employee-project* COMPOSITION (reusing appropriate information modeling constructs); the specification of the operation *create employee-project* COMPOSITION may be refined by writing a specification that includes, among others, the operation *insert tuple into employee-project table* (reusing appropriate relational DBMS contructs). Each of these levels represents a specification. Which specification represents the "computer program" depends, of course, on the capabilities of the target implementation platform (see Figure 2.1).

Each level in system development refines its specification into implementation building blocks appropriate to that level. Each level of refinement uses the same programming concepts. The operation *update B-tree pointers* is well known in traditional programming; algorithm inventors specified it in a precise and explicit manner (i.e., in the spirit of a contract) [Bayer 72]; file system implementors implemented it; and file system users (e.g., DBMS implementors) reused it. Likewise, the operation *create* COMPOSITION, less well known in traditional programming, has been specified using contracts (see Chapter 5 and Appendix D); it has seldom been implemented in a reusable manner (but is now in some object-oriented DBMSs); it has been reused by application modelers; had it been implemented, application programmers could reuse it instead of interfacing directly with the more primitive DBMSs (like relational). Likewise, the operation *transfer employee* (called a "business function" by some) is specified by an analyst using contracts; should be decomposed into generic information modeling operations (like *create employee-project* COMPOSITION) rather than represented as a (C) program interfacing with a DBMS; and may even be reused by other analysts under some

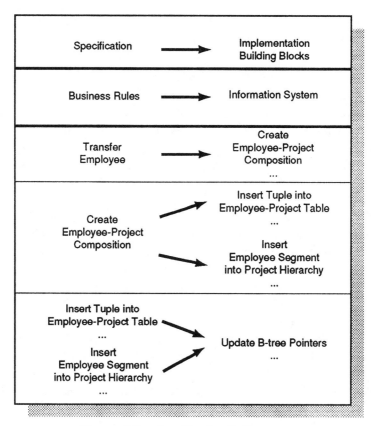

Figure 2.1. Specification Refinement

circumstances. An (oversimplified) information model for this enterprise is presented in Chapter 6.

A contract is a specification for all its lower levels and a part of the implementation of all its higher levels. Therefore, "ultimately, programs are contracts between the lowest-level programmers and the computer" [Morgan 90]. Contract properties at each level are to be formulated in terms common to and understandable by both parties—the SME and the implementor of this level. Therefore, the specifications of the properties at the analysis level should not use hardware or software terms like "records," "foreign keys," "normal forms," "customer codes," "communication lines," and so on. Although these latter properties are important—and some of them even essential—for the success of the system, they belong to the implementation rather than the topmost level of specification. Naturally, the same approach is used in everyday life: there exist different levels of (specifications of) a contract for buying a house (see Section 2.2.2).

2.3.2. Contracts and Properties

An information model defines business information by means of its properties. All properties of an object may be specified via its behavior (i.e., the set of available operations). The contract is the right approach for specifying behavior because it provides a way to ignore unnecessary details. These contracts state the pre- and postcondition for each operation and exist within an environment the most important properties of which are specified by an invariant.[9]

More often than not, contracts are not explicitly defined in analysis, which has traditionally been exempt from this type of rigor. Contracts are hidden within application programs and usually cannot be recovered from there. Had this information been explicit, businesses could have better understood and therefore maintained their systems. The approach of extracting information directly from application programs leads to contracts that are too implementation-specific. The other extreme is a very vague and too-general contract specification. A careful analyst avoids both extremes.

Contracts should be used for specifying properties that have traditionally been considered structural, for example, names and aliases (compare with features in Eiffel, where it does not matter whether a property is an attribute or a function: even notationally, and of course semantically, it is treated the same way [Meyer 92]). Therefore, the value of a structural property should be accessible (both for retrieval and update) only by means of executing an operation prespecified for this property. An attempt to apply a nonspecified operation (e.g., updating a record field) is a violation of the contract specifications and should be treated as such (e.g., result in an error message). These nonspecified operations are commonly available now, by means of applications—and even users—directly accessing the data structures in the implementation of the information model. There are various reasons for doing that, including performance, and the simplicity of a particular implementation. However, this results in violating information consistency: the consequences of these "simple" operations are usually not understood because of different levels of implementation and specification (i.e., very different frames of reference).

---

[9]Invariants may also be considered structural, since they belong to the definition of the valid "state" of the model. On the other hand, values of structural properties may be considered as results of valid operations. Therefore, the borderline between structural and behavioral properties is not really relevant.

Some of these ideas are well-known to programmers using abstract data types and object languages like Simula, Smalltalk, Eiffel, and so on [Dahl 70, Meyer 88]. In these languages, an object type is completely defined through a set of available operations. Each operation in turn is defined by its signature (operation name and parameter names and types) and semantics (pre- and postconditions). In information management, the signature and pre- and postconditions of an operation refer to properties of multiple associated objects that may belong to several types. They can and should be reused in a more complicated context: objects in information management do not exist in isolation, meaning that, as a rule, an operation spans several components of the model, and an invariant usually refers to several components as well. These relationships between model components are very important and should not be hidden in the application code or in the implementation (e.g., as "foreign keys"): they belong to the specification.[10]

As W. Kent noted in [Kent 83], it is difficult and irrelevant to differentiate between "attributes" and "relationships"; often, it is even impossible to find whether a property "belongs" to an entity. The "facts" that provide a framework for W. Kent's approach can often be generalized and considered as invariants. This approach has been among the very few clearly separating the business and computer-implementation-specific concerns in information management; unfortunately, not too many have used it.

2.4.   An Example of Information Modeling

Let us consider a "simple" world of personnel management with employees, projects, departments, dependents, and so on. This section is a general overview of how information modeling provides an understandable view of the world based on what is always true in that world (i.e., on invariants) and on what you can do in that world (i.e., on permitted operations).

2.4.1. Business Rules

In the world of personnel management, as in any other world, information modeling specifies the invariants and the set of permitted operations. Defining operations requires an understanding of objects and their associations. In other words, we need to know the consistent state of business information

---

[10]For instance, the inadequacy of attributes for understanding relationships between OSI managed objects led to the appearance of the ISO Draft Standard for general relationships [GRM 93].

(i.e., the invariants). They provide the most important part of the context for applicable operations. Each operation is defined by means of its contract.

Let's first try to get a handle on the world of personnel management by understanding the invariants, that is, the consistent state of business information. Here are a few of them. A more complete description of this world and a possible way of discovering its business rules is presented in Chapter 6.

2.4.1.1. Invariants

1. An employee must be either a technical employee or an administrative employee.
2. An employee's salary should be within the range for the employee's job title.
3. An employee belongs to exactly one department.
4. An employee cannot work on more than five projects.[11]
5. The identity of the project does not depend on the identities or the number of the employees who work on the project.

2.4.1.2. Permitted Operations

The business rules of personnel management require that only certain specific operations are permitted; these are often codified in the methods and procedures of the personnel department. Let us say that the following operations are the only allowed operations impacting an employee:

- *Hire an employee.*
- *Assign a new project to an employee.*
- *Assign an employee to a department.*
- *Raise an employee's salary.*
- *Terminate an employee.*
- *Assign a piece of equipment for an employee.*

Understanding these operations is more complex than it at first appears: *hire an employee* means much more than creating an employee record in a database. Most likely, the employee fills out many forms providing information not directly about the employee (e.g., taxes, medical insurance, and banking).

---

[11]In other words, the result of the operation *number of assigned projects* applied against an *employee* is greater than or equal to 0 and less than or equal to 5.

The information goes somewhere besides an implemented employee record. Appropriate changes must be made in other records, such as the department's and project's budgets. Only then is the database in a consistent state.

How the database is implemented is not important for understanding these operations; even the characteristics of the employee record may not yet be defined. The database need not even exist: for an appropriately-sized enterprise, filing cabinets and manila folders will do.

All permitted operations usually impact more than just the employee. For instance, terminating an employee also usually means that the dependents of this particular employee no longer interest the company.[12]

All other operations—that is, operations that are not explicitly specified—are prohibited: updating the salary in the employee's record may make information inconsistent and therefore should be impossible, because there are many other properties (e.g., budgets) to check and property values to be changed in the operation *raise an employee's salary*.

2.4.1.3. Contracts: Pre- and Postconditions

Specifying operations requires defining what must be true before performing the operation (preconditions) and what must be true after performing the operation (postconditions). These conditions must be true within the context of what must be true for all operations (invariants).

Let us specify one of the operations—*assign a project to an employee*—in a substantially complete manner. The invariants that have to be true immediately before and after every operation are presented above. We will need to consider only two of them: invariant number 4 and invariant number 5. We will—for a short while—ignore the cardinality-based invariant number 4.

In addition, the following postconditions should be true immediately after the operation *assign a project to an employee*:

1. The set of projects on which the employee works includes the old set of projects and this one new project.
2. The set of employees who work on the new project includes the old set of employees and this one new employee.

The following preconditions should be true immediately before the operation:

---

[12]For simplicity, we ignore the common need to retain information about the terminated employee, retain medical insurance for both the employee and dependents for some time, and so on.

1. The project and employee exist.
2. The employee does not work on this new project.

To add cardinality-based information, we consider invariant number 4 and also add (conjoin) the following precondition:

4. The employee works on less than five projects.

This precondition may be calculated from invariant number 4 and postcondition number 1. Thus, strictly speaking, it is redundant. However, we may explicitly specify it if the modeler together with the SME decide that the clarity of the specification will be improved (to rephrase [Potter 91], we may want to explicitly include conceptually significant aspects of the specification, even when some of these aspects are interdependent).

This behavior specification is clear, precise, and understandable. No picture is needed, and there is no handwaving about whether "employee-project" is a relationship with or without attributes, as often occurs in traditional ER modeling. The latter considerations are often alien to the SME and therefore are counterproductive for asking questions about the enterprise to be modeled (see Chapter 6).

2.4.2. Generic Business Rules

The specification of the operation *assign a project to an employee* is not that difficult: it reuses a more general specification of a "COMPOSITION" and its operation *create a COMPOSITION association between a composite and a component*. The concept of a COMPOSITION, however, did not appear out of a magic hat: it was developed and formulated by abstracting from lots of real-life cases like assigning employees to a department. In this manner, the concept becomes reusable. Instead of reinventing new concepts, the modeler picks and chooses from existing reusable concepts and renames their parameters.

The following is an incomplete specification of the reusable concept "COMPOSITION—PACKAGE" (more details are provided in Chapters 4 and 5 in the discussions about an Association and a COMPOSITION). The formal parameters are **boldfaced**.[13] Obviously, the formal parameters in this specification correspond to the actual parameters above.

---

[13]Because these assertions are formulated in a kind of English, the modeler or SME may want to also replace phrases such as "is associated with" or "add" with other more appropriate phrases, like "belongs to" or "assign."

ROBERT MORRIS
COLLEGE

Robert J. Skovira, Ph.D.
Associate Professor, Computer and Information Systems
600 Fifth Avenue, Pittsburgh, Pennsylvania 15219-3099
Narrows Run Road, Coraopolis, Pennsylvania 15108-1189
412-262-8257 | FAX 412-262-4049
Internet: Skovira@RMCNet.Robert-Morris.EDU

ecify the invariants.

of the **composite** does not depend on the identities or the s **components**.

consists of from **min** to **max** components.[14]

t while—ignore the cardinality-based invariant num-

ollowing postconditions should be true immediately *a component to a composite*.

onents associated with the **composite** includes the ents and this one new **component**.

osites associated with the **component** includes the of **composites** and this one new **composite**.

The following preconditions should be true immediately before the operation:

1. The **composite** and **component** exist
2. The **component** is not associated with this **composite.**

To add cardinality-based information, we consider the invariant number 2 and also add (conjoin) the following precondition:

4. The **composite** is associated with less than **max components**.

This precondition may be calculated from the invariant number 2 and postcondition number 1. Thus, strictly speaking, it is redundant. However, we may explicitly specify it if the modeler together with the SME decide that the clarity of the specification will be improved. To rephrase [Potter 91], we may want to explicitly include conceptually significant aspects of the specification, even when some of these aspects are interdependent.

2.4.3. Understanding

The example here shows how understanding is achieved through information modeling. We wrote down the business rules for the application that assigns a project to an employee, ignoring the details of a possible computer-

---

[14]In other words, the result of the operation *number of assigned components* applied against a *composite* is greater than or equal to **min** and less than or equal to **max**.

based implementation (abstraction). We did not rely on unstated assumptions about the reader's knowledge, and we meticulously wrote down everything we knew (precision). Finally, we did not need to invent concepts to describe these rules (reuse).

2.4.3.1. Abstraction

As you have seen from the formulation of the business rules for permitted operations in the previous section, they have no relationship whatsoever to the implementation of the information, that is, whether it is accomplished by a mainframe running a relational DBMS, a microcomputer running a file system (or another relational DBMS), or by an old-fashioned (and successful) filing system run on paper by clerks. As a result, the exact same rules are understandable by customer and implementor alike.

Representation aspects (e.g., records, fields, normalization, foreign keys, job title codes, and distributed systems) were not necessary to understand the business rules. They belong only to the implementation and should be introduced only at the implementation stage. (Some of them, e.g., patient numbers, should never be considered by a human at any stage [Gilb 77, Kilov 90]. As E. W. Dijkstra noted a while ago, when computers were first introduced people had to instruct computers, and now computers have to solve people problems.)

2.4.3.2. Precision

The business rules presented in our example are specified precisely. For every question of interest to the SME, these rules provide a definite answer. These rules are explicit: the reader does not have to infer them from examples. In addition, the rules, though written in structured English, are derived from logic and could therefore be written in any formal specification language. In fact, they have been: Appendix A (and also [Zave 91, Duke 91, Trader 92]) presents some rules of this kind written in Object Z; after that, these rules have been translated into English. And there are no defaults: all the rules are there, and there is no assumption that the reader will supply some of them.

2.4.3.3. Reuse and Extensibility

Some concepts are common to all applications. For instance, in this application, a project is considered as a composition of employees. Therefore, for example, the generic operation *create a COMPOSITION association between a composite and a component* (see Chapter 5 and Appendix D) is reused for assigning a project to an employee (and the corresponding pre- and postconditions for its contract were not reinvented: they were reused from the specification of the generic operation).

A library of things—fundamental generic concepts—appropriate for understanding business rules is described in Chapter 5. This library does not profess to present all generic concepts usable in information modeling. You, the reader, may find some additional concepts usable and helpful. We encourage you to do that by carefully adding new concepts to the library.

2.5.   A More Technical Discussion

This section presents a more technical viewpoint on the most important features of analysis—abstraction and precision. We have seen that the task of analysis is to understand the enterprise. Understanding implies that irrelevant aspects of the enterprise are ignored—abstraction. The result of careful analysis is an explicitly declared set of clear (contract) specifications—precision.

2.5.1. Abstraction

Abstraction tames complexity by making information intellectually manageable. As mentioned earlier, in programming we were urged to deal only with intellectually manageable problems [Dijkstra 72], and the same is true for information modeling. A problem may be made (more) manageable by means of abstraction (i.e., suppression of irrelevant detail). The idea of a hierarchy of layers where each successor provides an implementation for its predecessor and where the internals of the successor are invisible to its predecessor is known [Dijkstra 68] in programming and, again, may be reused in modeling (see our layered cake in Section 2.3.1). The underlying concepts at each layer are essentially the same. Each layer deals with a particular degree of granularity, with details suppressed and "squeezed into" the succeeding layer. The same is true for interrelationships between application-domain-specific information models within the framework of the corporate information model—at the top level, the internals of these constituent models may not be visible. Therefore, the problems of intersubsystem relationships may and should be solved in the same manner as the problems of interobject relationships (e.g., as proposed in [ODP 2]).

Requirements documents should communicate intent rather than pseudo-code. Precise declarative specifications of behavior are used exactly for this purpose: the intent of an operation is precisely specified in its postcondition. There are no pseudo-code details, and the developers are absolutely free to implement the intent in whatever manner they see fit, subject to providing a correct implementation. The implementation has to satisfy the postcondition (and the invariant) if the precondition is satisfied (i.e., true). The specification need not specify solutions: it specifies what is to be done, rather than how it is to be done. The level of abstraction in a specification is not fixed: it may be adapted to the problem at hand.

Finally, note that contracts for generic information modeling operations already exist in the generic information modeling library (presented in Chapter 5) and therefore are ready for reuse. However, application-domain-specific operations and their contracts must be discovered, understood, and formally specified. For some stable application domains (e.g., traditional banking), these constructs are more or less successfully found and even reused; for other domains, the situation is more complicated. The concepts and approach presented in this book may help.

2.5.2. Precision and Explicitness

At the beginning of analysis, when the modeler attempts to understand the enterprise, most of the requirements are vague and incomplete. This is tolerable at the beginning, and the reason is simple: the requirements are not yet precise and explicit. (A programmer would say: "You cannot program these, you need more information.") Precise formulation of the preconditions, postconditions, and invariants (in terms of the visible properties of things) is essential; otherwise, it will have to be invented by the implementor, because a program has to be precise anyway. This specification is declarative rather than operational (i.e., declares what rather than how). It is precise and therefore provides clear answers to questions ("yes," "no," "this question has no answer"). For this to be true, the specification must be explicit. (If "this question has no answer" is not acceptable, then the model should be extended, i.e., include more specifications.)

Explicitness means specifying everything, especially the "evident." There must be no undeclared assumptions. This is true both for "traditional" programming [Dijkstra 76] and for specification. Often, the most important problem is communications: extracting the "evident" information from the SME and explicitly specifying it. Both the modeler and the SME truly understand the problem only when the "evident" is made explicit.

A formal specification means that the problem is understood. It reveals gaps and inconsistencies in a prose or picture statement of the problem [Diller 90] and provides a concise, unambiguous, and exact means of communications for the specifier, user, and implementor. These specifications are enterprise-specific rather than implementation-specific and clearly separate the correctness concern (aka semantic integrity or business rules) from the efficiency concern.

It is difficult to provide precise formulations in English due to the inevitable imprecision of a natural language [Hehner 84]. However, it is well known how to formulate anything precisely—use mathematics. Indeed, there exist many notations based on predicate calculus that can be used for specifications. They are concise and readable; moreover, they are accessible to a first-year student rather than to a Ph.D.! This approach is recommended by many.[15] The 1992 Queen's Award was given to IBM and Oxford University Computing Laboratory for using formal methods, notably Z [Potter 91], in specifying the CICS™ system [Hayes 93]. Large telecommunications companies successfully use formal notations for declarative specification of their applications [Manning 90, Simon 91, Duke 91, Stocks 92]. The formal specification of the Trader in Open Distributed Processing [Trader 92] provided a substantially better understanding of its features. This experience suggests, in particular, that "natural language" specifications have been understood much better, and that inconsistencies and discrepancies in these specifications have been found and resolved only after the specifications in a formal notation (in this case, Z) have been produced. Specifying a small project is relatively easy; only for large or complicated products can the value of formalism in general and Z in particular be appreciated!

A correct specification is formal. The information to be specified exists in the head of a SME, and the information modeler should formulate appropriate questions that will help both of them understand the problem. These questions may cause discomfort because they may seem trivial to the SME. However, asking such questions is the job of the modeler: they may and often do uncover "obvious" parts of the specification that the SMEs have never formulated explicitly. A detailed and rather lengthy example of these questions is presented in Chapter 6. The process of understanding is informal, but its result is formal: a specification.

Of course, when trying to understand the problem, the information modeler will strive to reuse existing concepts (i.e., the generic association library). To do that, the questions should be expressed in terms of assertions for elements of this library. For example, the modeler may want to determine whether a particular association is a DEPENDENCY (see Chapter 5). To do that,

---

[15][Hehner 84, Meyer 88, Dijkstra 76, Ince 90, Kilov 91, Kilov 93, Wand 89, OODBTG 91, ISO ODP 91-3, GRM 93, ODP 4, ODP F, API 92, ACMF 92, OSI/NM Forum 91].

the modeler asks a question to determine whether the invariant for the DE-
PENDENCY is satisfied: "Is it true that for an instance of X to exist, a corresponding instance of Y should already exist?" If the answer is yes, then the
possibility of the association between X and Y being an instance of a DE-
PENDENCY should be carefully considered.

A lot is known about DEPENDENCY. For instance, when an object type X
is specified as a dependent entity with respect to its parent entity, the following invariant immediately follows and should be preserved by all contracts
for operations in which the dependent entity or its parent entity participates:

$$[\, x \in X \implies (\exists \, x.\text{parentOfInstance} \in X.\text{parentOfType}) \,],$$

meaning that the existence of an instance x of an object type X implies the
existence of a corresponding instance x.parentOfInstance (defined by the operation "parentOfInstance" applied to x) of a corresponding (defined by the
operation "parentOfType" applied to X) object type X.parentOfType.
(Square brackets mean that the formula is true for all instances x; see, e.g.,
[Morris 90].) In other words, the existence of an instance of a dependent type
implies the existence of a corresponding instance of its parent type.

Prose and pictorial explications of an information model should not be
discarded, even though they are not precise: they provide a sketchy roadmap
(like comments in a program) very useful to the reader of the formal specification. This approach is recommended by the authors of formal notations: a
Z or Object Z specification should contain English explanations. For example, every line in the Z specification of the Open Distributed Processing
Trader [Trader 92] is explained in English. Moreover, a formal specification
can usually be "translated" into a structured English one (just try to read it
aloud); perhaps even a mechanical way of doing this is possible. On the other
hand, due to the inherent ambiguity of a natural language, the reverse is not
true: providing a formal specification if a natural-language one is given is
highly nontrivial and often requires asking a substantial number of additional
questions. This is the job of a modeler!

How do you specify things that are "too complex to be formulated"? The
answer is simple: if it can be implemented, it can be formulated. Ultimately,
the program is the formulation, although it is too detailed and usually at the
wrong level of granularity for analysis. Moreover, the program may contain
subtle but important errors.

Consider an example of an operation formulated by a SME: *Delete all
friends of John from the database.* After asking some questions, it appears
that the intent of this operation is to delete all the people with the first name
John together with their friends. To do that, an existing SYMMETRIC RELA-

TIONSHIP *Is a friend of* is to be used. [An operational specification of this operation may lead to different and even incorrect results (consider John Smith being a friend of John Jones: in what order should they be deleted, due to either of them being John or a friend of John? What about their friends?[16])].

Let us try to provide a simple and precise way of understanding this problem, which may be very difficult to specify using traditional relational modeling and SQL. The specification we need should be declarative.

A precise declarative specification of this operation represents a contract. The contract deals with objects called *people*. We will see that the existence of the attribute *name* stands in the way of understanding. First, we don't care about the names of the friends we will delete, and more important, a *name* does not uniquely determine a *person*, so that the SYMMETRIC RELATIONSHIP *Is a friend of* should not be between *Person's First Name* and *Friend's First Name*, but rather between people (so that *Person's First Name* and *Friend's First Name* should not be properties of *Is a friend of*). We need different properties of *Is a friend of*, that is, not names, but something more unique than names.[17] Let's introduce *Person* and *Friend* as operations applied to *Is a friend of* (i.e., behavioral properties of *Is a friend of*; syntactically, dot notation will be used)—the values of these properties are (unique!) instances of *People*:

FriendsOfJohn = {x | x ∈ People ∧
  ((∃y ∈ Is a friend of ∧ y.Person.FirstName='John' ∧ y.Friend=x) ∨
  (∃y ∈ Is a friend of ∧ y.Friend.FirstName='John' ∧ y.Person=x))}.

Note that here we do not make any assumptions about the symmetricity of *Is a friend of*.

Now, the postcondition for the actual operation for the object *People* will be (the new state of *People* is primed):

People' = People \ (FriendsOfJohn ∪ {x | x ∈ People ∧ x.FirstName
                                                    = 'John'}).

(All Johns should be deleted as well, and we do not make any assumptions about the reflexivity of *Is a friend of*.)

And, finally, for *Is a friend of*, the actual postcondition will be lengthy

---

[16]Poorly specified systems often lead to inconsistencies and errors in information. For instance, the well-known anomalies in SQL referential integrity rules—finally resolved in the forthcoming SQL standard—are due to poor specifications [Horowitz 92]. These specifications use "intermediate states," that is, values that have not been specified in assertions and incorrectly attempt to satisfy invariants within operations that change properties referred to in the invariants. A declarative specification of pre- and postconditions both explains these anomalies and provides a solution.

[17]Object identifiers [OODBTG 91].

and therefore difficult to understand. But we don't have to explicitly state it[18] in the application model because it is already defined in the generic information model: thanks to *Is a friend of* being (a subtype of) a SYMMETRIC RELATIONSHIP, the postcondition we are interested in immediately follows from the SYMMETRIC RELATIONSHIP invariant (see Chapter 5). It demands that all instances of this SYMMETRIC RELATIONSHIP corresponding to the deleted instances of *People* should also cease to exist. There is no need to redefine this invariant for the application: it can and should be reused (inherited) from the generic model!

This example clearly shows the usefulness of the generic model and the importance and role of reuse of common constructs. (Here the common constructs already exist, and there is no need to invent them.) It would be much more difficult to formulate and understand a precise specification if its elements had a finer granularity, for example, if there were a need to deal with relational tables directly. Moreover, this example shows the importance of declarative specifications: it would be very difficult to understand the problem statement without the postcondition, for example, if it were formulated by means of SQL statements.

When a precise semantics of the enterprise is produced, it is quite difficult to retain as much of the "original semantics" as possible; to find out whether this has happened, the original semantics should have been precisely specified! It is possible, however, to show a "structured" English version of the specification to the SME for checking its correctness. It is even necessary to do this. The SME together with the modeler can determine when the model is ready: "With a view to requirements modelling, the purpose of a model is to ask questions and demonstrate that answers can be given entirely in terms of the model. If such answers can not be found then the model is inadequate" [Mac an Airchinnigh 91]. Probably, it is the SME who asks these questions, and probably these questions, from the viewpoint of the SME, are the "original semantics."

2.5.2.1. The Importance of Invariants

As we have seen in this chapter (and as we will see later), the pre- and postconditions for an operation applied to a collection of objects often follow from the invariants for this collection. It is quite reasonable to define a new operation and add it to the set of operations in which objects belonging to the

---

[18]Compare with domain subtraction in Z [Potter 91].

collection may participate. Generally, this new operation does not change the essential properties of this collection of objects. These properties are described by the invariant—an operation-independent predicate that must be true outside of any appropriate operation[19]. In other words, we may say that an invariant provides a context for operations. This approach has been used for isolated class invariants by Bertrand Meyer: "One should in fact consider that the invariant applies not only to the routines actually written in the class, but also to any ones that might be added later, thus serving as control over future evolution of the class" [Meyer 88]. Not only is such an approach applicable to invariants for collections of objects, but we may also say that the invariant for such a collection is formulated by crystallizing—abstracting from—the pre- and postconditions for various operations applied to this collection of objects.

The full precondition for an operation may therefore be viewed as the logical "ANDing" of the operation-specific preconditions and all the appropriate invariants[20]. If, however, an object can be modified only through specified operations (i.e., there are no backdoors through which individual property values can be altered), then the invariant would not need to be checked as part of the precondition: all permitted operations preserve the invariant!

On the other hand, the implementor of an operation can violate the invariant within the operation. The implementor will need to rectify this later, within the implementation of the same operation, to satisfy the invariant immediately after the completion of the operation: the postcondition of any operation should include all the appropriate invariants.

The user can invoke only predefined operations and, in doing so, can assume that the appropriate invariants are satisfied. Although the invariant is satisfied, the state of the system need not satisfy the preconditions for all permissible operations. Out of these, only operations for which the preconditions are satisfied may be executed. (If there is not enough money in a department's budget, an employee cannot be added to that department: the budget should be increased first.) If the precondition for an operation is not satisfied, the operation will not be executed, and an error message will be produced. After an operation is successfully completed, the system is in a new state, and the postcondition of the operation is true.

---

[19]In other words, outside of operations referring to properties mentioned in the invariant.

[20]In other words, all the invariants referring to properties mentioned in the pre- and postconditions of the operation.

This new state of the system will imply the preconditions for a new set of operations.

2.5.2.2. Co-ownership of Behavior

A modeler cannot meaningfully define an object without regard to other objects. The behavior of an object is defined, in large part, by its associations with other objects. (This statement clarifies the ER model statement, "Entities have relationships.") Associations of objects show up when assertions in which an object participates refer to properties of other objects. In our example, the specification of the operation *assign (employee, project)* applies to both the *employee* and *project* objects. This operation does not belong to the *employee* or the *project*: it is jointly owned by both. In a message-oriented approach such as Smalltalk, both of the following methods would exhibit the specified behavior:

> anEmployee Join: aProject
> aProject Include: anEmployee

An application written in Smalltalk may provide either or both of these. Whether an employee joins a project or a project includes an employee, or whether there is no notion of the "recipient of the message" at all, the pre- and postconditions of the operation are the same. Information modeling does not require choosing a message recipient, nor indeed a message-oriented or even object-oriented implementation platform. The behavior specified above could be implemented using Smalltalk, PL/I on top of a hierarchical DBMS, C++ on top of a relational DBMS, or even using a file system. This design decision is left to designers.

2.5.3. Generic Reusable Concepts

Specifying is hard! We try to make it easier. Fortunately, different application domains have some important constructs in common. Reuse is easier than reinvention. There is no need to explicitly specify assertions for reusable components: they are already there, and reading is much easier than writing. Common constructs can be defined only once and reused later. They can be reused, in particular, as the basis for formulating application-domain-specific constructs, as shown in the example about the friends of John (SYMMETRIC RELATIONSHIP) and in the example of personnel management (COMPOSITION). Precise (i.e., formal) definition of these constructs makes them accessible to users and implementors alike; as noted earlier, they need not be reinvented for each new application. In this manner, although these generic constructs do not belong to any particular application,[21] they provide a tremendous economy of intellectual effort for any application!

Invariants and primitive Create-Read-Update-Delete (CRUD) rules define business rules for associations between objects. These are not the only business rules of interest to the analyst: business rules include both CRUD (fundamental) rules and also more complicated ones (e.g., invariants and operations specific to a banking or telecommunications business). In the latter case, CRUD rules are the alphabet for representing application-specific business rules. The latter may change as requirements evolve, but the former are reasonably stable. This alphabet is simple and well-defined (see Chapter 5 and Appendix D); it is computer-system-independent. However, this alphabet is extensible.

2.6.   What Happened to ER Modeling?

The most important contribution of the ER approach is the acknowledgment that objects do not exist in isolation—"entities have relationships." Information modeling explicitly recognizes relationships between objects. However, we also recognize that there are several different generic kinds of relationships with properties differentiated by their behavior. These are very precisely defined in Chapters 4 and 5. In this manner, the ER and associated concepts are formalized: stated in an abstract, precise, and explicit manner.

From the point of view of a "classical" ER data modeler, there may be an argument: why bother? The association invariants and CRUD rules for operations may be—and actually have been—expressed in terms of cardinalities, mandatory/optional existence, attributes, and so on. Although this is true, a modeler may want to reuse a concept that has been invented or encountered in a different model. In this case, there are essentially two choices:

- Redefine it again using cardinalities, attributes,[22] and so on
- Formulate it in an implementation-independent manner (without overspecification), give it a name, and reuse

---

[21]These object classes are uninstantiated; compare with the concept of frameworks, for example, in [Johnson 91].

[22]"Attributes for representing relationships" often lead to excessive clutter and loss of conceptual clarity; see Chapter 6.

The former approach obscures the essential properties. The latter approach is preferable (as programming experience suggests). It is called "abstraction," and in programming languages it is called a "procedure."

2.6.1. Behavior

ER modeling is considered by some to lack behavior. Is this correct? Although ER is generally considered to specify only structural properties, these **"structural" properties** can be well specified in terms of operations. For instance, the most "structural" property—**cardinality**—can be expressed as an invariant (which will also show up, e.g., in the precondition of the operation *assign a new project to an employee*). Naturally, other operations that may change the number of projects for an employee should also satisfy this invariant, and therefore appropriate preconditions could be formulated.

Figure 2.2a is traditional. It (attempts to) show that an employee may work on from zero to at most five projects and that a project can be worked on by from zero to any number of employees. It is too low-level: it does not show that the subsystem represented is a COMPOSITION and that, therefore, the appropriate invariant is satisfied and appropriate contracts for CRUD operations are available. It also introduces an object—*Assignment*—that may not be considered as satisfying a business need by the SME. There is a better way represented by Figure 2.2b (where, of course, it is possible to add cardinalities if needed). The default cardinalities (like "any number") are not shown to avoid excessive clutter.

From the representation in Figure 2.2b it follows that this association

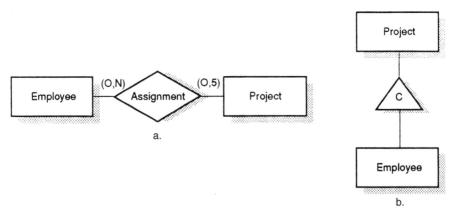

Figure 2.2. Two Representations of a COMPOSITION.

and its participating entities—*Employee* and *Project*—inherits all properties, including the invariant and contracts for CRUD operations, from the COMPOSITION generic association and its participating entities—Composite and Component. Alternatively, we may say that the formal parameters in the definition of COMPOSITION (i.e., Composite and Component) have been replaced with the application-specific actual parameters (i.e., *Employee* and *Project*). Of course, the properties of the Entity generic object class are also inherited by both the *Employee* and the *Project*.

More complicated cardinality constraints that are "difficult to express" in traditional ER models (e.g., "co-occurrence constraints" [Embley 92] that associate more than two entities) are very naturally expressed using assertions. The alleged "difficulty" probably exists just because it is difficult to draw these constraints on an ER diagram!

The assertions specified above for a COMPOSITION apply lock, stock, and barrel to this subsystem. What do these assertions define? Behavior, of course. If you still think there is no behavior in the ER model, think again.

2.6.2. Relationships

The goal of information modeling is to create an understandable and elegant specification of the business rules of an enterprise. Understanding and elegance are improved when we don't have to deal with too many details. Therefore, the details should be hidden in the building blocks of the model. What is the difference between COMPOSITION as a building block and an equivalent association as a building block, with an explicit set of rules dealing with cardinalities, mandatory/optional existence, and so on? As in programming, if the same pattern is recurring, a programmer names it and reuses it later (replacing formal parameters with actual ones) as a building block, instead of rewriting the same piece of code over and over again. In traditional programming, this is called a procedure; in information modeling, this is called a generic association. The benefits of this approach are especially apparent when compared with models that are developed using "relationships only" or even "restricted relationships only" (the concepts supported by some popular CASE tools). Understanding is improved, and more information is included in the same amount of square inches if a picture is used, because the library components (building blocks, molecules) used for modeling are of a higher level. (This can be compared with "lines of code" in programming: the same number of lines of code in Assembly language, C, and Smalltalk convey rather different information. Also the value of a program is in having not too many lines of code spent to express a solution!)

2.6.3. Pictures

Many ER modelers and users think of ER modeling primarily as drawing pictures. Information modeling is not about pictures.

When an association is shown graphically, it does not matter whether it is represented by a triangle, rectangle, or colored line. What matters is the need to show different associations differently, retaining the generic character of a construct called "association" (see Chapter 4). It is also necessary to show that associations are not symmetric, so that the "graphical link" should be directional. Also, it is necessary to separate the important concerns (e.g., properties that define the association type) from the unimportant ones (e.g., cardinalities that do not change this type). Finally, pictures are not necessary: for some people they help, and for some others hinder, understanding.

If pictures are used, it is important to have picture elements and their associations defined as precisely as any other (linear) notation. In this case, pictures may help and, even if they don't, will at least not make the specification ambiguous.

2.6.4. What's Not Needed

Some interesting features traditionally included in or associated with ER modeling are covered by information modeling concepts; some others do not belong to the specification of business rules in an information model. Let's describe the most important of those that are not needed.

2.6.4.1. Data Flow Diagrams and CRUD Matrices

One argument for the need of data flow diagrams and "CRUD matrices" (which traditionally go together with ER modeling) is the existence of processes that do not belong to one object. Such processes indeed exist and are essential for understanding the enterprise. However, declarative specifications of operations jointly owned by several objects serve the same purpose in a much cleaner, and therefore more understandable, manner. These specifications include the semantics of these collections of objects and of operations in which these objects participate. This semantics is often covered incompletely (if at all) in the more traditional approaches. Needless to say, the sheer size of "CRUD matrices" often makes them too complex to be understood.

2.6.4.2. Arity

The so-called problem of whether to use only binary relationships or to allow *n*-ary relationships goes away: behavior may be co-owned by more than two objects.

2.6.4.3. Foreign Keys and Normalization

Primary and foreign keys, normalization, and so on, which are often considered as part of an ER model, belong to a relational implementation (of this model) and are outside the scope of information modeling. These features are essential for the relational refinement of a business rule specification, but do not belong to this specification [ODP 2, Clause 8.6]. Appendix B shows a very simple implementation library: several ways of refining a construct (DEPENDENCY), defined by its business rules, into a relational implementation.

Object instances are distinguished (independent of their state or behavior) by implementation-free logical identifiers [OODBTG 91]. These identifiers may or may not be visible and may or may not be implemented as relational keys. It may not always be true that an instance of an object is distinguishable by a combination of values of a small subset of its visible properties. Moreover, the unstated assumption that the implementation will be relational may, of course, not hold: other DBMSs do and will exist!

Contracts

> *"**A** discrepancy between an abstract and physical machine was no longer interpreted as an inaccuracy in the manual, but as the physical machine not working according to specifications. This presupposes, of course, that these specifications were not only completely unambiguous, but also so 'understandable'—and orders of magnitude more simple than the engineering documentation of the machine—that everybody could agree that they described what was intended."*
> *[Dijkstra 76]*

In analysis, as in programming—and, indeed, in everyday life—contracts define and communicate rules of behavior. In analysis we call these rules business rules. When there are parties to an agreement over rules of behavior, and when the agreement is important enough and may be misinterpreted by its parties or by others, it should be represented as a formal contract.

Contracts exist at all levels of system analysis, design, and development, from top-level requirements to writing actual code. Some of them are used in traditional programming (contracts that define actual procedures written in a programming language), some others—to specify business rules (contracts that define an operation like buying a house or ordering a piece of software over the phone). The business rule contracts are used both by business system analysts and by all of us in day-to-day business.

Although properties of contracts differ based on their intended uses, all contracts have some properties in common. The essential property of a contract, whether it appears in a program or in an information model, is that it explicitly—and declaratively—defines an operation. All information about contracts should be explicitly available. A contract should describe both the parameters of an operation and their types (technically, this is called a signature) and also the semantics of the operation (i.e., what the operation has to achieve and under what circumstances).

The signature alone does not specify an operation because there may exist any number of very different operations having the same signature. As an example, consider an operation with parameters *name1, name2, address, money*. Such a signature may be used for buying a house (*name1* denotes the buyer, *name2* denotes the seller, *address* denotes the property address, and *money* denotes the price), lending money, hiring a person to mow a lawn, renting an apartment, and so on. Of course, a parameter name (e.g., "buyer" instead of "name") does not help much: its semantics is too vague to be of much help.

The semantics of each operation, therefore, must be precisely defined; this is accomplished by stating what conditions should be true before an operation can be successfully executed (the precondition) and also what the result, or goal, of the operation should be, that is, what conditions should be achieved immediately after the operation is successfully executed (the postcondition).

This aspect of operation specification has often been underestimated and led to unacceptable "specifications" in which the essence of an operation has been hidden in vague and slippery natural language comments or examples, if provided at all. All too often, the only way to find out what the operation really does is to analyze its implementation code. The deficiencies of this approach have been recognized by many, including, most recently, several bodies of the International Standards Organization [API 92].

Programming methodology shows how to declaratively specify the semantics of a state and of an operation in traditional programming [Dijkstra 76, Gries 81, Meyer 88]. Information modeling shows how the same approach may be used to specify the semantics of business rules. In particular, the generic association library presented in Chapters 4 and 5 is specified by means of invariants and pre- and postconditions that declaratively define the CRUD operations applied to elements of this library. In turn, when this generic association library is reused by an analyst to specify a particular enterprise, it nurtures precise, explicit, and declarative specifications.

Signature (operation parameters)[1] and semantics (pre- and postconditions) provide a complete description of a contract, but do not specify how it is to be implemented: the implementation may be unknown or of no interest

---

[1]Of course, types of operation parameters may be considered as belonging to semantics. However, there is much more to semantics than just operation parameter types!

to the contract definer and user. This ensures interoperability (implementation-independence) and also ensures understanding of the system (i.e., provides only the essentials without going into details inappropriate at the particular specification level). This approach makes reasoning about contracts substantially easier: implementation concerns are separated from the contract specification.

A contract for an operation exists within a context defined by the invariant for a collection of objects to which the operation is applied. Therefore, substantial parts of the contract definition immediately follow from this invariant. In particular, contracts for the primitive CRUD operations for the generic association library (some of which are presented in Appendix D) are implied by the invariants for the generic association types and their subtypes (presented in Chapters 4 and 5).

A contract may be refined. When an operation (and its contract) is refined, the contracts become more and more detailed. In the same manner, the signature (data referred to as operation parameters) corresponds to the level in which the operation is described.

3.1.   *Who Defines a Contract?*

Specialists are used to define contracts. In everyday life (e.g., when buying a house) these specialists are called lawyers. In information management, these specialists are called modelers at the higher levels, and programmers at the lower levels. They use the same approaches, formulating abstract and precise (formal) specifications.

"Debate and validation" [Swatman 92] about a specification should be done at the information modeling level rather than at the programming level, where too many irrelevant details stand in the way. These debates and validations should be done, in other words, in the proper frame of reference (**abstraction**). Very roughly speaking, programmers should not formulate business rules[2]—this is the work of SMEs and modelers. However, this is possible only if all the participants know precisely what they are discussing and if, for all the participants, the same words mean the same things. Therefore, to achieve this common ground, formal definitions at the appropriate level are essential (**precision**). (In fact, the existence of these definitions shows that a common ground is (being) achieved.)

---

[2]However, ideas for business rules may perfectly well be generated by programmers and accepted by business management! These ideas should not be based on a particular implementation; rather, they are generated by those programmers (or, better, abstractors) who know how to reason efficiently [Dijkstra 76].

Traditionally, to handle information semantics, certain specialists acquire some knowledge from both programming and subject matter and become indispensable, as they are the only ones who know the semantics of the contracts. If these contracts become explicitly formulated, then these specialists become less indispensable: "production of specifications of handcrafted products might mean that the painfully acquired intimate knowledge of the product, which may be the practitioner's real value to his or her employer, is now to be made generally available" [Potter 91]. Solving problems of this kind is outside the scope of this book.

3.2. Contracts in Information Management

Operations—and contracts for them—are different at different levels of information management. Operations at the topmost level describe functional requirements, whereas operations at the lower levels may describe updates of tuples in a database table and fields of records implementing these tuples (see Section 2.3.1). Accordingly, operations at the topmost level may deal with objects at the topmost level of enterprise modeling, whereas operations at the lower levels may deal with objects available only to the database (or file system) programmer. Therefore, an operation (or collection of operations) at the higher level is typically refined into several operations at the next lower level, in the same manner as collections of objects at higher levels are refined into collections of objects at lower levels.

Lower-level operations and objects are defined in more detail than operations and objects at higher levels. For example, contracts for operations at the information modeling (i.e., business rule) level will not consider such issues as the database management system used, notation used for contract syntax, development platform, data distribution mechanisms, and so on. In this manner, interoperability is achieved because contracts—and their interactions—may be understood and used without regard to their implementations.

The information modeling approach, which uses contracts at all levels of system development—from planning to construction—results in clear, precise, and complete specifications. This means that every operation should be specified as a contract.

In "real-life" contracts, an implementor and conformance tester usually apply common sense and reasonable subject matter knowledge in cases of doubt and incompleteness (unless they consciously look for loopholes). In information management contracts, as mentioned earlier, the implementor and often the conformance tester are not SMEs, so this "common-sense" approach too often does not apply. The contracts should be explicitly formulated and exposed to the implementor and conformance tester, or else they may simply not know what to do. Therefore, incompletenesses and inconsistencies in appropriately formulated information management contracts can be exposed much more easily than in real-life contracts.

3.2.1. Examples

Let us consider how behavior can be described at different levels of information management using appropriate contract specifications. One of our goals was to make behavior explicit, formalize (i.e., define contracts), and therefore be able to reuse—rather than reinvent—constructs encountered across applications.

Let us start with the traditional areas of information management.

For the relational approach, such concepts as tuple behavior, keys, and referential integrity are defining behavior (i.e., appropriate contracts). In fact, we may precisely define preconditions for at least certain relational operations due to the properties of primary keys (the invariant states that the value of a key uniquely identifies a tuple in the table), domains, and so on [Codd 70]. The contract for inserting a tuple into a relational table, even in the absence of referential integrity, preserves this invariant about keys; therefore, the precondition for such an insertion should state that a tuple with the same key does not exist in this table. (If there is a desire to replace such an old tuple with a new one, then the operation will be different—replacement—and should be so defined.) Therefore, it would be incorrect to state that relational databases, unlike object-oriented ones, store "data only": relational databases store precisely defined relational operations as well, although these operations—and their contracts—are usually on a lower level than object databases deal with.[3] By the same token, relational databases provide encapsulation, although, again, on a level usually lower than object-oriented ones deal with: a contract for a relational operation does not refer to its implementation by an underlying filing system.

As another example, consider a contract for assigning a sum of two numbers to a variable in a program. Here, again, the behavior is defined by precise rules of elementary arithmetic, and it is encapsulated, as these definitions do not (usually) rely on bit representation of the numbers in the

---

[3]As [Martin 92] correctly stresses, the relational model is conceptually different from the one used in analysis, design, and programming.

computer. We don't even need to assume that a computer is used: the contract remains the same, independent of whether a programming language, a calculator, or a pencil and paper are used.

Finally, let us consider traditional analysis—ER modeling. Here, things look different just because contracts in traditional ER modeling are usually absent; behavior is usually described in an implicit and vague manner. Nobody, for example, has precisely and explicitly formulated the invariant for a traditional relationship. As a result, it is not clear, for example, what a textbook example of a relationship *shipment* between entities *supplier* and *part* means. An instance of a *shipment* is supposed to associate an instance of a *supplier* and an instance of a *part*—or is it? This example does not recognize the difference between two things, a *shipment* and a *line item*. A *shipment* consists of several *line items*, and an instance of a *line item* really associates one instance of a *supplier* and one instance of a *part*. This example is considered in greater detail in Section 5.3.4. Such issues become clear only when you try to formulate contracts. However, no explicit contracts were available in the traditional ER model.

3.2.2. Interclass Associations

As mentioned in Chapter 2, the most important difference between a typical contract considered from a programming language viewpoint [Meyer 88] and from an information management viewpoint is the existence of explicit interclass relationships. In the relational DBMS world, for instance, they are implemented using "referential integrity."

For a typical information management contract, the pre- and postconditions in its specification refer to properties of several associated classes. In information modeling, this situation is a rule rather than an exception. In this manner, an operation for which a contract is specified usually spans several classes. Instead of an invariant defining an abstract data type and referring only to properties of instances of that type, an information management invariant usually includes visible properties of objects belonging to different classes, so that it is necessary to consider an interclass invariant. Such invariants are used for specifying the generic associations in Chapter 5.

Information modeling contracts define business rules using generic CRUD operations for several associated entities. An overview of this approach has been provided in Chapter 2. In fact, object classes may be defined as related (associated) if there exists an operation referring to a property of (instance of) one of the classes, such that its pre- or postconditions include properties of (instances of) the other classes. It is even better to use an invariant for this purpose: object classes are associated if their invariant refers to properties of all of these classes.

This approach to contracts may be used both at the generic level (e.g., "create a dependent entity"—see Appendix D) and at any application-domain-specific level (e.g., "transfer the ownership of a house"—see Chapter 2). Of course, contracts at any level of information management do not exist in isolation, in the same manner as objects do not exist in isolation.

Different levels of contracts (contract decomposition or refinement) should be distinguished from the interaction of peer contracts. A contract specified in terms of business rules may be decomposed into other contracts, also specified in terms of business rules. This decomposition is an essential part of analysis. It differs from implementation, where different levels of contracts use different object class libraries.

If an object is common to several applications, then each of these applications has its particular view of (i.e., set of properties applicable to) this object and associations the object participates in. In particular, each application has its own contracts in which this object participates. Information modeling harmonizes these applications, that is, describes a single object with possibly different application-specific properties—different application-specific contracts—rather than different application-specific objects for different applications.

3.2.3. Refinement (Layer to Layer)

At different layers of information management, and even at different sublayers within the same layer (e.g., within information modeling), different sets of contracts become visible as one peels off layers or sublayers. However, there is a need to distinguish between two kinds of refinements: one to be specified by the developer (e.g., which DBMS to use to implement an information model or which filing system to use to implement a DBMS), and another—only by the SME together with the modeler (e.g., which credit card to use or 13-digit vs. 16-digit card numbers).

The former refinements are between layers of information management; the latter are within the same layer. Information modeling is concerned mainly with the latter kind of refinements. In our house-buying example, all refinements are of this kind (see below). They correspond to creating/decomposing clusters in the information model. All contracts of this kind can and should be discussed by the modeler with the SME: the expertise of the latter will help to decide whether these contracts are correctly formulated. On the other hand, contracts that refer to refinements between layers are of no interest to, and should usually not be discussed with, the SMEs: in this case, the expertise of developers will help to decide whether these contracts are correctly formulated.

In our example of buying a house, the complete contract is quite a large document, with perhaps several hundred parameters. Even the signature of such a contract is overwhelming. However, not all of these parameters are equally important. Certainly, the identifications of the buyer, the seller, and the property are more important for the contract than, say, the sewer fee or the current credit card debt of the buyer on a particular credit card. Although, technically speaking, all of these parameters in the signature are mandatory, to understand the contract and its associations with other contracts it is necessary to abstract out the most important of these parameters. The expression "most important" is business-specific: some parameters are important for the mortgage lender, some others for the town in which the property is located, and so on. However, there exists the essential part of this contract, the one that is of interest to all participants, and it is very small. Its signature will probably consist of the identifications of the buyer, seller, property, dollar amount, and date of sale. Its semantics will also be quite simple. (A COMPOSITION of *property ownership* symmetric relationship objects, which associate an *owner* and a *property,* may be used as the starting point of modeling such an enterprise; this is described in more detail in Section 5.3.4).

3.2.4. Peer Contracts

As mentioned earlier, all information management contracts are specified in the same manner—using pre- and postconditions in the context of appropriate invariants. Many contracts explicitly refer to several objects rather than to one isolated object. Therefore, as mentioned earlier, there can be no "side effects" in a contract, and neither need there be a distinguished parameter in a contract specification.

Indeed, if a contract is specified completely, then all appropriate operation parameters are included in the specification, so that there is no need for a "side effect"—a change in state that is not specified explicitly. Of course, when peer contracts coexist, they may not be independent and may therefore lead to changes of state not specified by either of them. In other words, a contract becomes contextual. This problem of peer contract interaction shows that contracts, like objects, usually do not exist in isolation and may be composed to create higher-level ones. In such a composition, the invariants are conjoined [Zave 92], and the same may be true for pre- and postconditions of operations.

Another problem deals with information model changes. If an association between entities is added/changed/deleted, then naturally, assertions for some of the participating entities will have to be changed. In particular, it means that the correctness of the model change needs to be checked. It is clear that if, after the changes, the invariant for some collection of interrelated entities, or the precondition for some operation, will be FALSE, then the changes will have resulted in an invalid model and therefore should be reconsidered. At the very least, if the only result of the change implies that the precondition for some operation will become FALSE, then this operation will become impossible and should not be specified. Unfortunately, there exists no mechanical way of checking this condition.

Another important problem, with possibly serious consequences for information consistency, deals with contract decomposition that is orthogonal to encapsulation. If a contract is decomposed into a set of components at the same level (i.e., both the contract and its components have the same user—a situation quite often encountered in information management), and if the contract supports more sophisticated semantic integrity rules than its components, then the component user may violate integrity rules. In particular, it means that semantic integrity rules supported by a contract may not be supported by any of its components.

Entity-set-oriented vs. single-entity-oriented contracts (i.e., set-oriented contracts represented as sets of visible—to the same user—single-entity contracts) as well as contracts spanning several subsystems may belong to this category. For instance, if a certain goal may be accomplished by means of either one contract or (its decomposition into) a set of contracts with some additional actions, then the reuse of the latter may present problems because a human may not necessarily be willing or able to exactly repeat this decomposition, including all of these additional actions. This happens because specification and its decomposition exist at the same level (and is well known to programmers using procedures). This problem is to be acknowledged, and clear guidelines for disciplined reuse are needed for its solution.

Note that contract components are needed for reuse (e.g., subtyping or configuring of new contracts). Note also that, in some environments, a decision may be made to conceal the components of a composite contract, whereas in some other environments these components should be visible.

3.2.5. Contracts and System Correctness

Contracts define the rules for preserving a correct system state throughout the performance of operations. An operation may be performed only if its precondition, as specified in a contract, is satisfied. A precondition is a function applied to the current system state and returning TRUE or FALSE. If it returns TRUE, then—technically—it is satisfied. The result of a contract is a change of state of the system. Another function specified in an operation's contract, a postcondition, is applied to the system state immediately after the successful execution of the operation. This explicitly specified change of the system state is the only result of a contract. There are no side effects: any change of the system state is explicit.

However, contracts do not exist in isolation. An "elementary" contract may violate the system invariant (i.e., the semantic integrity of information) and therefore may not be executable by itself. Rather, such a contract may be executable only as a fragment of a non-decomposable collection of contracts that prescribes the collective behavior [ODP 2] of several objects. Quite a few examples will be provided in Chapter 4 when creation or deletion of an object is possible only in the same business process with creation or deletion of another object or objects. A business process is non-decomposable and implements an externally visible contract.

Some contracts do not change the state of the system. The common term for them is "read-only." In fact, the results of their implementation are often externally visible (e.g., output on paper or on screen). As for any other contract, a read-only one is valid only if its precondition is satisfied.

Contracts that are not read-only change the state of the system. They represent the only way to do so. Even if explicit human intervention is required, we are still dealing with contracts. Indeed, for some contracts, the preconditions may not be satisfied, but the result is not a rejection: rather, it is an overriding by a human being. Well-known examples are getting credit for the first time (i.e., without a credit history) and paying with an unspecified (e.g., out-of-state) check. The manager of a furniture store may decide whether to permit the return of a piece of a set bought some time ago, although by default it is not permitted. This kind of a contract is possible and, like any other contract, should be clearly and explicitly specified. In fact, it is always specified by means of clearly stated "company policies," but this is too often lost in the information model of the company.

Of course, a contract preserves an invariant, but a system state usually has more properties than satisfying the invariant. Naturally, in all cases the operations specified by a contract have to preserve the invariant, that is, an operation-independent predicate that should be TRUE outside of any operation. In other words, an invariant defines the context to be preserved by operations.

After a contract has been successfully executed, the system state has changed. In this manner, preconditions for some contracts may have become valid, and preconditions for certain other contracts may have become inalid.

Therefore, successful execution of a contract changes the set of contracts that are applicable to the (state of the) system.

Let's recall our example of buying a house. After successful execution of this contract, the buyer usually does not have too much money. Therefore, the precondition for buying another house is usually not satisfied. On the other hand, the buyer usually becomes eligible for various kinds of preferred treatment by banks (e.g., home-equity loans). Therefore, the preconditions for such treatment (and appropriate contracts) become satisfied.

This approach to contracts is in line with current requirements specified by national and international standardization bodies and industrial consortia. Details are described in Chapter 7, and we provide here just a short summary. The ANSI Object Data Management Reference Model [OODBTG 91] describes a general approach to specifying contracts using preconditions and postconditions for operations rather than the implementations of these operations. The same approach is used and described in greater detail by the OSI/Network Management Forum [OSI/NM Forum 91] as well as by the ISO standardization documents for Open Distributed Processing [ODP 2] and OSI Managed Objects, especially Managed Relationships [GRM 93]. The ISO Special Working Group on Modeling Facilities [ACMF 92] deals with exactly the same issues. Therefore, an information model based on contracts will make available standard-conforming descriptions of contracts that define the available behavior.

3.3.   Formalism in Contract Specifications

3.3.1. The Need for Formalism

Requirements documents should communicate intent rather than pseudo-code. Formal notations like Z [Potter 91, Spivey 92] or Object Z [Duke 91, Rose 92] are used exactly for this purpose: they provide a precise declarative specification of behavior, and the intent of an operation is precisely specified in its postcondition. There are no pseudo-code details, and the developers are absolutely free to implement the intent in whatever manner they see fit, subject to providing a correct implementation. In other words, the implementors have to satisfy only the explicitly formulated specification, no more and no less. This specification may serve for conformance testing as well.

As it is impossible to correctly specify the solution to a complex problem on the first try, a formal notation like Z need not specify solutions: it specifies **what** is to be done, rather than **how** it is to be done. The level of abstraction in such a specification is not fixed: it may be adapted to the problem at hand. Z and Object Z are among the most appropriate notations for information modeling because they have reasonable structuring facilities. As a result, a large specification is decomposable into small, and therefore more understandable, pieces. Such pieces can also be reused by other specifications.

In the same manner as formalization in "elementary" mathematics shows that most theorems formulated in geometry are wrong because they do not mention "obvious exceptions" [Dijkstra 92], formalization in information modeling shows that most models are wrong, at least for the same reason. (Actually, the "wrong" may be replaced with "incomplete," at least in some cases.) However, programmers who implement these models and are not SMEs may not know that! The results may be disastrous. However, the solutions of these problems are the same: use precise (i.e., formal) specifications because they require explicitness. It will be necessary to explicitly state in the specification all the "obvious" and "default" assumptions and exceptions.

This book shows how precise specifications are developed and used, and why they are essential for information modeling. Too many existing application models start their specifications with their own definitions of basic concepts, such as different extensions to the basic ER model. These definitions are often unclear or ambiguous, leading to inconsistent or ambiguous models. The generic association library used for information modeling (see Chapter 5) is formulated precisely, and its most important aspects are formulated using predicate logic. (An error in the generic association library—not noticed by any of its users and developers for a while—has been found only as a result of writing an Object Z specification for the association!) In this manner, questions about the type (e.g., COMPOSITION or SUBTYPING?) and therefore properties of a particular application association can be easily resolved. This library is specified only once and need not be respecified (and reinvented) by each application. Rather, it is reused by each application.

3.3.2. The Cost of Formalism

The substantial up-front investment in getting acquainted with a formal notation has been cited by several people and does exist. However, for a developer who knows, for example, the notation of C, a notation like Z will not represent any serious problems. Note that most concepts used in Z are taught in the first computer science courses. Moreover, the need to write precise specifications can cause many points of clarification to arise at the specification stage rather than to be invented by the developer at the developing stage.

For "traditional" specifications that use natural language + pictures, such an invention is needed because they are usually incomplete, ambiguous, or both. The reviews of such software documentation often overemphasize the typographical aspects of the document at hand [Potter 91], whereas specifications written using formal methods contain statements that have unambiguous meanings (or at least clearly defined ambiguity), and therefore the review process focuses on the meaningful content. The developer may not and need not be a SME, and therefore specifications created by the developer may lead to serious errors that will be dealt with later, during "maintenance," drastically increasing the overall cost of a project.

The problem of notation complexity is cited for any formal specification technique. Indeed, notations used in these techniques are based on (very simple concepts of) predicate calculus and therefore may not be understandable to the end user of a specification. Note, however, that the users of a class library specification do not have to completely understand all of its aspects. Specifications may and should be provided to their users on different levels of formality and detail.

Of course, using (reading) a specification component is not equivalent to being able to create (write) one, and in most cases specification authors and users refer to already existing specification components. Commonalities of specifications in seemingly different application areas can be understood only if the specifications are very precise (i.e., formal). This commonality facilitates reuse that can and does save time, effort, and money. This addresses the very real problem in industry: currently, too few teams are capable of producing and explicitly formulating good specifications.

3.3.3. Formal Notations

The Z and Object Z notations are currently considered by international standards bodies (see Chapter 7) and industry as the most appropriate for information modeling. Z is used in specifying telecommunications managed objects [Rudkin 91]. British Telecom and Telecom Australia [Stocks 92] refer to very positive practical experiences in using Z for understanding their enterprises. It appeared, in particular, that "natural language" specifications have been understood much better, and that inconsistencies and discrepancies in these specifications have been found and resolved only after the specifications in Z have been produced. Specifying a small project is relatively easy; only for a large product can the value of formalism in general and Z in particular be appreciated. Even a partial specification of a large product shows why the use of formalism is indispensable.

Consider the example used by [Zave 91]: a rather simple formal specification of one aspect of an actual product has exposed serious problems that have been overlooked in the development and "testing" of this product. Another good recent example is the 1992 Queen's Award to IBM and Oxford University Computing Laboratory for using formal methods and Z in specifying CICS.

The use of Z or Object Z does not mean that this particular choice of notation is crucial. As long as a formal notation is appropriate for specifying an information model and convenient for human use, it is acceptable. Many modelers independently acknowledged the strengths—and some weaknesses—of Z in formulating actual specifications, and their general feeling has been in favor of using Z with possible object-oriented extensions to better support abstraction and reuse. An example of specifying some generic associations in Object Z is presented in Appendix A.

Programming notation is based on mathematics, and therefore the distinction between formal and informal is much clearer and physically visible. In information modeling, we may go either way, that is, we may or may not decide to expose the formal specification in, say, Object Z. However, we should base our specifications on mathematics, even if these mathematical formulations are not exposed to every user. It is almost always possible to translate from such a mathematical formulation into "structured English," so that a specification will look like an informal one but will in fact be formal: it will use only carefully chosen expressions in carefully chosen contexts. In addition to those found in this book, examples of such "structured English" specifications are provided by the reference model for Open Distributed Processing [ODP 2, ODP 3, ODP 4].

3.4. Some Guidelines for Contract Specification

This section will describe guidelines for specifying contracts. These guidelines will be separated into three groups: general guidelines applicable to all contracts, guidelines for contract refinement and use, and guidelines for interrelated contract specifications.

3.4.1. General Guidelines

- *Contract specifications should be implementation-independent (encapsulation).* (For instance, information model contracts should not include DBMS-specific information such as tables, primary and foreign keys, normalization, codes, etc.). In this manner, semantic integrity of information will be supported because information will be understood by both clients (including SMEs) and implementors in the only appropriate—implementation-independent—manner. In particular, this approach leads to platform-independent software development: the specification is not platform- and vendor-specific. As a corollary, "data modeling" will not be artificially separated from "process modeling": representation-specific information will be considered only at the implementation level—where it belongs—whereas both structural and behavioral properties of the collection of information objects of interest will be considered and specified uniformly.[4] As an example of this approach, the generic association library (see Chapters 4 and 5) does not use structural properties (a.k.a. attributes) for its specification: explicit associations are implementation-independent, whereas attributes of associated entities may be used as an implementational (relational) way of representing associations. In the latter approach, semantics is often lost. For another example, the General Relationship Model standardization documents explicitly state that the semantic properties of relationships should be specified independent of how the relationship is represented [GRM 93]. In this manner, the semantics of a relationship can be easily understood.

These considerations apply to reverse engineering—the activity of understanding a system by uncovering appropriate contracts that are already there, but are not explicit. Accomplishing this goal requires separating contract specification from implementation-specific details, including details about particular databases and DBMSs used. The difficulties encountered here are both technical (specifications may not exist and therefore may have to be extracted from application code) and educational (the analysts may be too close to the implementation and therefore may encounter serious difficulties in separating the specification from implementational concerns, e.g., in organizing information, specifying operations, etc.). Our experience suggests that mechanical extraction of design information from code may miss critically important information, and that, therefore, various "design generators," "flowcharters," and the like provide only a very limited amount of help, if it is provided at all.

- *Technological information* (response time, commitment of transactions, etc., as well as contract establishment issues) *included in the*

---

[4]There exist no "thingless events" (i.e., just process) or "eventless things" (i.e., just data) [Wand 89].

contract specification should be clearly separated from the correctness (semantic) information. Correctness of the contract (i.e., its precondition, postcondition, and invariants for object classes participating in the contract) should certainly be stressed as its critical aspect. Otherwise, symptoms may appear that are well-known in a "usual" programming environment—things clearly go wrong if the correctness and efficiency concerns are considered either simultaneously or even as being of equal importance. ([Weinberg 71] noted a while ago that if a program does not have to be correct then it can easily satisfy any other criteria.) These considerations do not mean that technological concerns are unimportant; they do mean, however, that a contract specification may need to be split into a semantic part and a technological part, and if the semantic (correctness) part is not satisfied, then the technological part is irrelevant. Of course, the semantic and technological parts of a contract may be written by and discussed with different persons: the expertise for reasoning about these parts is quite different. Moreover, these parts will reuse rather different libraries.

• *Contract specifications should include pre- and postcondition and should preserve invariants for object classes participating in the contract.* They are to be specified in a precise and explicit manner, usually based on predicate calculus with possible extensions. ("The notion of a contract is important to capture the idea that the behavior of an application or an object must be evaluated against precise expectations" [ODP 2, 11.2.2].) This approach is essential for open systems because only these specifications are vendor-neutral and permit software (application and data) portability [Overcoming Barriers 91]. There exist several specification languages for doing this (e.g., Z [Spivey 92], Object Z [Duke 91], etc.), but the contract users and implementors may have problems in understanding such specifications.[5] A natural language (or graphical) explanation may guide the user (as a bird's-eye view?) through the rigorous formal specification, although the former should be used very cautiously due to often imprecise and incomplete definitions of its elements. (Of course, it is possible to define a graphical notation in a precise and explicit manner, but in quite a few cases it is able to represent only some fragments of an information model.) It is possible, however, to translate the specifications from a formal notation into "structured" English (e.g., read the formal specification aloud). Such a quasi-natural-language specifica-

---

[5]Appropriate educational efforts are necessary, not least of which is reusing a good reference list.

tion helps understanding a lot and may often be considered sufficiently precise. For example, the descriptive model of Open Distributed Processing [ODP 2] is specified in this manner. The invariants defining the generic associations in Chapter 5 are also presented in this manner.

Only when contracts are clearly specified can an information model be understood: it has been our experience that some modelers could not answer questions about their own models because precise contracts were not (yet) specified! Without understanding of the model, it cannot be correctly implemented and used; programmers will have to "introduce" their own understanding because a program has to be precise (and in this manner a programmer will have to become a modeler, usually without the benefit of reusing the class libraries of information model components).[6] As a simple example, consider the generic integrity rules for an information model based on contracts for primitive CRUD operations. They define generic associations in a precise and unambiguous manner: when an object is specified as belonging to a particular generic association, appropriate semantic integrity constraints (i.e., preconditions and postconditions for CRUD operations and invariants for the association) are immediately clear because they follow from (and in fact constitute) the definition of the generic association. Note that both set-oriented and single-entity-oriented access specifications are formulated in a uniform manner, using appropriate assertions.

- *Only predefined operations should be available to the client.* Exposing "data" to the client by allowing, say, a client's access to an SQL interface to a relational DBMS may lead to violating business rules and therefore should be prohibited. Every operation available to the client should be specified using a contract, but only by those who know the business rules, that is, by the modeler together with the SME (on the client's request), rather than by the client or by the developer. This approach is used, for example, in specifying generic associations in Object Z, which provides facilities for explicitly enumerating operations available to the user (visibility list). Naturally, new operations can be added to the set of operations available to the client, but they should be clearly and carefully specified.

---

[6]Only exceptional programmers can do that; however, they work within a certain application domain, and the problem of redundant and inconsistent data across different application areas will not be solved in this manner.

- *Ad hoc queries[7] should be disciplined.* Operations that retrieve, but do not change, values of any and all **visible** properties[8] of an object or a collection of objects should be predefined. A particular combination of these properties may be visualized as a relational-like selection and projection of unneeded property values from a retrieval of all visible properties of several entities associated by means of their semantic "links" defined in the information model. This approach is preferable to user-specified "joins" for several reasons. It controls arbitrary user access (which may result, e.g., in compromising secure or private data), tames complexity (formulating a query is difficult for the end user), ensures consistency (an existing explicitly specified query—unlike a named predefined one—may have to be changed when the information model is changed), and improves the information model (links between entities that are not related in the information model may suggest a defect in the model). However, in some cases a new combination of properties—not a selection or a projection of an existing one—is needed, and therefore, there may be a need to define new retrieval possibilities. It is recommended that this activity should be accomplished by an application modeler—rather than by an application customer—for several reasons, including integrity, security, and performance. It may lead to improvements of the model.

3.4.2. Refinement and Use of a Contract

- *A higher-level contract is to be decomposed into (i.e., refined as) a set of contracts on a lower level.* Sometimes this refinement uses the same object class library (e.g., procedures in a programming language use both other procedures and various ways of combining them prescribed in the programming language; legal contracts use both other legal contracts and various ways of combining them prescribed in the law). Sometimes refinement uses a different object class library, and then it becomes an implementation (e.g., a program can be compiled, or an information model "programmed" into a set of data definition and data

---

[7]In relational terms, semantically meaningless joins will be impossible because corresponding operations will not exist: all associations between entities will be predefined in the schema. On the other hand, an application-specific contract may use the values of visible properties of objects in any semantically meaningful manner, and this manner is defined by the modeler (specifier) of this particular application.

[8]Note that a visible property (often a.k.a. attribute) of an entity need not correspond to a field of the entity record! See also [OODBTG 91].

manipulation language statements). Some considerations about refining the generic association library into a relational implementation (using an implementation library) are presented in Appendix B.

One level's specification is another level's implementation. The implementation of a contract at the lowest level is an actual program [Morgan 90] (i.e., its user is a computer system), whereas the implementation of a contract on any other level is a set of contracts on a lower level (i.e., its user may be a human being). In particular, it is possible to visualize "subsystems" as (very large) composite objects and apply operations to these objects in the same manner as operations are applied to their components: building blocks interact in the same manner as entities do. Of course, it is possible to jump from an application-specific contract directly to its "database" implementation, but in this case the jump distance will be too large, and common generic contracts will have to be reinvented, possibly with errors, each and every time: they will not be reused. On the other hand, semantic integrity (correctness) depends upon the context (level): "As soon as a model allows an application to combine operations, consistency is in the eyes of the application developer" (N. Ballou). A trivial example of such an approach is provided if the get and set methods for all attributes of an object are available: by (in)appropriately combining these methods, consistency is violated.

- *Each contract implementation should implement the corresponding specification, no more and no less.* All "defaults" and other implicit assumptions including information about the global environment, if they are to be implemented, should be explicitly specified. However, globals (objects that are referred to within a contract and exist also outside of the contract, but are not contract parameters) should be used very sparingly if at all because they lead to assertions that are elaborate, difficult to formulate, messy, and difficult to verify. In contrast, the assertions for a "parameterized" contract specification—if neither the specification nor the implementation use globals!—should involve a small number of parameters (thin and visible interface, E. W. Dijkstra), and therefore the assertions and invariant must only describe the relationship among a few objects rather than the relationship among all the objects in the system. In this manner, the assertions and invariant become intellectually manageable (see also below). This guideline is also essential for contracts considered within a certain context (environment); see the following section.

- *Lower-level contracts are invisible to the client of a higher-level contract, and therefore each contract should have a well-defined set of its possible users.* This approach supports encapsulation, a precondition for making complex systems intellectually manageable. In other words, circumvention of the contract methods should not be possible for the contract user[9] (otherwise, there may exist both opportunities for the malicious and traps for the unwary; compare [Conrad 91]). These ideas have been well known in programming since the second half of the '60s: Dijkstra suggested "to confine ourselves to the design and implementation of intellectually manageable programs" [Dijkstra 68, Dijkstra 72]. It is conceivable to imagine registration of permissible properties of potential clients of a particular server (e.g., the property of belonging to a particular level): only a client with these properties may be served by this server (a conjunction to the appropriate preconditions). This may be done, for example, in the context of a Trader.

3.4.3. Interrelated Contract Specifications

- *Composite contract specifications should be intellectually manageable.* If a contract is decomposed into a set of component contracts at the same level (i.e., both the contract and its component contracts have the same users) then a component specification may be very long and complex; therefore, a composite contract specification, in order to be intellectually manageable, may be less detailed than the sum of its component contract specifications. In this manner, such a contract may be visualized as a cluster of its components where irrelevant details of their specification are suppressed in order to establish a simplified model, in accordance with the definition of abstraction in [ODP 2]. Any cluster of generic associations from the corporate information model provides a good example: the "top level" of the information model consists usually of "top-level" entities each of which may be visualized as a cluster (usually represented as a composite or a supertype) of interrelated entities at a more detailed level. This clustering establishes the separation of concerns essential for understanding the information model as a whole rather than the particularities of its components (a "typical" specification document for an information model often does not separate concerns as the user has to read what he

---

[9]Evidently, an *implementor* of higher-level contracts may—and need—see and reuse lower-level contracts: implementations of different higher-level contracts may reuse the same lower-level ones.

or she does not need). Even the need for composite contracts may be explained by the limitations of our brains (E. W. Dijkstra).

- *Properties that exist in the information model should be reused in a contract specification.* In fact, the act of creating an information model may be considered as an act of reusing a set of appropriate generic contracts for primitive (CRUD) operations (see Appendix D) specified by means of assertions and invariants. The contracts defining generic associations for the information model need not be copied: only the names (and subclasses) of the generic associations should be specified because these specifications immediately and unambiguously imply the corresponding contracts.

  The information model includes both the specification of the stable state (the invariants) and the specification of contracts for the applicable operations. These specifications are complete, that is, they define all properties that exist in the information model.

  A pictorial representation of an information model is not required for its use. Not every business rule in the information model need be graphically specified. Some properties of the generic associations may not be shown in a picture. Trying to show everything in a picture will lead to clutter and therefore to intellectually unmanageable diagrams.

- *Assertions for an operation usually imply changing more than one instance, possibly of more than one class.* In particular, these assertions may appear as a result of the need to maintain the invariant(s). These assertions for the CRUD operations applied to the generic association library are presented in Chapter 5 and Appendix D. Several nontrivial problems appear to exist in the context of implementing this guideline. Should all these updates be made known to the contract specifier or contract user? Could they? Theoretically, the answer to all of these questions is "yes," but in "real life" the result may be very complicated due to the need for intellectual manageability.[10] Explicit specifications of all these changes may lead to unacceptable clutter, and therefore the approach well-known from programming—separation of concerns—should be used. If, however, the answer is "no," then there should be some source of information about these updates, and this source should not be an application program. The information

---

[10]One of the possible solutions explicitly specifies assertions (and changes) only for the closest neighbors (first-degree relationships or direct associations) of the object class rather than for the transitive closure of its associations (see also [Kilov 90-1] and the discussion of nonelementary molecules in Chapter 5).

model represents such a source for generic changes, that is, changes enforced by generic information modeling contracts. These changes (creates, updates, and deletes) themselves need not be specified by all operations that use them: only the generic association (and their participating object) names are sufficient, because assertions for these operations follow from the generic association definitions (see, e.g., the example about *FriendsOfJohn* in Chapter 2). Note that these changes should certainly be known to the contract implementor, unless they are automatically taken care of by, say, the DBMS.

3.5. Separation of Concerns

Because contracts are used at all levels of information management, we need to identify not only the features of any contracts, but also the characteristics of contracts specific to the information modeling level. As usual, we will have to separate our concerns. The most important concerns to be separated in discussing information modeling contracts are:

- Technical vs. marketing (e.g., how to sell a contract or a collection of contracts to a client)
- Correctness vs. technological
- Semantic vs. syntax
- Generic vs. application-specific

As shown above, information modeling stresses the technical, correctness, semantic, and generic concerns. These same concerns have been stressed by programming methodology.

Associations

*"**A** scientific discipline emerges with the—usually rather slow!— discovery of which aspects can be meaningfully 'studied in isolation for the sake of their own consistency'—in other words, with the discovery of useful and helpful concepts."* [Dijkstra 82]

This chapter describes properties common to all generic associations between objects. In particular, it discusses an elementary association—the concept common to all elements of a generic association library for analysis (information modeling), presented in more detail in Chapter 5 and Appendix 4. It shows how to precisely specify the properties of an elementary association in a declarative manner. It introduces the components of such an association—source and target. It also shows how the declarative specification of behavior represents "classical" ER modeling notions—such as mandatory/ optional participation and cardinality—in a simple, explicit, and unambiguous way.

4.1. Basics

We will use the term "object" or "entity" to denote the type,[1] and the term "object instance" or "entity instance" to denote the instance. In the same manner, we will use the term "association" to denote the type, and "association instance" to denote the instance.

Joseph Morabito contributed to the text of this chapter.

[1]To be more precise, a "type" defines a protocol shared by a group of objects called instances of the type, whereas a "class" defines an implementation shared by a group of objects [OODBTG 91]. Related, but different, definitions are provided by [ODP 2] (a type is a predicate, and a class is a set of objects satisfying a type). However in many cases we will use these terms interchangeably, as in [OODBTG 91].

A generic object is defined only within the context of its associa-tion(s). For example, stating that a particular entity (a *performance history*) is a "dependent" one makes sense only within the context of the "DEPEND-ENCY" association, that is, the association between the "parent" (an *em-ployee*) and "dependent" (a *performance history*) entities. **An association is a collection of objects the invariant of which refers to the properties of all the participating objects.** The invariant of each association, as stated earlier, is the condition that should be TRUE all the time outside of an oper-ation on this association or on the associated objects. The invariant should be preserved by each operation, and therefore it can be considered as conjoined to the precondition and to the postcondition of each operation.

A generic association—like any other association—is defined by its in-variant. For a generic association, this invariant is not specific to any partic-ular application: a generic association may be encountered in any applica-tion. Generic associations are distinguished by different invariants (e.g., the invariant for COMPOSITION differs from the invariant for SUBTYPING). How-ever, some properties of generic associations are common to all of them. These properties represent the invariant of (i.e., they define) an elementary generic association. They will be described in the following sections. In par-ticular, we will show how traditional ER constructs like "mandatory or op-tional participation" and, more generally, "cardinality" may be precisely and unambiguously specified as components of the invariant for an association.

The invariant of an association implies that only certain operations are permitted for the association and its participants. An operation applied to a collection of objects[2] within the context of its invariant can be described by a contract the specification of which is a business rule for the operation. A con-tract defines an operation declaratively: it precisely specifies the postcondi-tions ("what should be true after") and preconditions ("what should be true before") for the operation. The implementor uses these declarative specifica-tions as the only source of information for a successful implementation. This book is not about implementation; many good books and papers have been written about this topic. However, some hints about a possible implementa-tion library are presented in Appendix B.

Various representations, including graphical ones, may be used as tools for expressing associations. However, information modeling concepts—including associations—are tool-neutral, in the same manner as program-ming concepts are language-neutral. An algorithm can be specified in any programming language, and in the same manner, a generic association can

---

[2]The collection may consist of one object.

be specified in any notation, be it graphical or linear. The choice of a notation is sometimes dictated by a mixture of technical and nontechnical considerations, and this book will not try to discuss the relative merits, if any, of this choice.

4.2.   Objects (Entities) and Their Properties

This section will present properties common to any and all objects.

An object in information modeling is also known, in more traditional approaches, as an "entity." This is a basic notion and, to be precise, it is best of all to leave it undefined.[3]

Some properties of an entity type are "owned by" the entity itself and describe only a particular entity isolated from any other entities. A typical example of such a property is an *employee's name*. However, most properties of interest to an information modeler do not describe an isolated entity; rather, they are "jointly owned" by several associated entities and are therefore used to define this association. In other words, a jointly owned invariant or operation is applied to a collection of instances rather than to a single isolated instance. It describes the collective behavior of these instances. A typical example of such a property is the operation *assign employee to a project*. This is not a property of an *employee*, and neither is it a property of a *project*: it is jointly owned by both.

Every object instance has some properties (i.e., satisfies some predicate). The same predicate may be satisfied by different entity instances (e.g., "is an employee," "works for project 1234567," "is an integer"). Such a predicate ("typical" for these instances) is usually called a "type" [ODP 2] and may have a name. **An object instance can satisfy several types** (e.g., the same *person* can be an *employee*, a *male*, a *teacher*, a *student*, a *Republican*, a *stamp collector*, a component (of a *project*), a parent (of a *child*), etc.).

Every application-specific object participates in associations. These application-specific associations are subtypes of generic ones. In our example above, the *person* is a component (in an *employee-project* COMPOSITION) and a parent (in a *parent-child* DEPENDENCY). An application-specific association inherits the properties of its generic supertype. Therefore, an application-specific object participating in application-specific associations inherits the

---

[3]"If there are 10 people in a room, and each is asked for definitions of the term ... 'entity' ..., 20 different definitions are likely to be supplied." [Codd 90]

properties of the generic objects—participants in corresponding generic associations. In our example, the *person* inherits the properties of a component in a COMPOSITION and of a parent in a DEPENDENCY. In addition, every object is a subtype of the generic object type "entity" (described below) and therefore inherits its properties.

Traditionally, properties have been separated into structural (values) and behavioral (operations). This borderline is rather fuzzy. Indeed, behavioral properties of an object are defined by the set of operations in which the ob-

> *"A class is characterized by its features. Every feature describes an operation for accessing or modifying instances of the class.*
> *A feature is either an attribute, describing information stored with each instance, or a routine, describing an algorithm . . . A feature of a class describes an operation which is applicable to instances of the class." [Meyer 92]*

ject participates. Structural property (state) values should also be available only by application of predefined operations (see Chapter 2, [OODBTG 91], and [ODP 2]): *ad hoc* handling of isolated structural property values often does not have a reasonable mapping back to the semantic modeling level.[4] Whether structural property values are or are not stored in an implemented database is not important for information modeling. (Compare with **features** in Eiffel [Meyer 92]. As mentioned above, there is also an important difference: Eiffel's features belong to a particular class, whereas information modeling captures properties that are usually jointly owned by more than one entity.)

As a simple example, consider an "innocent" operation, "set the value of *number of employees for project 1234567* to *5.*" This operation, taken in isolation, may violate the invariant[5] of the system, that is, leave the system in an inconsistent state. Therefore, such an operation should not be permitted in

---

[4]A structural property of an entity may be implemented (e.g., in a relational database) as one attribute, several attributes, or even a part of an attribute of a corresponding relation. These attributes and relations are not visible at the information modeling level (and should not be discussed at that level). This idea is not new: E. F. Codd discussed in [Codd 79] several ways of implementing, for example, a dependency (in Codd's terms, a characteristic entity). Appendix B deals with these issues in more detail.

[5]Stating that the budget of a project equals the sum of salaries of its participants plus some other precisely specified expenses, and so on.

this context. The semantically meaningful—and therefore predefined and permitted—operation would be *"assign 5 employees to project 1234567,"* with preconditions including the availability of employees, the availability of money in the budget, and so on, and with changing the values of such structural properties as *project budget, department budget, and internal office addresses of employees.*

Often, structural properties of the same or different object types are similar. For instance, an *employee* may have a *home address* and a *business address*, a *customer* may have a *customer address*, a *telephone service* can have a *service address* and a *listed address*, and so on. These properties have common (and therefore reusable) characteristics; most important, they have the same pool of possible values from which they draw their values. This pool may be defined either extensionally (by enumerating the values) or intensionally (by stating their properties). The set of possible values from which a structural property draws its values is called its domain, and is described in more detail in Chapter 5. In describing a structural property, its domain should be specified.

To find objects, consider the properties of associations between objects. In finding generic associations, structural properties of association participants are of secondary importance. Indeed, the concepts of DEPENDENCIES, SYMMETRIC RELATIONSHIPS, COMPOSITIONS, and so on can be easily explained without the use of structural properties. (Invariants for all generic associations do not include particular structural properties.) However, in finding application-specific entity types (such as *employee, department*, and *equipment*) representative structural properties are important because they help to identify this type.[6]

Among the most important properties of an object are the operations in which the object participates. An operation is usually applied to more than one object; that is, its parameters include properties of several objects.

A complete specification of an **operation** includes:

- Its **signature**, that is, the (values and types of the) operation parameters—structural properties of the objects participating in the operation
- Its **semantics**, that is, pre- and postcondition for the operation

Naturally, **the signature alone is not sufficient for describing an operation** [API 92]: **it does not specify what the operation is going to accom-**

---

[6]In a relational implementation, these representative properties may correspond to the collection of attributes constituting the primary key.

plish! The signature of an operation *assign employee to a project* is exactly the same as the signature of an operation *remove employee from a project*, although the semantics of these operations are quite different.

As mentioned earlier, every operation should preserve those invariants in which its objects participate. Therefore, to understand an operation we should start with invariants. Let's formulate the invariant for any object.[7]

> **Invariant**. Each object instance is unique and can be identified independent of its behavior or state. An object is not isolated: there exists at least one association of this object with some other object.

Each object instance is unique; the values of visible structural properties of different object instances may or may not be different, but each object instance should have a unique identity [OODBTG 91, Codd 79, ODP 2]. This may be realized by means of a "unique identifier" [OODBTG 91], the value of which distinguishes between object instances and may not necessarily be visible to the user.

An object is not isolated: the generic association(s) in which the object participates define some of the invariants associating an object with other objects; other invariants may be defined by the application.

Note. Considerations about the presence of "key attributes," "partial keys," "foreign keys," and so on belong to a possible (relational) implementation, that is, to a frame of reference different from information modeling (see Chapter 2). ("Specifications and their refinements typically do not co-exist in the same system description." [ODP 2])

4.3.   Association

This section considers features of an elementary association. All elementary generic associations mentioned below and described in more detail in Chapter 5 have these features.

There are not too many generic association types. They are encountered in, and reused by, all applications. The next section will enumerate all elementary generic associations discussed in this book. You have encountered most, if not all, of these associations in the previous chapters and in your everyday work.

Invariants for the generic association types are provided in Chapter 5.

---

[7]This invariant consists of two clauses, both of which should be TRUE. In other words, they are conjoined. In what follows, we will use the same approach.

They precisely express the business properties of these association types. Contracts for CRUD operations applied to (the elements of) these association types follow from these invariants. Some of these contracts are presented in Appendix D.

The invariant of an association (e.g., a COMPOSITION corresponding to an application-specific COMPOSITION between a *project* and a set of *employee*s) describes the properties of the "collective state" of the participants of the association. An entity may participate in several elementary associations. For example, the *employee* may be both a component in a COMPOSITION association (*project-employee*) and a parent in the DEPENDENCY association (*employee-child*). Such an entity therefore becomes a participant in a nonelementary (application-specific) association, the invariant of which is generally a conjunction of the invariants of its participating elementary associations. Therefore, a contract for an operation in which such an entity participates will also follow from this (more complicated) invariant. The extended example in Section 6.1.2 shows that formulating such a contract specification is rather straightforward.

These elementary generic associations constitute the top level of the **generic association library** to which a modeler should refer when specifying an information model. The *entity* is a supertype, and all other generic objects—participants in generic associations—are its subtypes. Therefore, each generic object inherits all properties of an entity. By the same token, the elementary association is a supertype, and all generic associations are its subtypes. Therefore, each generic association inherits the properties of the elementary association. Therefore, we are describing these properties only once, below.

4.3.1. The Association Invariant

An elementary association (in what follows, we will call it "an association") is a binary (asymmetric) relation. An association type—a relation type—relates a source type to a target type [Potter 91]. Any of these types may be nonelementary (e.g., an instance of such a type may be a set, a set of sets, etc.). If a nonelementary type is a set, then its corresponding elementary type will be an element of this set. An instance of a relation generally exists if and only if there exists an instance of its source type and an appropriate instance of its target type (for the only exception, see below).

Let's apply these features to all generic association types:

- A DEPENDENCY association (see Section 5.1.1) may be represented as a relation between the source type (parent) and the target type (dependent). Both the source and the target types are elementary. An instance of the DE-PENDENCY association exists if and only if corresponding instances of the parent and dependent types exist. In other words, the existence of an instance of the DEPENDENCY association is equivalent to the existence of corresponding instances of the parent and dependent types. For example, the existence of an instance of an *Employee-Performance History* DEPENDENCY is equivalent to the existence of an instance of an *Employee* and the existence of a corresponding instance of *Performance History* (for this *Employee*).

- A REFERENCE association (see Section 5.1.2) may be represented as a relation between the source type (maintained) and the target type (reference). Both the source and target types are elementary. An instance of the REFERENCE association exists if and only if corresponding instances of the maintained and reference types exist. In other words, the existence of an instance of the REFERENCE association is equivalent to the existence of corresponding instances of the maintained and reference types.

- A COMPOSITION association (see Section 5.1.3) may be represented as a relation between the source type (composite) and the target type (set of component types). In this case, the source type is elementary, and the target type is not. Indeed, an instance of the composite type corresponds to a set of sets of instances for each of its component types. The cardinality of each set of instances of a particular component type may be arbitrary. Consider a *document* composed of *text*s, *picture*s, and *table*s. An instance of the *document* corresponds to a set consisting of three elements. Each element, in turn, is a set of instances of pieces of *text*, *picture*s, and *table*s, correspondingly. Each of these sets may be empty.

- A SUBTYPING association (see Section 5.1.4) may be represented as a relation between the source type (supertype) and the target type (set of subtypes). Again, the source type is elementary, and the target type is not. However, for any given SUBTYPING association instance, the sets of instances of its source and target types will have a nonempty intersection (this does not hold for any other association). In fact, the set of instances of the target type will be a subset of the set of instances of the source type. Consider a supertype *employee* and subtypes *technical employee* and *managerial employee*. An instance of an *employee* may be an instance of either a *technical employee* or a *managerial employee*. The set of all instances of *technical employee*s and *managerial employee*s will be a subset of the set of instances of *employee* (if the SUBTYPING is exhaustive, then the union of these sets of subtype instances will be equal to the set of supertype instances).

• A SYMMETRIC
  RELATIONSHIP   association (see Section 5.1.5) may be represented as a relation between the source type (symmetric relationship object) and the target type (set of participating—regular—entity types). For this association (unlike, e.g., the COMPOSITION association), the number of elements in the set must always be more than one; if it is equal to two, the SYMMETRIC RELATIONSHIP is traditionally called "binary," whereas if it is greater than two, the SYMMETRIC RELATIONSHIP is traditionally called "*n*-ary." The number of elements in each set of typed participating entity instances is equal to one (again, unlike COMPOSITION).

In all cases, except a COMPOSITION-PACKAGE (see below), an instance of the association (i.e., relation) is created simultaneously with the creation of its element(s). Similarly, in all cases, except a COMPOSITION-PACKAGE, the association instance (i.e., relation) is deleted only simultaneously with the deletion of its element(s).

The exception to the association instance rule mentioned above exists for a certain kind of COMPOSITION (PACKAGE, see Section 5.1.3). For a PACKAGE—and only for a PACKAGE—instances of the source and target types may exist independently, without the existence of a corresponding instance of the COMPOSITION association. On the other hand, for an instance of the

COMPOSITION association to exist, naturally, corresponding instances of the source and target types have to exist.

The following **invariant** is valid for all associations, **except COMPOSITION-PACKAGE**:

> **The existence of an association instance is equivalent to the existence of corresponding instances of its source type and its target type.**

For a COMPOSITION-PACKAGE, the equivalence does not hold and is replaced by an implication: the existence of a COMPOSITION-PACKAGE instance implies the existence of an instance of its Composite type and an instance of its Component type.

This general invariant implies that a separate operation for creation or deletion of an association instance is not needed and not available, except for a COMPOSITION-PACKAGE, where instances of participating Composite and Component types may exist in isolation, so that separate operations are needed and available to create or delete an association between these entity instances. These operations are described in Appendix D.

This is not the complete invariant for a generic association: we know more than that!

As we stated above, for any given SUBTYPING association instance, the sets of instances of its source and target types will have a nonempty intersection—and we also stated that this is an exception. The rule is quite different.

For all associations, **except SUBTYPING**, the following **invariant** holds:

> **For any association instance (and its transitive closure), the sets of instances of its source and elementary target types have an empty intersection.**

In other words, an instance that belongs to a source type cannot belong to an elementary target type in the same association instance. (Don't forget that a target type may be a set, so that an elementary target type is an element of this set.) Indeed, in an instance of DEPENDENCY, a parent instance cannot have itself as a dependent; in an instance of COMPOSITION, a composite instance cannot have itself as one of the components; and so on. Moreover, a parent instance cannot have itself as an indirect dependent; and a composite instance cannot be, directly or indirectly, its own component.

More formally, the relation between a source type and its elementary target type is irreflexive. The same is true for the transitive closure of this relation.

Finally, let's discuss an invariant satisfied by all associations (no exceptions this time). Let's consider the sets of types of an instance of a source type and an instance of an elementary target type (recall from Section 4.2 that an object instance can satisfy several types). These sets should be different, although they may have a nonempty intersection. For example, in a DEPENDENCY association, a parent instance and a dependent instance may satisfy a common type, *person*, but they will satisfy other, different, types as well: the parent instance will satisfy the *employee* type, and the dependent instance will satisfy the *child* type. For another example, in a COMPOSITION between *widgets*, both a composite instance and a component instance will satisfy the *widget* type, but the composite instance will also satisfy the *assembly* type.

Therefore, for all associations, the following **invariant** holds:

> **For any association instance, the set of types for an instance of its source type is not equal to the set of types for a corresponding instance of its elementary target type.**

The conjunction of all these boldfaced invariants constitutes the invariant for the generic association. In the description of particular generic associations, this discussion (and this invariant) will generally not be repeated. They have just been abstracted out.

The invariant of an association should be satisfied by the pre- and postconditions for (CRUD) operations applied to the participants of this association. The CRUD operations cannot be executed arbitrarily. An operation usually changes the state of the system, and therefore—as a result—makes possible the execution of some operations and makes impossible the execution of certain other operations. Only those operations for which the preconditions in a particular state of the system are TRUE may be executed in that state of the system.

4.3.2. How an Operation Changes Sets of Associated Instances

Recall from Section 2.4.2 that adding a component to a composite leads to a change in the set of composites associated with this component and also to a change in the set of components associated with this composite. The elements of the new set include all elements of the old set and one new element. This property (postcondition of the create operation) may be generalized for all generic associations. Moreover, a symmetric postcondition exists for the delete operation. This section will formulate appropriate generalizations, so that we will not repeat them in discussing particular generic associations in Chapter 5.

An instance of the source type may be associated with several instances of the target type (don't forget that these types need not be elementary). By the same token, an instance of a target type may be associated with several instances of the source type.[8] For example, a parent instance may have several dependent instances that participate in several different instances of the DEPENDENCY association. Similarly, a dependent instance may have several parent instances that participate in the same or several different instances of the DEPENDENCY association.

What happens after an instance of an association between an instance of the source type and an instance of the target type is created? Naturally, the new set of instances of the target type corresponding to this instance of the source type will consist of the old set of instances[9] of the target type and this new instance of the target type. By the same token, the new set of instances of the source type corresponding to this instance of the target type will consist of the old set of instances of the source type and this new instance of the source type. If the source or target types are not elementary, then this also applies to each element of the set of instances of these types. For example, in a SYMMETRIC RELATIONSHIP association, a new instance of a symmetric relationship object (source type) may be created and associated with an existing instance of a target type (i.e., a set of typed participating entity instances, see above). As a result, we may refer to either the new set of instances of the source type corresponding to this instance of a target type, or the new set of instances of the source type corresponding to a particular element of the target type. In the first case, we may refer to "all symmetric relationship instances corresponding to this set of participating entity instances," and in the second case to a potentially larger set of "all symmetric relationship instances corresponding to this participating entity instance."

Symmetry considerations suggest that analogous rules are applicable for deletion. For example, after an instance of the association between an instance of the source type and an instance of the target type is deleted, the new set of instances of the target type corresponding to the instance of the source type will consist of the old set of instances of the target type minus this instance of the target type. As a result, this new set of instances of the target type may become empty.

---

[8]In either case, we may deal with more than one association instance.

[9]Obviously, the old set may be empty, consist of one element, and so on.

Consider our document example again. If a table is added to a particular document, then:

- The set of documents of which this table is a part will include the old set of such documents and this particular document.
- The set of tables for this document will include the old set of its tables and this particular table.

(A table may be used by, i.e., be a part of, several documents, and a document may use several tables.)

In the description of particular generic associations, including their invariants and CRUD rules, this discussion will not be repeated. It has just been abstracted out.

4.3.3. Graphical Representation

We will propose a simple graphical representation and use it—sparingly—throughout. We will try to make this representation as convenient as possible, and also as close to the "conventional" as possible ("notation is a tool for thought," E. W. Dijkstra). As mentioned above, our notation should denote the asymmetricity of an association and also be able to distinguish between different association types.

In Figure 4.1, an application object is represented as a rectangle, with its name inside the rectangle. To denote the asymmetricity of an association, we

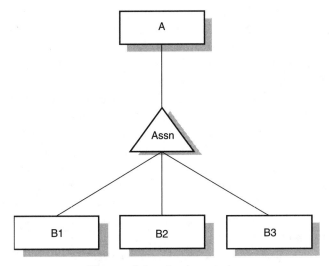

Figure 4.1. An Association.

have chosen a triangle on the link between association elements. This triangle points to one of the association elements, its source. To distinguish between different association types, we have chosen to put the type name into the triangle. A triangle does not denote any application object. These choices are quite straightforward and are by no means the only possible ones.

This picture represents an association Assn between a source type A and a target type—a set of three types, B1, B2, and B3. Clearly, the source type here is elementary, and the target type is not. The triangle with the name Assn in it is positioned on the link between the source type and the target type. Observe that several rectangles (with names B1, B2, and B3) constitute the target type. An instance of this association (instances are not shown in the picture) may relate an instance of A (say, a) to a set of three sets of instances of B1, B2, and B3 (say, {{b11, b12}, {}, {b31}}—the first set consists of two instances of B1, the second is empty, and the third consists of one instance of B3). This example may be compared with the example of a *document*—a composite corresponding to *text*s, *picture*s, and *table*s (its components) (see above).

You will see a few pictures of this kind in the book, with Assn replaced with a particular association name (like "D" for Dependency, or "C" for Composition). We will not repeat this picture in the definitions of generic association types in Chapter 5: pictures used for denoting these association types are the same as the one above. Of course, a picture is not necessary to understand; if you hate pictures, it is quite possible to formulate a specification without them, as shown in the small example below (see also examples in Chapters 5 and 6 and Appendix A).

A graphical representation may also be used to specify mandatory/optional participation of an object in an association and, more generally, "cardinalities." A consistent way to do this is proposed below. Again, a linear representation can perfectly well be used for this purpose; as you will see, the predicate representing this information can be conjoined with (and becomes a constituent of) the invariant for the association.

To distinguish between different application-specific subtypes of the same association type, on a graphical representation we may use different (suffixes for the generic) names inside the triangles. Pretty often, we don't need to do that: we can "show" the association of interest (i.e., point to it). On the other hand, in a linear representation, names of different application-specific subtypes of the same association types will have to be explicit. For example, a graphical representation of an application-specific Composition between an *employee* (component) and a *project* (composite) will look like Figure 4.2.

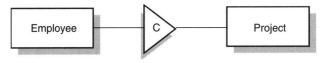

Figure 4.2.   A COMPOSITION.

A linear representation of that same association may look like:

```
PE: Composition (Project, set of Employees).
```

The graphical representation does not explicitly name the application-specific COMPOSITION, whereas the linear representation does (the name is PE). The triangle on the graphical representation contains the generic name of the COMPOSITION and "points to" the composite—the association is asymmetric. Of course, any model consists of several, perhaps many, associations (see Chapter 6).

For large models, as for large programs, it is often necessary to use more than one level of model development and presentation. On the coarsest graphical level, a model should usually fit on one page. This model can be decomposed into several submodels, each of which should fit on one page.

There exist quite a few tools for modeling and, more generally, for information management. Our experience suggests, however, that using pencil and paper or simple object-based software drawing tools often leads to very good results: the essence of the high-level model is captured.[10] Some modelers prefer not to use a graphical representation at all. Our approach agrees with their preferences: a linear approach can perfectly well be used for a specification.

4.3.4. Subtypes of a Generic Association

As mentioned earlier, every generic association is defined by its properties—the business rules for the association. It is possible to define these properties in somewhat greater detail than using the taxonomy above and still remain application-independent (i.e., generic); there exist only a small number of possible variations of these properties for each of the generic as-

---

[10]It may happen that a tool chosen for some particular reason corresponds to lower levels of information model development, that is, levels that are much closer to the implementation than proposed here. In such a case, the modeler may choose for modeling any appropriate higher-level graphical representation and translate it afterwards into the chosen notation. In the same manner, if a programming language chosen for implementation happens to be inappropriate then programming is done using an appropriate notation, which is afterwards translated into the chosen one: "program into a language and not in it" [Gries 81].

sociations. These variations are defined by subtyping the invariant for the association. As an example, consider the COMPOSITION association: as for any other generic association, its (generic) subtypes are defined by refinements of its generic invariant (see Chapter 5). An important generic subtype of a COMPOSITION—CONTAINMENT—is defined by the COMPOSITION invariant conjoined with the predicate stating that the existence of a Component instance implies the existence of exactly one corresponding Composite instance. Of course, there exist other generic refinements of the generic COMPOSITION invariant described in Chapter 5. These refinements define other generic subtypes of COMPOSITION.

In this manner, every generic association can be considered as a supertype for several generic subtypes defined by refining the supertype invariant. As this invariant defines the business rules for the association, we may choose a subtype of the generic association by choosing a set of particular additional business rules. Mandatory or optional participation of an entity in an association is very important in this choice of business rules, and therefore will be described in some detail. These considerations will be applicable to every generic association.

4.4.   Mandatory/Optional Participation; Cardinalities

Let's refine the invariant of an elementary association presented in Section 4.3.1. To do that, we will precisely define the traditional concepts of mandatory and optional participation.

The participation of an entity in an association may be mandatory or optional. An **entity** has mandatory PARTICIPATION in an **association** if *the existence of an instance of the entity implies the existence of a corresponding instance of the association*. In other words, the **association** for this entity has mandatory EXISTENCE. The italicized predicate conjoined with the invariant of an elementary association defines the invariant for mandatory participation of an entity in an association. For example, a dependent entity, in accordance with the DEPENDENCY invariant (see below), cannot exist in isolation, and therefore the DEPENDENCY association satisfies this invariant: a dependent entity has mandatory participation in a DEPENDENCY association. On the other hand, a parent entity can exist in isolation and therefore does not have to satisfy this invariant: a parent entity need not have mandatory participation in the DEPENDENCY association.

However, in many cases, PARTICIPATION of an **entity** in an **association** is optional. In this case, *the existence of an instance of the entity does not imply the existence of a corresponding instance of the association.* Unlike the previous case, the italicized predicate should follow from the invariant for the association. To continue our example, a parent entity has optional participation in the DEPENDENCY association. If the invariant of the association implies mandatory participation of an entity in this association, then the italicized predicate for this entity will violate this invariant and therefore cannot be satisfied.

If the invariant of the association implies optional participation of an entity in an association, then this association may be subtyped. For some application-specific entities in an application-specific instantiation of this association, their participation may be mandatory, that is, the invariant will be (satisfied and) strengthened. This invariant describes a subtype of such an association—an association with mandatory participation of an entity. For example, the DEPENDENCY invariant implies optional participation of a parent. It is possible, therefore, to consider a subtype of DEPENDENCY with mandatory participation of a parent.

This subtyping can be performed for any association with optional participation of an entity in the association. It implies—thanks to its invariant—corresponding sets of permissible operations applicable to the participants of the association. It leads, in particular, to the need to distinguish between the Create operations for the first and non-first instances of this entity participating in the association, and the need to distinguish between the Delete operations for the last and non-last instances of this entity participating in the association. Again, thanks to the invariant, contracts for these operations will have substantially different specifications. These specifications follow from the invariant in a straightforward manner.

4.4.1. When an Isolated Instance Can and Cannot Be Operated Upon

The invariant for an entity with mandatory participation in an association implies that both the entity instance and the **first** corresponding association instance must be created in the same business process.[11] As shown earlier, the existence of an association instance is equivalent to the existence of the in-

---

[11]An indivisible unit of work [OODBTG91] (a transaction) consisting of possibly several single-entity CRUD operations. Within the context of generic information modeling, an operation constituting a business process preserves the invariant of the appropriate association, and no suboperation of this operation preserves this invariant. In other words, an invariant holds only outside of a business process that uses entities referred to in this invariant.

stances of associated entities that belong to its source type and its target type. Therefore, to create the first association instance it will be necessary to create, in the same business process, corresponding first instance(s) of other entities with mandatory participation in this association. Similarly, the **only** instances of the associated entities with mandatory participation in this association should be deleted in the same business process.[12] Violation of these rules leads to violating the invariant of the association (i.e., the semantic integrity rules of the association) and is therefore inadmissible.

Recall from Section 4.3.1 that the only exception to the association-instance-related invariant for the elementary association is provided by the COMPOSITION-PACKAGE. This generic association subtype always has optional existence, and therefore the reasoning of the previous paragraph is not applicable to it.

The invariants for mandatory/optional participation of an entity in an association naturally imply corresponding preconditions for Create and Delete operations. Therefore, only certain Creates and Deletes are permitted:

- Optional participation of an entity in an association implies the possibility of creating an instance of this entity separately (in a separate business process) from an instance of its associated entity. For example, an instance of the parent (with optional participation) may be created independent of its dependent instances, so that this creation will not violate the DEPENDENCY invariant.

- Mandatory participation of both the source and the target in an association implies the requirement for creating the first associated instances (or deleting the last associated instances) of these associated objects in the same business process. It also implies the possibility of creating the not-first (i.e., not-only) associated instances, as well as deleting the not-last (i.e., not-only) associated instances of one of these objects separately.

These generic CRUD rules will be reused for all generic associations.

Business rules for a particular application may require simultaneous creation (or deletion) of associated entity instances belonging to both the source type and the target type, independent of whether these entities have mandatory or optional existence in this association. In this case, the creation (or

---

[12]Both the creation of the non-first instance and the deletion of the non-only ("non-last") instance by itself do not violate the mandatory participation invariant. Therefore, in these cases there is no need to create/delete instances of both associated objects in the same business process.

deletion) of the instances of the source type and the target type will happen in the same business process (for deletion, the traditional name of the operation is **Delete cascade**). In other words, this business process will have to appear as an indivisible operation at the chosen level of abstraction. Moreover, for deletion, some of the objects to be deleted may not be explicitly mentioned in the operation's signature, but will be explicitly mentioned in the operation's assertions (i.e., in the definition of its semantics)!

Consider, as a simple example, the DEPENDENCY association between an *Employee* (a parent) and a *Performance History* (a dependent). The DEPENDENCY invariant is instantiated for this association as follows:

> The existence of an instance of *Performance History* implies the existence of at least one corresponding instance of an *Employee*.

(In our case, the invariant is stronger: the number of parent instances for each dependent instance is exactly one.) If an *Employee* has optional participation in this DEPENDENCY, then an instance of *Performance History* can be created only **after** its corresponding parent instance of *Employee* has been created, because the existence of the latter is a precondition for the creation of the former. Similarly, an instance of *Performance History* may be deleted **prior** to deleting its corresponding instance of *Employee*: the corresponding instances are deleted in separate business processes.

Let's consider a different situation. If this DEPENDENCY association illustrated a parent with mandatory participation (i.e., if the existence of an *Employee* instance would have implied the existence of at least one instance of *Performance History* for this *Employee*), then this different invariant would imply (preconditions for) different operations. Here, it would be possible to delete either one object instance—*Performance History*—if it is not the only *Performance History* for this *Employee*, or both object instances—*Employee* and *Performance History*—in the same business process for the only instance of *Performance History* for this *Employee*.

4.4.2. Providing More Detail When Needed: Cardinalities

In most cases, specifying mandatory/optional participation of an entity in an association is sufficient for further analyzing an association of a particular generic type. As we have seen, this specification refines the invariant of the association (and may define its subtype).

To be even more specific—if the need arises—the concept of "cardinality" may be used.[13] The cardinality of an entity in an association refers to the minimum and maximum number of instances of this entity that may participate in the corresponding association instance. The minimum cardinality for an entity with mandatory participation in an association is greater than zero, whereas the minimum cardinality for an entity with optional participation is zero. Naturally, this specification belongs to the invariant of an association: it specifies a property of the association and its associated objects that should be TRUE outside of any operation on this association.

Default cardinalities may be defined for each generic association: they are implied by the corresponding invariants. (For example, the default—both minimum and maximum—cardinalities for a parent in a DEPENDENCY is "exactly one," whereas the default cardinalities for a dependent is "any number.") Therefore, these cardinalities need not be respecified for application-specific associations. However, in some cases additional non-default "numeric" information may be needed. Here, an explicit specification of cardinalities has to be introduced.

How do we specify cardinalities?

Assertions specify all properties, including cardinalities, in a precise and explicit manner. In particular, they precisely show the meaning of mandatory/optional participation of an entity in an association and, more generally, cardinality. Based on these definitions, it is possible to create a consistent graphical representation, if one so wishes. Cardinality information, in the same manner as the information about mandatory/optional participation of an entity in an association, belongs to the invariant for the association. This invariant may be represented graphically, and in what follows we will show how it can be done. Of course, there may be other **semantically equivalent** ways of doing that; we do not pretend to be graphic artists. By convention, default cardinalities are omitted from the **actual** diagrams in order not to overload them with clutter.

Let us again consider DEPENDENCY as an example. The generic invariant for the DEPENDENCY association formulated below, and described in our examples earlier, implies that **a dependent instance always has mandatory participation in the DEPENDENCY association**. On the other hand, **a parent instance has an optional participation in a DEPENDENCY association,** that is, a parent instance need not have a mandatory associated dependent in-

---

[13]Cardinalities are defined in somewhat different ways by different sources. Our definition is close to the ones traditionally used in ER modeling. However, the developers of the OSI Managed Relationship Model [GRM 93] considered, in addition, a useful concept of "relationship cardinality"—the number of instances of a specific relationship in which a particular entity instance can participate. Naturally, this concept, as well as any other definition of cardinality, may easily be represented using invariants.

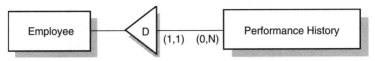

Figure 4.3.   A Parent with an Optional Dependent

stance. Figure 4.3 graphically represents the example we have already discussed.

This is the default for DEPENDENCY. An *Employee* here may have any number of *Performance Histories* (naturally, including 0)—this is shown on the picture by "(0,N)" closer to the *Performance History*—and a *Performance History* may be owned by exactly one *Employee*—this is shown on the picture by "(1,1)" closer to the *Employee*. We do not need to show these default cardinalities on our graphical representation.

Here and elsewhere, the first number in parentheses means minimum cardinality, and the second, maximum cardinality. "(0,N)" means the minimum cardinality of 0 (i.e., optional participation). The maximum cardinality is unknown: the invariant does not refer to "N." If the maximum cardinality is not precisely constrained, it cannot be specified; this has traditionally been achieved by using "N" on ER diagrams. Actually, this "N" stands for an unknown value.

Usually, maximum cardinality is application-specific. Certain applications may be interested in the precise specification of maximum cardinality. When the maximum cardinality **is** known, it is stated in the association invariant. In this case, a number is used (i.e., "(1,1)" or "(1,2)"). Naturally, if the minimum cardinality is different from "0" or "1," then it is also stated in the invariant. (A trivial example is a composite that has to consist of two components—a *cable pair* consists of two *cables;* the cardinality here will be "(2,2).")

What happens if the parent does have a mandatory associated dependent? Another version of our example is shown in Figure 4.4.

Here an *Employee* must have at least one *Performance History,* while a *Performance History* must be attached—as earlier—to exactly one *Employee*. Again, the default cardinalities (in this case, "(1,1)") need not be shown.

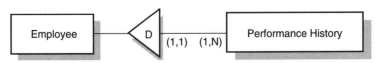

Figure 4.4.   A Parent with a Mandatory Dependent

Let us consider a more complicated association, a COMPOSITION: a composite entity *Document* consists of *Text*s, *Picture*s, and *Table*s. This is an example of a COMPOSITION-PACKAGE: each Component may exist independent of whether the Composite exists and vice versa. Moreover, each Component may be associated with any number of Composites and vice versa (e.g., the same text may be (re)used by several documents). Therefore, the cardinalities for each of the entities will be "any number," that is, "(0,N)"—the default ones. This is illustrated in Figure 4.5.

This picture is somewhat cluttered: it contains too much (default) information. As mentioned earlier, the default cardinalities are usually not shown, and therefore, on this picture no cardinalities need be shown at all.

Let's consider a small change: imagine that the SME wants to discourage *Document*s with too many *Picture*s and therefore prohibits *Document*s with more than five *Picture*s (a somewhat arbitrary constraint). In this case, the appropriate cardinality "(0,5)," stating that there may be at most five *Pictures* in a *Document,* will have to be explicitly stated in the invariant. Conjunction of this predicate to the general invariant for a COMPOSITION can be shown as in Figure 4.6.

The type and subtype of the association (in our case, COMPOSITION-PACKAGE) does not change when any of the **maximum** cardinalities change. However, the mandatory/optional participation of an entity in an association

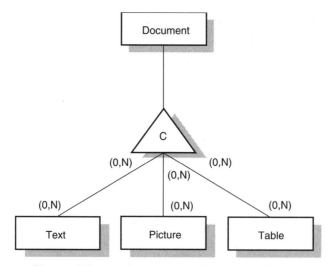

Figure 4.5. Optional Participation of Components

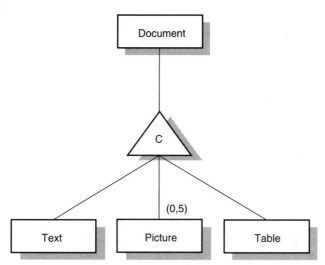

Figure 4.6. Optional Participation of Components: Non-Default Maximum Cardinality

may change the subtype of the association: the invariants of different subtypes of the same generic association have different predicates referring to mandatory/optional participation. As mentioned above, these invariants define which CRUD business rules (i.e., which contracts) are applicable to the association and its elements.

Naturally, if another graphical representation is accepted, then it should be able to represent the same information about cardinalities.

4.4.3. Instance-Specific Rules: A Detailed Example

Let's recall our example of the *Employee-Performance History* DEPENDENCY. Let's postulate that an *Employee* has to have a *Performance History*. We will see how this mandatory participation of an entity in an association (represented in the invariant) will constrain the create and delete operations (i.e., the choice of contracts) applicable for a specific entity instance. Again, we have to consider the state in order to determine what preconditions are satisfied, that is, what operations may be applied. (Naturally, if a precondition for an operation is FALSE, the operation cannot be applied.)

Below, we show how an invariant and a business requirement define which of the operations described in the generic contract library (part of which is shown in Appendix D) should be used to satisfy this requirement.

Invariant

The general Dependency invariant (the existence of a dependent instance implies the existence of its parent instance) AND

The existence of a parent instance implies the existence of at least one of its dependent instances

1. **Requirement:** Add a performance history to a new employee
   Precondition
   The parent instance and all corresponding dependent instance(s) do not exist
   Postcondition
   The parent and corresponding dependent instance exist
   Operation
   Create parent and first corresponding dependent instance

2. **Requirement**: Add a performance history to an existing employee
   Preconditions
   A corresponding parent instance exists
   The dependent instance(s) does not exist
   At least one dependent instance already exists
   Postcondition
   The dependent instance(s) exist
   Operation
   Create a dependent instance(s)

3. **Requirement**: Delete a performance history for an employee who will retain some other performance history(ies)
   Preconditions
   The dependent instance(s) exists
   At least one other dependent instance exists
   Postconditions
   The dependent instance(s) does not exist (the formerly corresponding parent instance exists)
   Operation
   Delete a dependent instance(s)

4. **Requirement**: Delete the last performance history for an employee
   Preconditions
   The parent and corresponding dependent instances exist
   This is the only remaining dependent instance
   Postconditions
   The parent instance and corresponding dependent instance(s) do not exist
   Operation
   Delete dependent with parent instances

4.5.   Beyond Elementary Associations

The associations referred to in Section 4.3.1 and described in detail in Section 5.1 are "elementary": they are the smallest building blocks for creating an information model. These associations are reusable in any model, for any application. However, these are not the only reusable associations. There exist other, less elementary, associations that are still generic and reusable for any application—consider, for example, associations representing multiple inheritance, or a "recursive COMPOSITION." These associations should be specified at the generic level because many application-specific models include them. Naturally, they should not be reinvented from scratch for every application in which they are used. They are not elementary because it is possible and easy to show how they are composed from simple, elementary building blocks.

Section 5.3 describes in more detail some typical simple nonelementary associations. These nonelementary associations are described in the same manner as elementary ones. An invariant defines the static properties of the association and associated entities, and the pre- and postconditions define contracts for operations. These definitions are rather simple: they are obtained by conjoining the assertions for the component elementary associations. As their assertions are rather straightforward, complete definitions will not be presented.

4.6.   Usage of the Library:
Application-Specific Assertions

Every application-specific object class belongs to one or more application-specific subclasses of elementary generic associations. For example, an *employee* may be a component in an *employee-project* COMPOSITION and a parent in an *employee-child* DEPENDENCY. Therefore, it inherits the assertions for the appropriate elements of those generic object associations that are supertypes of these application-specific associations. Naturally, additional application-specific assertions may also exist. They will be conjoined with the generic ones. This is a usual property of SUBTYPING: any subtype inherits the properties of its supertype(s) and, in addition, has subtype-specific properties of its own. Application-specific invariants should not contradict the appropriate generic ones: if they do, then the model is inconsistent and should be repaired.

Consider a simple example of an *employee-project* COMPOSITION. If the participation of an *employee* in this COMPOSITION is mandatory, then the precondition for creating an instance of the *employee* (i.e., adding this instance to an instance of the *project*) will imply, in particular, the existence of a corresponding instance of the *project*. This application-specific precondition is obtained by replacing, in the generic precondition, formal parameters (Component and Composite) with actual parameters (*employee* and *project*). However, in a particular application there might be a need for an "additional" application-specific precondition: an *employee* added to a particular *project* must have security clearance. This additional predicate is conjoined with the generic one to obtain a complete application-specific precondition for adding an *employee* to such a *project*. Naturally, the generic precondition has not changed. For another (or the same) *project*, there may be a need for another application-specific precondition: the *employee* should be willing to travel 50% of the time. Certainly, this additional predicate is again conjoined to the generic precondition to obtain a complete application-specific one.

Naturally, these considerations apply to the invariants as well. In fact, the preconditions for creation discussed above immediately follow from the invariants, and these invariants are formulated in the same manner: by conjoining the generic clauses and the application-specific ones. Although it is preferable to use invariants in modeling, for some SMEs it may be substantially easier to reason in terms of (contracts for) applicable operations. This is acceptable; the resulting model will be the same.

This example is sufficiently simple. However, it shows that the generic association library can be reused in different application-specific situations, and that, for different applications, additional application-specific assertions will be conjoined to the generic ones.

The Library

5

> *"In many situations, it is not extreme freedom that yields progress, but well-considered restriction.... Complexity is equivalent to huge quantities of details. Neither their design nor their documentation are sufficient for economic administration of work and utilization; a sea of details confuses not only the ones who approach the system from outside; it confuses as well the development team, the ones who are supposed to know the plans and the work from inside."* [Zemanek 90]

This chapter defines the generic associations belonging to the library (re)used in all applications. All these associations are subtypes of the elementary association type described in Chapter 4. Therefore, they inherit the properties of the elementary association. These properties may be referred to here, but will not be described in detail again: they will be reused.

The general approach and concepts underlying the library have been presented earlier, in Chapters 2 and 3. The components of this library deal with generic information modeling constructs encountered in all applications.

The definition of each association is based on the invariant of this association. The operations applicable to the association and its elements should preserve this invariant, and therefore their definitions follow from this invariant. For each association we provide an overview, including the description of properties of both the association and its elements (these properties are based on the **invariant** of the association), and some typical examples of using the association in particular applications. Most associations can be

---

Joseph Morabito and Naidu Guttapalle contributed to the text of this chapter.

subtyped (e.g., a COMPOSITION may be hierarchical or nonhierarchical), and the description of the association includes the definition of its subtypes. We use a graphical representation for each association described in Chapter 4: a triangle on the link between the source and the target, pointing to the source. However, as noted earlier (and later), this book is not about pictures: any other graphical representation may be used, as long as it differentiates between different associations, shows that they are not symmetrical, and does not impose the need to specify implementation-dependent constraints.

The elementary generic associations are used to build other reusable constructs. Some of these may be encountered in (almost) all applications. The presentation of elementary associations is followed by a less detailed description of some of those reusable nonelementary ones.

The definitions of the elementary associations are followed by a short description of domains—constructs used for specifying sets of values of structural properties of objects. These sets are often the same for different structural properties of possibly different objects, and it would be unreasonable to define them more than once.

The set of generic associations described here is not intended to be complete; it can be extended if it appears that different applications have certain other constructs in common. These constructs will have to be understood, specified, and then reused—in the same manner as the constructs already described in the specification of this generic library of reusable information modeling components.

The (extensible) generic association library described here consists of only a few (uninstantiated) association types and their immediate subtypes. Any application-specific object (e.g., an *employee*) may belong to more than one of these association types (e.g., be a parent in a DEPENDENCY, a component in a COMPOSITION, etc.): see below, Chapter 3 on peer contracts, and Chapter 6.

The contracts for CRUD operations follow from the invariant of the (subtype of the) association. Some of these contract specifications are outlined here; some are provided in Appendix D. Other contract specifications can be provided, rather straightforwardly, in the same manner. Therefore, for those readers who want an overview of the generic association library, reading this chapter is sufficient; for those who want to use the library, reading this chapter is necessary, but not sufficient. The latter category of readers will have to use Appendix D as well.

Naturally, Appendix D is not supposed to be read from cover to cover. Rather, as with any reference, it should be consulted by its users, that is, by modelers, model reviewers, SMEs, developers, and others, when a specific need arises to understand, create, criticize, or refine an information model.

5.1.   Elementary Associations

5.1.1. Dependency

The existence of an entity instance may be declared to depend on the existence of another entity instance: if the latter is deleted, then the former must disappear as well. This construct represents a DEPENDENCY association between a parent entity and a dependent entity.[1] For instance, a dependent of an employee is of interest to the application only as long as the employee exists within the scope of the application. An instance of a dependent entity may depend upon more than one instance of a "parent" entity: a child may have two parents working for a company. The instances of the parent entity, however, should belong to the same type. Properties of a parent entity do not depend upon properties of its dependent entity.

A dependent entity instance is not necessarily automatically deleted when its parent instance has to be deleted: sometimes the deletion of a parent instance is not permitted if dependents exist. On the other hand, a dependent instance cannot be created unless a parent instance already exists. These considerations imply appropriate contract specifications for CRUD operations. For example, the contract specification for creating a dependent instance should include, as its precondition, the existence of a parent instance for this dependent instance.

In some cases, a parent entity has mandatory participation in a DEPENDENCY association (see Chapter 4), that is, has to have a mandatory associated dependent entity. For such a kind of DEPENDENCY, the first instance of a dependent may be created only together with (in the same business process as) the instance of its parent. Therefore, the operation "create [only] a dependent instance" is not applicable for this kind of DEPENDENCY if this dependent is the first one for this parent. Naturally, this operation is applicable for the non-first dependent of this parent.

> **Invariant (generic).** A parent type corresponds to one dependent type. The existence of a dependent instance implies the existence of at least one corresponding instance of its parent type.[2] The existence of an instance of the DEPENDENCY association is **equivalent to** the existence of instances of both the corresponding dependent and parent types. (The

---

[1] Also called "weak entity" (P. Chen) or "characteristic entity" (E. F. Codd).

[2] If the existence of an entity depends upon the existence of exactly one instance of each—rather than only one—of its "parents," then this construct represents a SYMMETRIC RELATIONSHIP: these parents belong to different types (see below).

last statement is inherited from the invariant for the elementary association, see Chapter 4.)

Invariant for mandatory. If a parent entity has mandatory participation in the DEPENDENCY association, then the existence of an instance of a parent entity implies the existence of at least one corresponding instance of its dependent entity.

Possible graphical representation. A triangle with a "D," pointing to the Parent, on the link between the Parent and the Dependent.

EXAMPLES

1. **Accounts and account transactions.** A (real or potential) *bank customer* may have several *accounts*. An *account* has (a non-empty history of) several *transactions* associated with the *account*. An *account* has to have at least one (mandatory) associated *transaction,* so that for the *account-transaction* DEPENDENCY the invariant for mandatory (see above) should be satisfied. Therefore an account can be created only in the same business process with creation of its (first) transaction ("deposit"). An *account*, in turn, is a dependent entity with respect to its *customer*. An *account* may be jointly owned by more than one *customer*, and therefore should not necessarily be deleted after an owner of the *account* decides to discontinue being a *customer*.

2. **Beneficiary.** In a *savings plan for salaried employees*, the *beneficiaries* are dependent instances with respect to the *plan* instance. However, the *main beneficiary* can be deleted only together with cancelling the *plan*.

5.1.2. Reference Association

A REFERENCE association associates a reference entity with a maintained entity. A reference entity in this association represents **read-only** instances used for creating/updating/deleting instances of other, maintained, entities.[3]

---

[3]This is a good example of tolerating imprecision. The particular rules for using the reference entity instances as input information for creating/updating/deleting instances of maintained entities are application-specific. However, these rules have some important properties in common, and these properties are encountered often enough to warrant their abstract formulation and reuse.

A reference entity has its own operations (not just read-only) within another generic association, possibly outside of the particular application area. In other words, a particular entity is a reference entity only within the context of a REFERENCE association.

Operations applied to an instance of a maintained entity in a REFERENCE association should leave instances of its reference entity unchanged. A separate instance of a reference entity need not exist for each instance of the maintained entity. In other words, more than one instance of a maintained entity may refer to the same instance of a reference entity. Moreover, an instance of a maintained entity may refer to several instances of a reference entity.

Reference entity instances may be used both to validate the preconditions for, and as information sources[4] for, creating/updating/deleting instances of its maintained entity. Values of some properties of an instance of the latter entity should agree with (in the simplest case—but not always!—be equal to) values of some properties of an appropriate instance of the reference entity. The particular appropriate instance need not be prespecified in the operation.

When a reference entity is changed—as a result of an operation in the context of another association—all instances of its maintained entities will have to be examined (triggering condition) and, if necessary, changed. This should ideally take place in the same business process, to satisfy the invariant for the REFERENCE association (see below). However, in practice there may be a delay, in which case you may want to keep more than one version of the reference and maintained entities (and update the values of maintained entity instances later—"lazy update"). If more than one (e.g., both the "old" and the "new") versions of reference entity instances will simultaneously be of interest to the application, then an immediate massive update of "maintained" entity instances may not be needed.

This approach leads to the need to solve the problem of simultaneous existence of more than one (possibly time-dependent) version of information (both for instances and for classes) [Casais 90]. The update of a reference entity instance may lead to the need for updating a large number of instances of its maintained entity. However, it may be acceptable for an application not to update these instances immediately (in fact, it may be the only realistic possibility, due to the need for the application to be constantly on-line). In this

---

[4]By providing parameters and possibly an algorithm (postcondition).

case, a "lazy update" may be triggered when an instance of a maintained entity is updated only after it is referred to by any operation. As a result, the "mass update" of a large number of maintained entity instances is diluted in time, and the delays become acceptable: instead of one long delay, the application will suffer many very short delays that its users will not even notice.

A REFERENCE association should be distinguished from an association between a structural property value and its domain (see Section 5.2). A maintained entity instance refers to a set of properties of a reference entity instance rather than to one of these properties. On the other hand, one structural property value refers to one domain instance. A maintained entity instance may use more than one reference entity instance of different types (see the *speeding ticket* example in Section 5.3.2); a reference entity instance may be used by more than one maintained entity instance of the same or different types. This is very different from the property-domain association: a domain may be used by more than one property, but a property may use only one domain.

There exist two subtypes of the REFERENCE association. One, ORDINARY REFERENCE association, is supported during the lifetime of its associated entities. Therefore, a change (i.e., creation of a new version) of a reference entity instance will immediately or eventually lead to corresponding changes (i.e., creation of new versions) of associated maintained entity instances.[5] Another subtype of the REFERENCE association, the REFERENCE FOR CREATE, is of interest only during the create operation. In this case, an instance of a maintained entity may be created when the criteria described by the properties of the corresponding reference entity instance are satisfied (possibly by an instance of another reference entity, see the example in Section 5.3.2). After the maintained entity instance has been created, any change in the property values of the corresponding reference entity instance does not affect this instance of the maintained entity. In other words, the invariant for the REFERENCE association applies only to the version of the reference entity that existed when the maintained entity was created (i.e., "lazy update" of the maintained entity instance will never happen). REFERENCES FOR CREATE usually participate in notifications (see Section 5.3.2).

For an ORDINARY REFERENCE, the creation of an instance of the maintained entity is the result of a user-initiated operation. For a REFERENCE FOR CREATE, this creation may be either user-initiated, or the condition for creation may be a triggering condition, in which case the creation is "system"-initiated.

---

[5]The concept of versions need not be used for immediate changes of maintained entities.

If the participation of a maintained entity in a REFERENCE association is optional (see Section 4.4), not every maintained entity instance requires a corresponding reference entity instance. However, after creation of a maintained entity instance, the reference-maintained instance correspondence may subsequently be established.

The updating of maintained entity instances initiated by a change of the reference entity instance is accomplished as follows: The validation of each maintained entity instance is an application operation. If this validation operation indicates property correspondence between a reference and maintained instances (i.e., the invariant for the REFERENCE association is satisfied), nothing happens (i.e., properties of these instances remain unchanged). If there is no correspondence, then the invariant has to be satisfied: the maintained instance is updated, deleted, or a new version is created for it.

Invariant. A maintained type corresponds to one reference type. The existence of a maintained instance implies the following:

> If a corresponding instance of the reference type exists, then the property values of the instance of the maintained type shall correspond[6] to property values of an appropriate version of the corresponding instance of the reference type. The appropriate version of the reference type should be its current version, or, in the case of a "lazy update," a prior version, or, in the case of REFERENCE FOR CREATE, the version that has been used for creating an instance of the maintained type.

As follows from the invariant for the elementary association (see Section 4.3.1), the existence of an instance of the REFERENCE association is **equivalent to** the existence of instances of both the corresponding reference and maintained entities.

Possible graphical representation. A triangle with a "Ref," pointing to the maintained entity, on the link between the reference and the maintained entities.

EXAMPLES

1. **Validation (use in a precondition).** To be able to create an instance of the *employee* entity, it is necessary to validate the properties of the potential instance with respect to the corresponding instance of the

---

[6]The result of an appropriate Boolean function with properties of the reference and maintained entities as parameters should be TRUE.

job classifications reference entity, in order to find out whether the combination of values of the following properties is acceptable: *job title, level, salary, degree, years of experience.* (An instance of the *job classifications* entity corresponds to a *job title.*)

2. **Validation (equality) (use in a precondition).** To be able to create an instance of an *inventory item* (e.g., before accepting a shipment), it is necessary to check whether an instance of a *catalog item* reference entity with the corresponding set of property values exists. In other words, a potential instance of an *inventory item* is not acceptable unless its description exists in the catalog.

3. **Information source (use in a postcondition).** While creating/updating the *taxes withheld* set of properties of an *employee* entity, the corresponding instance of the *tax withholdings* reference entity is to be referred to, in order to define the parameters for (or even the algorithm and parameters for) this operation. When an instance of the *tax withholdings* entity is changed, a mass update of the corresponding instances of the *employee* entity is to be accomplished.

4. **REFERENCE FOR CREATE.** See the notification example (Section 5.3.2) for a nonelementary molecule.

Note: It is possible for an entity to be clearly outside of the scope of the current application area, but to have (REFERENCE) associations to entities in this area. A reference entity may, but need not, be out of the scope of its application area.

5.1.3. Composition

A composite entity "consists of" (in other words, is an "aggregate of") component entities. A component may or may not exist independent of the composite entity. A composite entity may or may not exist without components. Structural properties of a composite are not inherited by components. Some operations applied to a composite entity propagate to its components. For instance, if a *document* consists of chunks of *text* and *pictures*, then operations such as "read," "copy," "move,"[7] and so on propagate to all components of the document. There exists at least one property of the composite entity such that changes in some properties of its component entities will change its value. Such property of the composite is known as its resultant or

---

[7]Considered as "updates," as certain property values will be changed.

hereditary property.[8] In our *document* example, creating a new version of a component or changing the number of pages in a component will result in changing the values of appropriate resultant properties of the composite (*document*). Properties of a composite that are independent of components' properties are known as emergent properties.[9] A composite must have at least one emergent property (of identity), or there would be no reason for its existence.

A composite type corresponds to one or more component types, and a composite instance corresponds to zero or more instances of each component type. The sets of application-specific types for the composite and its components should not be equal (irreflexivity).[10] In other words, there should exist at least one type of the composite such that it is not, at the same time, a type of its components. Creating, updating, or deleting a component does not change the identity of the composite.

In our example of a COMPOSITION association between a *document* and its components, changing a chunk of *text* in a *document*, adding a new *chapter*, or even adding a new type of component (e.g., *table*) does not change the identity of the *document*. However, when, for example, the identity of a participating entity instance in a SYMMETRIC RELATIONSHIP association instance is changed, the SYMMETRIC RELATIONSHIP association instance is deleted and a new one is created (see Section 5.1.5).

A component instance may belong to zero or more composite entity instances (e.g., the same *picture* may be a component of zero, one, or more than one *document*). A component entity may belong to more than one type of composite entity; for example, a *picture* may belong to a *document* or a *viewgraph*.

A COMPOSITION association may be subtyped by means of several mutually orthogonal hierarchies.

- Serializability
  - Nonordered components (**default**).
  - Ordered components (i.e., a sequence for which it is possible to determine whether a certain component is *before* another compo-

---

[8]Note that a parent of a dependent entity does **not** have any resultant properties.

[9]See [Wand 89]. Wand assumes, however, that a resultant property depends upon only one constituent, and that all emergent properties of a composite object are "linked by object laws" to properties of several of its constituents.

[10]This follows from the invariant for the generic association (see Section 4.3.1). This should also be true for the transitive closure of the COMPOSITION association.

nent). The components may be ordered (i.e., the predicate *before* is defined) either only within a component type or across component types of the same COMPOSITION.

Due to the possibility of using *before* in the pre- and postconditions of operations for ordered components, it is possible to define operations like: *get next component after a given component, insert a component before a given component,* and so on. The definitions of these operations are straightforward and will not be provided here. For nonordered components, these operations are not permitted.

- Changeability[11]
  - Static components—After a COMPOSITION has been established, no dynamic entry/departure of components into/from the COMPOSITION is possible.
  - Variable components—Dynamic entry/departure of components is possible (**default**).

    Changeability refers to whether or not the collection of components becomes frozen. For static components, the COMPOSITION is established and frozen: there exists an operation *freeze* that prohibits any further creations/deletions of components. The specification of *freeze* is straightforward and will not be discussed here. For variable components, an operation *freeze* is not permitted.

- Hierarchy
  - Hierarchical—A component instance may be associated with not more than one composite instance.
  - Nonhierarchical—The COMPOSITION association is a network, that is, a component instance may be associated with more than one composite instance (in different instances of the same COMPOSITION association) (**default**).

    "The COMPOSITION is hierarchical" is equivalent to "for every component instance there may exist at most one corresponding composite instance." This is, of course, an additional conjunct of the COMPOSITION invariant for the hierarchical COMPOSITION.

- Linkage
  - ASSEMBLY—COMPOSITION is associated with the composite.
  - SUBORDINATION—COMPOSITION is associated with the component.
  - PACKAGE—COMPOSITION is not associated with either the composite or component (**default**).

---

[11]The concepts of dynamic entry and dynamic departure are also used in [GRM 93].

- LIST—COMPOSITION is associated with both the composite and component.

  The existence of a composite instance for the ASSEMBLY implies the existence of at least one corresponding component instance. The existence of a component instance for the SUBORDINATION implies the existence of at least one corresponding composite instance. There are no additional rules for the PACKAGE. The PACKAGE is the only subtype of COMPOSITION for which the operation "Create a COMPOSITION association" for existing composite and component instances is defined. Moreover, the PACKAGE is the only association for which such an operation is defined.[12] In other words, the PACKAGE is the only association for which the existence of an instance of the association is not equivalent to the existence of the associated object instances. Finally, for the LIST, the existence of a component instance implies the existence of at least one corresponding composite instance, and the existence of a composite instance implies the existence of at least one corresponding component instance.

All subtypes of COMPOSITION are orthogonal. As different COMPOSITION subtypes are orthogonal, they may be combined by explicitly picking one of the possibilities from several (not necessarily all!) of these subtypes. We may define, for instance, a hierarchy of variable ordered packaged components. Some of these combinations are more likely than others and may therefore be named; for instance, a ***containment***[13] (see below) is a hierarchical subordination (with the other two subtypes being default, i.e., nonordered and variable). A particular COMPOSITION association inherits properties of the appropriate subtypes from each of its participating SUBTYPING hierarchies (i.e., multiple inheritance). In this example, a containment inherits properties of both subordination and hierarchy.

It may happen that component entities associated with the same composite entity in the same COMPOSITION have different properties (e.g., instances of one component type can be associated only with this particular composite, and instances of another with any composite), and therefore belong to different subtypes of COMPOSITION. This situation becomes not wor-

---

[12]Naturally, the same is true for "Delete a COMPOSITION association."

[13]The OSI Management Information Model, before the appearance of the General Relationship Model draft standard [GRM 93], stressed only this subtype of COMPOSITION [OSI/NM Forum 91, ISO/IEC 91-1, Kilov 92].

thy of classification because of the extraordinary complexity of the case analysis. Naturally, in every particular application-specific case it is straightforward to combine (conjoin) the existing COMPOSITION subtypes described in this section (compare [Zave 92]). Although every such case is straightforward, the enumeration and analysis of all of them is almost beyond human understanding.

> **Invariant (generic).** A composite type corresponds to one or more component types, and a composite instance corresponds to zero or more instances of each component type. There exists at least one resultant property of a composite instance dependent upon the properties of its component instances. There exists also at least one emergent property of a composite instance independent of the properties of its component instances. The sets of application-specific types for the composite and each of its components should not be equal.

Identity is an emergent property of a composite, and therefore creating, updating, or deleting a component instance does not change the identity of the composite instance.

As follows from the invariant for the elementary association (see Section 4.3.1), the existence of an instance of the COMPOSITION association—for all subtypes of COMPOSITION except PACKAGE—is **equivalent to** the existence of an instance of the corresponding composite and a set of corresponding instances of its component entities.

The generic invariant permits a component instance to belong to any number (zero or more) composite entity instances. Certain subtypes of the generic COMPOSITION association are more restrictive.

The invariants of subtypes of the generic COMPOSITION follow. (Naturally, the generic invariant for COMPOSITION is inherited by each of its subtypes.)

> **Invariant for ordered components (serializability).** For two component instances in an ordered COMPOSITION association instance, it is possible to define whether one is **before** the other.
>
> **Invariant for static components (changeability).** After a static COMPOSITION association instance has been **established**, the preconditions for creating or deleting a component are FALSE.
>
> **Invariant for hierarchical COMPOSITION.** For every component instance, there exists **at most one** corresponding composite instance in a given hierarchical COMPOSITION association.

Invariants for linkage subtypes. For an ASSEMBLY, the existence of a composite instance implies the existence of at least one corresponding component instance. For a SUBORDINATION, the existence of a component instance implies the existence of at least one corresponding composite instance. For a LIST, the existence of a composite instance implies the existence of at least one corresponding component instance, and the existence of a component instance implies the existence of at least one corresponding composite instance.

EXAMPLES

1. **Document**. A *document* consists of chunks of *text*, *pictures*, and *tables*. The same chunk of *text* (e.g., biography of an author) may belong to more than one *document*. The same *picture* (e.g., a slide) may also belong to more than one *document*. The number of chunks of *text*, *pictures*, and *tables* is not predefined, although it may (but need not) be stated that a *document* should contain at least one chunk of *text*.

2. A certain ***personal computer system***, in accordance with its Owner's Manual, consists of a *"main unit,"* monitor, *keyboard*, *mouse*, *cables*, *system software*, and *documentation*. The *main unit* includes, in particular, *memory*, (possibly) an *internal hard drive*, a *floppy drive*, and various *cards*. Any of these components may be changed, but the identity of the *computer system* will remain the same.

3. ***Road layers***. A paved *road* is typically composed of a *static part* (a COMPOSITION that, once created, is never changed) and a *dynamic part* (a *layer* or layers that can be added or removed). The static COMPOSITION consists of a *concrete base*, *asphaltic concrete*, and *sheet asphalt*. The dynamic part consists of *sheet asphalt layers* that can be deleted (removed) or added (resurfaced). In other words, a road is a COMPOSITION of two components (*static part* and *dynamic part*), and each of these components, in turn, is a COMPOSITION of other components.

4. ***Journals***. All issues of a particular journal on a library shelf associate into a COMPOSITION. Certainly, the components within this COMPOSITION are ordered (by date).

5. **ASSEMBLY**. In an automobile assembly plant, an information model may contain a composite *Car* with components such as *Engine*,

Transmission, and so on. Each component instance exists independently before being "assembled" into a composite instance of *Car*. The corresponding instance of the composite *Car*, on the other hand, does not exist prior to at least some assembly; that is, an instance of *Car* does not exist until at least one corresponding component instance has been associated with it.

6. ***Supermarket*** (PACKAGE). In a supermarket, instances of various *products* sold to a customer may be modeled as components that are eventually packaged or associated with a corresponding composite instance of a *shopping bag*. In this case, corresponding instances of the composite (the *shopping bag*) and components (*products* sold) exist independently, and a composition is created by associating (packing) them. Similarly, a composition association may be deleted by unpacking; the result of such a deletion is that all corresponding instances of the *shopping bag* and *products* bought still continue to exist.

Possible graphical representation. A triangle with a "C," pointing to the composite, on the link between the composite and the components.

5.1.4. Subtyping

Object instances can be grouped together using the notion of types. All instances of a type possess the same properties, so that a type may be described as a predicate that defines these properties [ODP 2]. In other words, these instances satisfy the type. Different types may have common properties. They may be abstracted out into a "supertype," whereas the types themselves are called "subtypes." On the other hand, subtypes may be obtained by adding interesting properties to the properties of a supertype. (SUBTYPING may be considered as being on the borderline between generic and application-specific information modeling.) An instance belongs to a (sub)type because it satisfies the (sub)type's predicate. An instance of a subtype has properties that distinguish it from an instance of another subtype. In other words, an instance of a subtype satisfies the invariant of (i.e., the predicate that defines) this subtype, in addition to the invariant for its supertype. Such an invariant may be application-specific. The predicate for a type may or may not be formulated by means of other explicitly specified properties. In the latter case, type membership becomes a predicate (of the type) to be explicitly specified by the user during "create" (i.e., by extensional inclusion)—compare with "enumeration types" in some programming languages.

A SUBTYPING association need not be **static**. This happens when a new type (a supertype) may be dynamically attached to an instance of another type (a subtype). Of course, this **dynamic** supertype may also be detached from such an instance. The identity of an instance does not change when a new supertype is attached or detached[14] (an *employee* can become a *patient* and therefore acquire properties of a *patient*, but the identity of this *employee* will remain the same). A type can participate in several different static or dynamic SUBTYPING hierarchies (see below). The default SUBTYPING is static.

For static SUBTYPING, the set of instances of a subtype is a subset of the set of instances of its supertype. In other words, if an instance belongs to a subtype, then it belongs to its static supertype(s). Properties of a (static or dynamic) supertype are inherited by its subtypes.[15] (In particular, a supertype and all its subtypes belong to the same element of a generic association; e.g., if a supertype is a dependent entity in a particular DEPENDENCY, then all its subtypes will also be dependent entities in the same DEPENDENCY.) Therefore, a subtype's properties are a superset of its supertype properties. For dynamic SUBTYPING, this is true only for those instances of a subtype that are also instances of its dynamic supertype.

A subtype may have different supertypes within different SUBTYPING associations (multiple inheritance). In this case, the conjunction of all predicates defining all of the supertypes should not be false.[16] More than one classification hierarchy for the same supertype may exist (e.g., an employee may be subtyped by gender or job classification). This nonelementary association is described in Section 5.3.5.

A well-known example is a supertype *employee* with subtypes *technical employee, managerial employee,* and *support employee*. As another example, consider the same supertype *employee* with subtypes *full-time employee* and *part-time employee*—a different classification hierarchy for the same supertype. Observe that all subtypes of an *employee* inherit properties of the *employee*: have dependents, immediately participate in a COMPOSITION (with respect to a composite *department*), refer to a reference entity (with respect

---

[14]Although a new object identifier may appear: object identity and the existence of a particular object identifier are not equivalent.

[15]To quote [OODBTG 91], inheritance means deriving new definitions from existing ones. This approach includes both restriction and extension [Dahl 90]. It does not guarantee that an operation defined for the supertype will be available for the derived type: although a natural number may be derived from an integer, subtraction is not always defined for natural numbers. Derived types are not considered as subtypes (see, e.g., [Cusack 91]). They will not be discussed in this book.

[16]Different ways of dealing with property name clashing exist [Booch 91, Meyer 88].

to the *job classification* reference entity), etc. A subtype may also have additional properties of its own: for example, a *technical employee* may participate in a SYMMETRIC RELATIONSHIP (see Section 5.1.5):

```
author: SymmetricRelationship (authorship, {technical
    employee, book})
```

The associations between a supertype and its subtypes give rise to two orthogonal constraints: the "exclusiveness" of the subtypes and the "exhaustiveness" of the subtypes.

The exclusiveness refers to whether or not a given supertype instance can belong to (i.e., have the properties of) more than one subtype. If it can, we say the subtypes are **overlapping**; if not, the subtypes are **disjoint** (consider the supertype *employee* with overlapping subtypes *in-house lecturer* and *in-house student*). For disjoint SUBTYPING, an instance of a supertype may have properties of, at most, one of its subtypes. The default SUBTYPING is disjoint.

The exhaustiveness refers to the participation of all supertype instances in the SUBTYPING hierarchy. If every instance of a supertype belongs to (i.e., has the properties of) at least one subtype, we say the hierarchy is **exhaustive**; if not, the hierarchy is **nonexhaustive**. The latter is probably an incomplete specification; an instance of a supertype should generally belong to its subtype. The default SUBTYPING is exhaustive.

As mentioned earlier, SUBTYPING may also be static or dynamic. For dynamic SUBTYPING, if an instance of a subtype belongs to its dynamic supertype, then—as for any SUBTYPING association—all properties of a supertype are inherited by its subtype (i.e., a subtype instance will acquire new properties—the properties of its new dynamically attached supertype). As an example, consider *furniture*, *computers*, *cables*, *software*, and so on, in a company. These types are very different and modeled differently. However, instances of each of these types become *inventoried items* when they are assigned to some employee. This happens dynamically, so that the properties of an *inventoried item* are dynamically attached to an instance of *furniture*, *computers*, or others. Of course, properties of an *inventoried item* can be dynamically "detached" from such an instance (when the employee leaves the company or does not need the instance anymore). If, however, the company decides to attach the properties of an *inventoried item* to only one type (e.g., *computers*), then it would be reasonable to model *inventoried item* as either a dynamic supertype, or a nonexhaustive static subtype of a *computer*. Certainly, repetition of the exactly same nonexhaustive static SUBTYPING for several different types is not advisable; dynamic SUBTYPING should be used instead.

For multiple inheritance, there may be more than one supertype associated with a given subtype. In this case, for static SUBTYPING hierarchies, one business process will usually have to handle all these hierarchies. For example, an instance of a given subtype will have to be created, together with properties of all its supertypes and this subtype, in the same business process. This construct is a nonelementary molecule (see below). The same approach applies to deletion of an instance of such a subtype: after deletion, the instance will not exist anymore, and therefore will not have properties of any of its supertypes; naturally, this should happen in one business process.

Dynamic SUBTYPING implies multiple inheritance. When an instance is created, it has (the properties of) some static type (i.e., it satisfies the predicate of this type). When another (super)type is attached to this instance, the existing predicate is conjoined with the new one—with the predicate that defines the dynamically attached (super)type. As in static multiple inheritance, the conjunction of these predicates should not be false.

Dynamic SUBTYPING cannot be exhaustive because it does not satisfy the invariant for exhaustive SUBTYPING.

Invariant. A supertype may participate in several SUBTYPING associations; a subtype may participate in several SUBTYPING associations. A supertype in a SUBTYPING association corresponds to one or more subtypes. The set of instances of a subtype is a subset of the set of instances of its static supertype. If an instance of a subtype belongs to its supertype, then the structural and behavioral properties of a subtype constitute a superset of the structural and behavioral properties of its supertype. (This is property inheritance. It is always true for a static supertype. If SUBTYPING is dynamic, then it is true only for those instances of a subtype that belong to its dynamic supertype.)

As follows from the invariant for the elementary association (see Section 4.3.1), the existence of an instance of the SUBTYPING association is equivalent to the existence of an instance of a supertype having the properties of one of its subtypes.

Invariant for exhaustive. The union of sets of instances of all subtypes is equal to the set of supertype instances.

Invariant for overlapping. There exist two different subtypes such that the intersection of the sets of instances of these subtypes may be not empty.[17]

---

[17]The careful reader will have noticed that these expressions are translated from a formal specification (e.g., written in Z) into English.

These invariants imply that it is possible to attach a subtype to, or detach a subtype from, an instance of a supertype if and only if the SUBTYPING is overlapping or nonexhaustive. It is possible to attach a supertype to, or detach a supertype from, an instance of a subtype if and only if the SUBTYPING is dynamic.

EXAMPLES

1. **Library loan**. A *borrowable item*[18] (with properties like *inventory number, catalog code, name, price*, etc.) can be borrowed by a *library patron*, so that there exists a symmetric relationship object *borrowing* that associates these two regular entities (with properties like *date due*, etc.). However, usually within a library, borrowed items are classified into *books, computer programs, cassettes, videos,* and so on, with corresponding properties of interest to the library (e.g., *maximal borrowing time*). Therefore, each of these subtypes will have the properties of the *borrowable item* and perhaps some other ones. Moreover, each of these subtypes will immediately participate in a SYMMETRIC RELATIONSHIP association with *borrowing*, so that *borrowing* will become a supertype as well. This SUBTYPING may or may not be explicitly shown in the model.

   If *library patrons* are subtyped into *town residents* and *out-of-towners* (with different borrowing privileges), then *borrowing* will be subtyped into a Cartesian product of subtypes of its participating entities (i.e., *town residents borrowing books, town residents borrowing cassettes, . . . , out-of-towners borrowing books,* etc.).

2. **Student/Lecturer**. An *employee* may be an *in-house student* or *in-house lecturer*. These subtypes are overlapping, as the same *employee* (instance) may be a *lecturer* for one course and a *student* for another course. If the *employee* ceases to be a *lecturer,* then its instance need not be deleted.

3. **To subtype or not?** A *document,* which is a COMPOSITION of *texts, pictures, tables,* and so on, may be considered instead as a COMPOSITION of *document components.* In this case, the modeler together with

---

[18]A *borrowable item* is a particular instance of an item rather than an item with a particular title. For instance, ten copies of this book are ten—and not one!—*borrowable item*s. Moreover, each subtype of a *borrowable item* (e.g., *book*) may also be a subtype of some other supertype (e.g., *computer science information sources*).

the SME decided that it is reasonable to abstract common properties of *texts*, *pictures*, *tables*, and so on, into their supertype—a *document component*. As a result, a *document* becomes a COMPOSITION of *document components*, which are, in turn, subtyped into *texts*, *pictures*, *tables*, and so on.

Possible graphical representation.   A triangle with an "S," pointing to the Supertype, on the link between the Supertype and the Subtypes. For overlapping subtypes, a "+" is added to the contents of the triangle; for exhaustive subtypes, an "E" is added. For dynamic SUBTYPING, a "D" is added to the contents of the triangle.

5.1.5. Symmetric Relationship

A symmetric relationship object associates two or more "equal," "symmetric" regular objects. An instance of a symmetric relationship object corresponds to exactly one instance of each of these regular (participating) objects. A regular object instance, on the other hand, may participate in more than one instance of a SYMMETRIC RELATIONSHIP association of the same or different types. The symmetric relationship object has its own properties. They provide information about the symmetric relationship object itself, and not information about any of its participating objects. There exists at least one such property—the property of identity.

A SYMMETRIC RELATIONSHIP is a subtype of an association[19]—in the same manner as DEPENDENCY and COMPOSITION are. Not too much is known about an association (see the association invariant in Chapter 4); when particular properties of an association are known, they define its subtype. A SYMMETRIC RELATIONSHIP is (a subtype of) an association of which the particular properties are known: there exist at least three associated objects (the symmetric relationship object and at least two participating entities), and a symmetric relationship object instance corresponds to exactly one instance of each participating entity. Anecdotal evidence (quite a few complicated models) suggests that SYMMETRIC RELATIONSHIP associations are encountered much more seldom than the other associations. We may even suggest that a SYMMETRIC RELATIONSHIP association is often used as "none of the above," when "the above" have been considered inappropriate (see Chapter 6).

An instance of a symmetric relationship object can exist only if all its

---

[19]The terminology (symmetric relationship) used here is the same as that in the OSI General Relationship Model [GRM 93].

participating entity instances exist. Therefore, after the deletion of an entity instance, the corresponding symmetric relationship instance(s) should not exist. Such a deletion of a symmetric relationship instance may occur after or before the deletion of the entity instance: a business rule may permit deletions of certain entity instances only if they are isolated, that is, if they do not participate in SYMMETRIC RELATIONSHIP association(s). If an entity instance is replaced by another entity instance (i.e., having a different identity), then the corresponding symmetric relationship instance(s) will also have to be replaced by another symmetric relationship instance(s).[20]

If one or more of the entities participating in a symmetric relationship have subtypes (see above), then the symmetric relationship may have subtypes as well. These subtypes may or may not be of interest to the particular application.

A symmetric relationship object may participate in other SYMMETRIC RELATIONSHIPS, have dependents, components, and so on, and therefore its behavior in a SYMMETRIC RELATIONSHIP association is the same as the behavior of the "traditional" ER construct known as an associative entity.

The regular entities participate in their SYMMETRIC RELATIONSHIP association in a symmetric manner: first, the regular entity instances may be created separately from the symmetric relationship instance and from each other; second, when a regular entity instance is deleted, the corresponding symmetric relationship instance is deleted, but the other regular entity instances in this SYMMETRIC RELATIONSHIP association instance are unaffected.

By default, a regular entity may optionally participate in a SYMMETRIC RELATIONSHIP association. As noted before, it means that an instance of a regular entity may exist in isolation, without participating in an instance of the SYMMETRIC RELATIONSHIP association. However, some regular entities may have mandatory participation in their SYMMETRIC RELATIONSHIP association, whereas some others may have optional participation in the same SYMMETRIC RELATIONSHIP association.

Invariant. A symmetric relationship type corresponds to two or more participating entity types, and a symmetric relationship instance corresponds to exactly one instance of each of these types. The existence of a symmetric relationship instance implies the existence of exactly one entity instance for all participating entity types.

---

[20]The reader may wish to compare these considerations with the ones for a composite entity (see above).

As follows from the invariant for the elementary association (see Section 4.3.1) and from the previous paragraph, the existence of an instance of the SYMMETRIC RELATIONSHIP association is equivalent to the existence of an instance of the corresponding symmetric relationship object and of exactly one entity instance for all immediately participating entities.

As follows from the invariant for the SYMMETRIC RELATIONSHIP, creation or deletion of an entity instance immediately participating in a SYMMETRIC RELATIONSHIP instance does not lead to creation or deletion of instances of other entities immediately participating in this SYMMETRIC RELATIONSHIP. It means that entities within a SYMMETRIC RELATIONSHIP are independent of each other.

EXAMPLES

1. **Ownership**. An *employee* owns *office equipment*. There exist properties of *ownership* that are properties neither of the *employee* nor of *office equipment* (e.g., *acquisition date*, *usage (public or private)*, etc.). When an *employee* leaves the company, all the corresponding instances of *ownership* are deleted. However, the *equipment* stays with the company. Symmetrically, if the *equipment* is destroyed, the *employee* does not leave the company.

2. **Product entry**. A *Customer directory product entry* in a hypothetical telephone company directory is a symmetric relationship object, with *Format specification* and *Customer directory data* as its regular entities. The page layout of the *Customer directory product entry* is not a property of either *Format specification* or *Customer directory data*.

Possible graphical representation. A triangle with a "Rel," pointing to the symmetric relationship object, on the link between this object and its participating entities.[21]

---

[21]Graphical representations of SYMMETRIC RELATIONSHIPS and "associative entities" have been used since at least 1976. They distinguish between an "entity" and a "relationship," that is, try to graphically show that a relationship is allegedly not an entity, but rather something different. Often, they use the same graphical representation for the relationship object and for the relationship association. This approach leads to serious problems; the need to introduce an "associative entity"—needlessly trying to distinguish between a "relationship" and an "associative entity"—is just one of them. There is no compelling reason for using the traditional representation. In fact, the association between a symmetric relationship object and its immediately participating entities, and the association between, say, a composite entity and its immediately participating components, differ only in the assertions defining the association. The object approach suggests finding (and using) a supertype for things having common properties, and a generic association (see Chapter 4) is just that. There is no reason to state that one kind of association (SYMMETRIC

5.2. Domains

A domain is a set of all possible values from which a structural property of an entity draws its values. This notion was introduced by [Codd 70] within the context of the relational model: it is the glue that holds the (relational) database together (C. J. Date). In information management, domains have been used less often [Codd 90, Kent 79, Kilov 83, Kilov 89, Date 90]. Domains support business rules for structural property values (most often, names of "things" and their aliases of different nature) and maintain the integrity of these values in a centralized manner. Domains are specified by abstracting out and reusing common characteristics of different properties of possibly different entities: **one fact** is put **in one place**. A good example is a domain composed of the 50 states of the Union: on creating/updating an entity, the property of which is defined on top of this domain, the new value of this property has to belong to the domain and not just be a two-character alphabetic string. (Naturally, different properties of different entities may be defined on top of this domain.)

In finding objects, the role of structural properties and domains is subordinate, as usually only the "representative" structural properties are considered. However, in both the final stages of semantic modeling and, especially, application-specific modeling, all structural properties, and therefore domains, should be examined. Domains may help to find interesting associations between objects. **The concept of domains is**, of course, **generic**.

Most systems support trivial domains equivalent to base types: integers, reals, strings, and sometimes booleans, date, and time. This approach only scratches the surface of a deep concept. Thanks to abstraction and reuse, user-defined domains [Kilov 89] provide not just better property checking, but better understanding of the information model, in particular, by getting rid of redundant and inconsistent property definitions.

As noted earlier, there exists an analogy between domains and reference entities. However, these concepts differ: a reference entity instance is used for "maintaining" several properties of an entity rather than values of a single property of perhaps several different entities. As a rule, related properties of a reference and a maintained entity are defined on the same domain.

RELATIONSHIP) is more equal than any other kind of association (e.g., SUBTYPING, COMPOSITION, DEPENDENCY, etc.) [Kilov 91-1]. Therefore, the generic pictorial representation for all kinds of associations should be the same, with some distinction between association subtypes. The graphical representation proposed here is certainly not conventional. However, as E. W. Dijkstra noted, "As long as numbers are only used to chisel on buildings the years in which they were built, Roman numerals are fine; as soon as we want to do arithmetic with numbers, the Hindu/Arabic decimal system—though unconventional when it was introduced in Europe—is objectively more convenient" [Dijkstra 89].

A domain can be defined intensionally (i.e., by means of a set of explicit rules for domain elements) or extensionally (i.e., by means of actually enumerating domain elements). In the latter case, an analogy exists with Pascal enumerations. The sets of possible values for domains may be fixed, as in Pascal (e.g., "yes," "no," "maybe"), almost fixed (e.g., countries of the world), and varying (e.g., colors). (The method of physical storage is irrelevant, although the temptation to store fixed sets in the "program" should of course be resisted!)

Domains may be used for supporting different user-defined names (i.e., aliases) belonging to different classes (e.g., "short names," "official names," "nicknames," "foreign language names," etc.) for the same thing. For instance, within the domain "50 States," "New Jersey" may have aliases "NJ," "N.J.," and "nj," with "NJ" being the preferred one. As a result, the correctness of property values on bulk data entry/update may be verified in a centralized manner by the "system" rather than by "applications." All values (including aliases) should be manually checked only once, when they are entered into their domains for the first time (naturally, there may be many aliases belonging to the same class; some of them may be defined—for input convenience—even by a data entry clerk). Afterwards, the existence checking will be done by the system. As a very useful side effect, domains make new manual coding unnecessary, check the correctness of existing codes,[22] and use actual—rather than "computer-oriented"—names. Coding, if it is needed at all, is better done by a computer system than by a human being!

The character set of a domain refers to the external representation(s) of a domain value. This would permit, for example, the same value to be expressed in several languages. There is a default character set for each domain. Some domains may be composed of other domains. For instance, a domain *Address* may be composed of the subdomains *Number, Street, City, State,* and *ZIP Code®.*[23]

Domains for "system" data (i.e., entity names, property names, domain names, and so on), may be defined in the same manner as user-defined ones. For instance, aliases for these data may be handled in exactly the same manner as aliases for user-defined data.

A domain is usually defined "on top of" some other domain. As a trivial

---

[22]It is easy to err when manual codes are entered, as they have no semantics and are close to each other. A wrong code that differs slightly from a correct one has a good chance of being accepted because it may well correspond to another correct name. However, if "actual names" are entered, then a wrong name has a good chance of being rejected by the system because name-state space is much larger than code-state space.

[23]ZIP Code is a registered trademark of the United States Postal Service.

example, base types (see above) are used in the definition of any domain. As a more semantically meaningful example, consider subdomains as subtypes (of a domain, and not of an entity!). (For instance, there may be a subdomain "East Coast States" of the domain "50 States.") A subdomain inherits all characteristics of its parent domain and has some extra characteristics (e.g., membership in a set). All elements of a subdomain are elements of its parent domain.

Domains are a primary notion with respect to properties: property values belong to a user-defined type, and this type is a domain. Therefore, it is recommended to define domains first and always include a domain name in a property definition. Domain names (unlike property names) should be unique within an application.

A domain definition includes its ancestors (starting from base types) and explicitly specified characteristics of domain elements (rules or enumeration, see above). The conjunction of these characteristics should unambiguously define, for each value, whether the value belongs to the domain. Typically, for a domain with a numeric base type the rules will include range(s) of acceptable values, range(s) of prohibited values, and user-specified functions (e.g., "even"). For a domain with a text base type, the rules will include the acceptable alphabet, maximal length, and alias class characteristics. One of these classes is marked as "privileged" and will be, by default, used for information output.[24] CRUD rules for domain elements (and property values) do not depend on a particular domain name: they depend on the extensional or intensional way of specifying domain elements. For instance, operations such as "add an alias," "change name," and "delete an alias" are applicable to any domain with extensional specification of its elements, whereas "is an element?" is an important operation applicable to any domain.

A domain is a generic concept that describes the value space of structural (state) properties. It is *not* an association between objects. A domain has assertions that govern its behavior.

A property value that refers to a domain instance value does not refer to a particular alias. The alias is used when the property values are to be shown to the user or input by the user.

> **Invariant**. The existence of a structural property value implies the existence of a corresponding domain value or correspondence with a rule for this domain. (The existence of a domain value does not imply the existence of a corresponding property value for any entity with a corresponding property.)

---

[24]An output specification can require the "main" alias from a specified class (e.g., foreign language output).

5.3. *Beyond Elementary Associations*

Some associations are encountered in many applications, and therefore can and should be reused. This idea is not new, and the library of Section 5.1 described several of these associations. However, a generic reusable association may be more complicated than one of these elementary associations. It will be composed of (or built from) these elementary ones. This section presents a library of such nonelementary associations that are still generic and therefore reusable in any application. Each of these associations may be visualized as a big molecule composed from elementary ones. Usually, the invariant for a nonelementary molecule is straightforward: it is a conjunction of the invariants for the elementary molecules—components of the nonelementary one.

It is possible to hide information about the components of big molecules, although not completely desirable: in the same manner as objects and elementary molecules, these big molecules do not exist in isolation either. Therefore, when these molecules are associated, their components should be visible because they will be referred to in the invariants for these associations and also in the contracts for their operations. Information hiding for nonprimitive molecules (using clusters) is desirable in an overview of the model for better understanding. This information should not be hidden in more detailed contract specification (refinement). This happens because invariants and contracts for operations are often jointly owned by several components of several nonprimitive molecules, rather than confined to only one of these.

In what follows, we will present some "typical" nonelementary associations encountered in quite a few applications. We will not formulate their invariants as these are straightforward, and we will often restrict ourselves to the graphical rather than linear representation: these nonelementary associations are providing examples of the use of elementary ones. "In presentations like these the best a picture can do is to give an example, an instance" [van Gasteren 90]—exactly what the pictures below will be doing.

5.3.1. Recursive Associations

A "recursive association" is an association between two instances of the same type. This association type is an association between an entity type and the same entity type. One of the traditional representations of this construct looks like Figure 5.1.

Such an approach is unnatural (compare [Kalman 91]). It is not clear which entity instance is associated with which (this representation misses information). In fact, any association associates distinguishable entities. Even

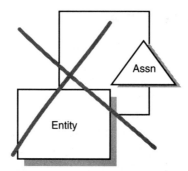

Figure 5.1. Recursive Association—A Traditional Representation

if an entity instance may belong to both, it is not associated with itself: an association instance associates different entity instances each of which exhibits distinguishable behavior. Figure 5.1 excludes this behavior. Clearly, the *entity* may be subtyped on the basis of these criteria, and the construct becomes cleaner and easier to understand (see Figure 5.2).

An entity instance may belong to both *SubA* and *SubB* (this is possible because the SUBTYPING is overlapping).

The invariant for this molecule may be expressed as follows: each instance of the *entity* is an instance of at least one of its subtypes. An instance is not associated with itself.

The invariant for this molecule has been obtained by conjoining the invariants of its primitive molecules. The same instance of an *entity* may par-

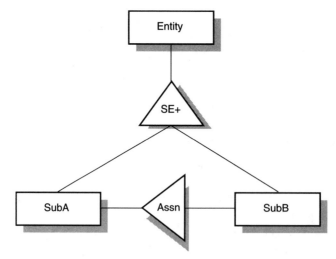

Figure 5.2. Recursive Association—A Better Representation

ticipate in different instances of the association ASSN—for example, in one case as an instance of *SubA*, and in another case as an instance of *SubB*.

Consider a simple (and well-known) example. An *employee manages* an(other) *employee*. This is certainly a SYMMETRIC RELATIONSHIP. The two regular entity types are not identical: the symmetric relationship object *manages* associates two subtypes of an *employee*: *supervisor* and *supervisee*. An *employee* may participate in this SYMMETRIC RELATIONSHIP both as a *supervisor* (in one instance of this association) and as a *supervisee* (in another instance of this association) (see Figure 5.3).

The same approach is used for representing "recursive COMPOSITIONS." A typical example of such a construct represents an assembly (*BigPart*) composed of subassemblies (*SmallParts*), as in Figure 5.4.

Of course, properties of a *Part* when it participates in the COMPOSITION as a *BigPart* will differ somewhat from the properties of the same *Part* when it participates in the COMPOSITION as a *SmallPart*. For instance, an instance of a *Part* that participates in an instance of the COMPOSITION association as a

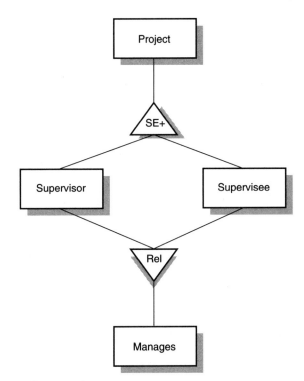

Figure 5.3. Recursive SYMMETRIC RELATIONSHIP

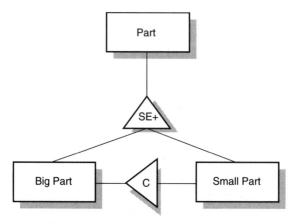

Figure 5.4. Recursive COMPOSITION.

SmallPart is considered atomic[25] in this COMPOSITION instance. This same instance of a *Part* that participates in another instance of the COMPOSITION association as a *BigPart* is not considered atomic in this COMPOSITION instance.

Additional modeling considerations related to this molecule are presented in Chapter 6. Naturally, this molecule need not be implemented as three different relational tables (see Appendix B).

5.3.2. Notifications

A notification is "emitted" (in other words, an event "happens" or a notification operation is executed), when a certain condition is satisfied. This is different from executing an ordinary operation. An ordinary operation is executed when the user requests its execution and if its precondition is satisfied. We do not discuss in this book the particularities of the user request. When the precondition for an operation is satisfied, the operation may, but need not, be executed. For a notification, things are different: when the notification condition is satisfied, the notification operation will be executed (if its precondition is satisfied). This notification condition is called "triggering condition" by some.

To model a notification, we can use REFERENCES FOR CREATE. Usually, the only result of a notification operation is the creation of an instance of some entity (often called a *notification*). This instance of a *notification* is never changed after creation. Therefore, a *notification* becomes a maintained

---

[25]That is, indivisible at the chosen level of abstraction.

entity, and its REFERENCE association is a REFERENCE FOR CREATE. However, the *notification* has two reference entities: the properties of one of them are monitored, and the properties of the other define the notification criteria.

In this construct, the creation of a notification instance is implied by satisfaction of the notification criteria by the state of the monitored object. Update and delete operations for a notification instance are not defined in this molecule. A precondition for creation may be conjoined if needed.

In the same manner as any other construct, a notification can be represented either graphically (as in Figure 5.5) or linearly. In a linear representation (equivalent to the graphical one), we will have to include two elementary associations:

```
monitored-to-notification: reference for create
(monitored object, notification)
criteria-to-notification: reference for create
(notification criteria, notification)
```

In other words, the invariants for both instantiations of the REFERENCE FOR CREATE will have to be satisfied; these invariants will be conjoined. Of course, the invariant for a REFERENCE FOR CREATE is reused from Section 5.1.2.

As a simple example, consider a *speeding ticket* (notification) issued if the speed of the *automobile* (monitored object) at a particular place of the

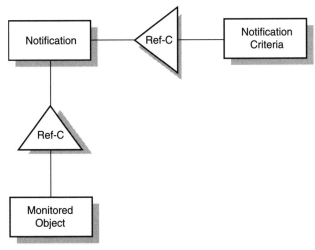

Figure 5.5. Notification

road exceeds the *permitted speed at that place* (notification criterion). If the *permitted speed* will subsequently change, the *speeding ticket* that has been issued (created) earlier will still exist and will not be changed. A precondition for creation of a speeding ticket is: "the automobile does not belong to a diplomat."

5.3.3. Exclusive OR

This molecule defines a case where an entity participates in either one set of associations, OR another one, but never in both simultaneously (see Figure 5.6). To model that, we need to use disjoint subtypes of the entity, with each subtype participating in its corresponding "exclusive OR" association. This kind of SUBTYPING is natural: a SUBTYPING association is based on some properties of an entity, and in this case the property "participation in a particular association." Whether this property is implemented as an attribute value is irrelevant—this is not an information-modeling issue.

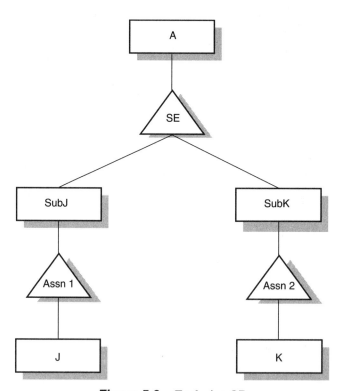

Figure 5.6.   Exclusive OR

The invariant for this molecule can be expressed as follows: every instance of an object participates in exactly one of a given set of associations.

The entities *SubJ* and *SubK* in Figure 5.6 are not artificial: they represent logical subtypes of entity *A* that appear because of different properties of different instances of *A*. It does not mean that entities *SubJ* and *SubK* should (or should not) be implemented as different physical objects (see Appendix B). This implementation issue is decided by the developer, who takes into account system-specific considerations.

5.3.4. A COMPOSITION of Symmetric Relationships

A typical example of a SYMMETRIC RELATIONSHIP provided in many texts is a "supplier-part-shipment" one. It is presented, informally, as "a supplier supplies parts; a part may be supplied by many suppliers, and a supplier may supply many parts." Consider, then, an instance of a shipment—what is it? Is it a shipment of a particular part from a particular supplier, or, rather, a collection of parts shipped by the same supplier? Certainly, it cannot be both. Therefore, the original "specification" is incomplete. **An object is missing** from it: this object is a "line item," that is, an elementary shipment of a particular part from a particular supplier. Naturally, a shipment is a COMPOSITION of such line items. Each line item may have its own properties (e.g., quantity, discount, name of responsible person, etc.). Each shipment, in turn, has its own properties (e.g., discount, order number, total cost, etc.). A correct specification for this simple model will graphically be represented as in Figure 5.7.

The invariant for this nonelementary molecule is straightforward: it is a conjunction of the invariants of its elementary molecules (i.e., of the SYMMETRIC RELATIONSHIP and COMPOSITION).

Molecules of this kind are encountered in a substantial number of applications. Of course, the "SYMMETRIC RELATIONSHIP" may be replaced with any other association.

5.3.5. Multiple SUBTYPING Hierarchies

A SUBTYPING association between a supertype and its subtypes exists because instances of these subtypes satisfy the supertype predicate and, in addition, some other predicates. In other words, these instances have all the properties of the supertype and some other, additional, properties. To separate different concerns of the enterprise, it is convenient to collect semantically related subtypes together. Several such orthogonal collections (multiple

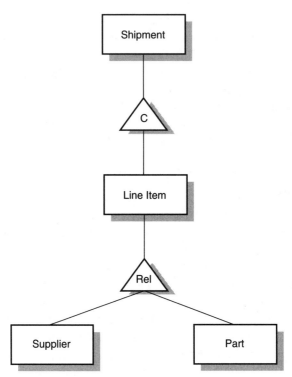

Figure 5.7.   Supplier-Part-Line Item-Shipment

SUBTYPING hierarchies) may exist for a given supertype. A simple example is provided by a supertype *employee* that can be subtyped into a gender SUB-TYPING hierarchy and a job classification SUBTYPING hierarchy.

The invariant of this molecule states that the existence of a supertype instance implies the existence of a subtype instance for each of its SUBTYPING hierarchies corresponding to static exhaustive subtypes. In other words, the conjunction of the predicates for each of these subtypes has to be satisfied. The create operation creates an instance of such a supertype and attaches to it properties of subtypes for each of these multiple SUBTYPING hierarchies (of course, if the subtypes are static and exhaustive). In our example, when an employee instance is created, we "take" one subtype from each of its SUBTYPING hierarchies (i.e., one gender subtype and one job classification subtype).

Let's try to show a graphical representation. First, the gender SUBTYPING hierarchy is shown in Figure 5.8.

Next, the job classification SUBTYPING hierarchy is shown in Figure 5.9.

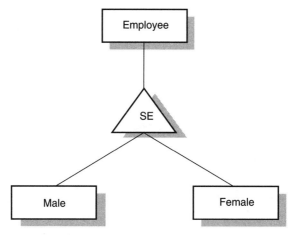

Figure 5.8.   Gender Hierarchy

To create a nonelementary molecule that combines these hierarchies, we may do what is shown in Figure 5.10.

Of course, we may also choose to consider the job classification hierarchy first and create a different-looking but semantically same graphical representation. However, this unnecessary choice is not needed; even more important, the exact same information is repeated here more than once, leading to loss of clarity. However, it is possible, even graphically, to show one fact in one place (see Figure 5.11).

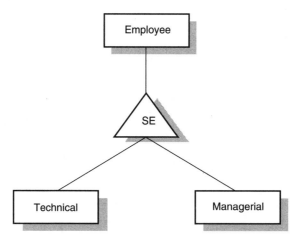

Figure 5.9.   Job Classification Hierarchy

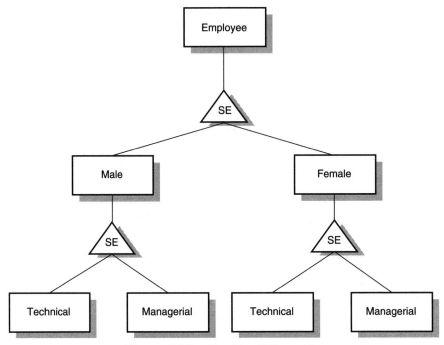

Figure 5.10.   Combined Hierarchies

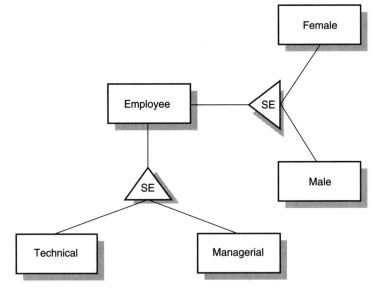

Figure 5.11.   Combined Hierarchies: One Fact in One Place

Here no unnecessary choices are to be made, and no information is repeated.

Of course, if a linear representation instead of a graphical one is chosen (like the one elsewhere in this chapter), it is only natural to write a specification of two (named) SUBTYPING associations:

```
gender: SubtypingExhaustive (Employee, {male, female})

jobClassification: SubtypingExhaustive (Employee,
   {technical, managerial}).
```

No information is repeated here.

Guidelines

6

*"**W**ith a view to requirements modelling, the purpose of a model is to ask questions and demonstrate that answers can be given entirely in terms of the model. If such answers can not be found then the model is inadequate." [Mac an Airchinnigh 91]*

This chapter is about mastering some fundamental concepts of information modeling. In Chapters 2 and 3 we have established the basic approach, and in Chapters 4 and 5 we have presented the library to be used. However, application of this approach using the library requires intellectual effort and practical wisdom. This chapter attempts to help: it shows an extended example, together with the process of creating an information model, and also shows certain reusable patterns of reasoning. When we create an information model, we have to extract, understand, and formulate relevant information. The key to being able to do that is to formulate questions that can be reasonably discussed and answered, without "using a computer as a crutch" [Reynolds 81]. This chapter shows some of these questions and an example of their use.

Although it is not a science (yet?), information modeling certainly has some aspects of science: you can formulate explicitly and learn the basic principles. However, information modeling is much more than knowledge of these basic principles. You have to master their application if you wish to manage complexity. Like many crafts, this mastery is often gained through apprenticeship—working with a master. However, there is a better and more logical way—make the effort to write down explicitly what a good master does. Naturally, there is no one right way to model (as there is no one right way to program): different masters may use the same concepts differently.

Our exposition is not a miraculous all-encompassing methodology that provides all the questions to ask and pretends that the questions it does not provide do not exist. What follows is not and cannot be 55 steps to create a good model, just as there could not and should not be 55 steps to create a good program. Although a model can be discovered through a series of explicit questions, an experienced modeler will recognize and reuse patterns and try to justify or discredit a hypothesis built on these patterns. Naturally, patterns are recognized and reused at all levels of information management (see Chapter 2). The patterns relevant to the craft of information modeling describe how objects interrelate.

This chapter will show a rather simple, but reasonably complete, example of developing a model using a walkthrough. It will discuss how to use the association library described in Chapter 5. It will present some important reusable patterns of reasoning. Finally, it will present some considerations about existing models and tools.

6.1. An Example

Let us start with a simple example to understand how to manage information about employees, projects, and departments. In this scenario, subject matter experts[1] (SMEs) walk through a reasonably trivial enterprise (where the modeler and you, the reader, will not have to spend time understanding the subject matter area itself; in particular, you don't have to spend time finding the objects).

The model discussed here will be used to explain how elementary associations are found and why a particular association is a COMPOSITION, REFERENCE, DEPENDENCY, and so on (see Chapter 5). When a modeler succeeds in finding elementary associations, they will become established patterns of reasoning in walking through more complicated enterprises. This is how traditional programming is taught: elementary programs are shown first, to keep the technicalities of basic building blocks out of the way when creating the complete application.

In this example, the goal is to discover the business rules about employees and departments. In particular, we need to understand what is always

---

[1]Preferably, there should be more than one SME. As they are likely to have different and even contradictory viewpoints, such deliberations help to crystallize the understanding.

true, regardless of any business operations and regardless of whether the information system for our enterprise will ever have a computer-based implementation. In technical terms, we need to discover the invariants that will define the context for rules that govern the applicable operations. The use of abstraction generally suggests looking for one building block—one elementary molecule—at a time and abstracting away the others. Of course, these molecules do not exist in isolation: an object may participate in more than one such molecule. The interaction of these molecules can be understood later.

6.1.1. Questions and Answers

A typical modeling session has a question-and-answer format. Modelers ask questions, and SMEs answer them.[2] The questions that help to discover objects, associations, and their properties are facilitated by a walkthrough, during which the SMEs introduce the enterprise. The process of understanding is informal, but its result is formal—a specification.

Quite a few of the questions are driven by the generic association library. These questions are an almost direct reuse (with formal parameter substitution) of the invariants for the generic associations and pre- and postconditions for operations applied to their elements.

In the following, the modelers' questions are numbered, the SMEs' answers follow them, and the modelers' decisions and comments are *italicized*.

Some basics.

0. *Q* What is this enterprise about? What are the most important things there?

A Employees, departments, and projects. Employees work for departments.

Comment: It seems that there should be three objects—employees, departments, and projects. They are not isolated. However, there should exist no modeling objects without a business purpose (participating in message passing as a message, message sender, or message recipient is not a business purpose by itself). For example, a relational modeling concept (e.g., the relation "works for" with two foreign keys introduced to satisfy the relational modeling rules) is also not an object on the information modeling level. Thus, "works for" or "assignment" is not a

---

[2]A modeler and a SME might be the same person.

thing and therefore should not be introduced as an object in our model. Probably, the association between departments and employees is a COMPOSITION and not a SYMMETRIC RELATIONSHIP. Let's test that assumption. Also, let's forget about projects for a moment (abstraction).

1. *Q* Are there departments that have no employees?

  A Yes, but only during "start-up."

2. *Q* Are there **ever** employees that are not assigned to a department?

  A No, never.

*Comment: To force the SME to think carefully about the answer, we stress **ever** in the question.*

3. *Q* Is the department considered the same department as employees come and go?

  A Yes.

4. *Q* Are there properties of a department that depend on properties of its employees?

  A Yes; for example, the budget is a function of the number and job titles of employees.

Comment: Employees and departments are not peers (i.e., are not independent) (because first, properties of a department depend upon properties of employees; and second, employees cannot exist without a department). But even if they were, we prefer COMPOSITION over SYMMETRIC RELATIONSHIP because the SME has not identified "assignment" as a thing. We try to create modeling objects that correspond to the things the SMEs want to talk about (i.e., those things the business manages). An inexperienced programmer or modeler will say: "OK, but in a relational DBMS you will have to create a table for 'assignment'." The answer is: "Maybe,[3] but we don't care since we are modeling. Business rules are implementation-independent." Question 4 is based on one such generic business rule—the invariant for the COMPOSITION (see Chapter 5). Other questions or collections of questions are also based on such generic business rules.

---

[3]Or maybe not. In a relational implementation, it is possible to have three tables—for "employee," "department," and "assignment"—or two tables (with appropriate foreign keys), only for "employee" and "department," or even one (non-normalized) table, for "employee." The information model remains the same and does not depend on this choice.

5. *Q* Are employees **ever** assigned to more than one department?

  A No.

6. *Q* If a department is dissolved, what happens to the employees that are assigned to it?

  A They must be assigned to another department or terminated.

Comment: These questions define a particular subtype of a COMPOSITION—CONTAINMENT. They correspond to the definitions of the components of the generic association library (see Chapter 5).

Another comment: We could, but choose not to, find out whether a maximum number of employees per department exists (maximum cardinality). These details will be dealt with at the next pass through the model.

Still another comment: At this stage we could, but again choose not to, draw a simple picture of this COMPOSITION.

And now let's recall that projects exist. We'll try to discover whether they are associated with employees or departments.

7. *Q* Are projects assigned to people or to departments?

  A People.

Comment: The SME does not want to consider this "assignment" as a thing, either. (Compare with the Comment to Question 0.) Moreover, projects and people are not independent.

8. *Q* Are there ever projects that are not assigned to anyone?

  A Yes, I think so.

9. *Q* Are there employees that have no project assigned?

  A Yes, but there are not many of them.

Comment: This is probably a COMPOSITION-PACKAGE, but we decide that we are not too much interested in COMPOSITION subtypes during the first pass because we have seen these things before, and because at this stage of modeling more important things need to be covered.

10. *Q* Are projects worked on by employees from more than one department?

  A Yes.

Comment: The hypothesis here is that projects are COMPOSITIONS of employees, just as departments are. If the answer to Question 10 were "No," then departments could be considered as COMPOSITIONS of projects, which, in turn, could be COMPOSITIONS of employees. This is not the case here.

Another comment: Question 10 is nontrivial. It tries to establish the associations, if any, between employees, projects, and departments.

Still another comment: Now is probably the time to draw a simple picture, because there are too many things to be captured in a fairly complex situation (see Figure 6.1).[4]

For those modelers and readers who hate pictures, it is possible to express the same information in a linear form, for example:

```
C1: Containment (Department, set of Employees)
C2: Composition (Project, set of Employees).
```

As noted in [BETA 91], "the graphical notation and the textual notation are two alternative representations of the same language." Either notation may be used for analysis (i.e., information modeling).[5] Because our graphical representation is equivalent to a linear one, drawing an appropriate pic-

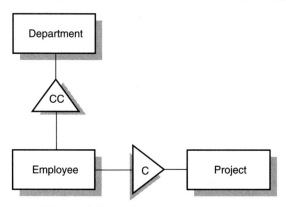

Figure 6.1. The Specification So Far

---

[4]An interesting question arises: Does this picture show one association or two? We prefer to separate our concerns by considering two associations (elementary molecules), each with its own properties. These molecules may even be modeled by different applications (see below). However, one entity (*employee*) belongs to both, and therefore these associations are not completely independent: there exists an invariant that refers to both.

[5]However, in certain cases a graphical notation may be inadequate (See Section 6.6) because the picture becomes too cluttered.

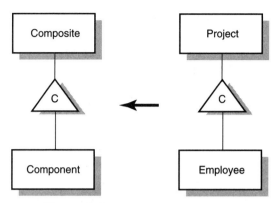

Figure 6.2.   Parameter Substitution

ture with named objects and associations is in fact a parameter substitution. In a picture, however, we may, but don't need to, denote different instances of the same association type by different identifiers. In other words, we may point to "this COMPOSITION" on a picture, but we have to name it—as above—when we use a linear representation.

In Figure 6.2, "Project" and "Employee" are substitutions for the formal parameters, "Composite" and "Component."

If the answer to Question 10 were different, it would represent a different business decision—to concentrate all work on a project within a single department. In this case, the specification would also have been different. Figure 6.3 represents this specification (to be supported by the "system") of a different real world (where there exists a hierarchical COMPOSITION between *Department* and *Project*).

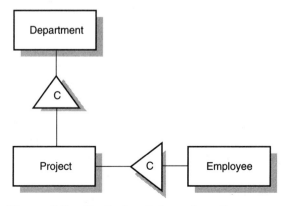

Figure 6.3.   If a Project Belonged to a Department

Some subtypes should be there.

11. *Q* Are there different types of employees, projects, and departments?

　　A Well . . . what does that mean?

12. *Q* Do you group employees in some way?

　　A Aha! Yes, by job functions. There are technical and administrative employees.

Comment: At this stage, we will not go into the details of SUBTYPING. We will have to find out later whether the SUBTYPING of interest will be exhaustive and try to convince the SME that it should be.

Let's try to uncover References that are sure to be there . . .

13. *Q* When an employee is hired, many properties of the future employee must be gathered and stored. Are these properties (e.g., salary) to be checked for acceptability?

　　A Yes; for instance, a new employee's salary cannot exceed an amount that depends on their job title, experience, and area.

Comment: This is almost certainly a REFERENCE. Of course, salary is not the only such property, and we would explore them, but we will not here. Here, the modeler, with the help of the SME, introduces and names a REFERENCE entity, "Job Classifications."

14. *Q* Are there properties of the employee that are generated automatically rather than input?

　　A Yes, default W4 information; for example, payroll deductions.

Comment: Another REFERENCE entity introduced by the modeler with the help of the SME.

Are we finished?
Our current specification is summed up in Figure 6.4.

15. *Q* Look at the figure (i.e., at the current model), and tell us what is incorrect or missing.

　　A Wait . . . where's the equipment that is provided to each employee? We keep track of that.

16. *Q* What kind of equipment?

　　A I'm thinking of office equipment like desks and computers.

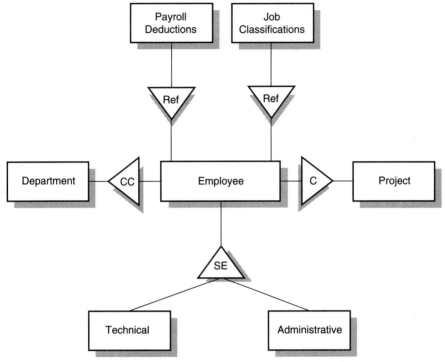

Figure 6.4. Current Specification

Comment: This is probably a SYMMETRIC RELATIONSHIP, unless equipment depends somehow on employees or vice versa.

17. *Q* Are there properties of an employee that may change when this employee gets new equipment or changes the equipment or no longer has the equipment?

A No.

Comment: We ruled out a COMPOSITION. Thus, the remaining possibility is a SYMMETRIC RELATIONSHIP. Let's verify that.

18. *Q* What happens with equipment when the employee quits or goes to another department?

A The equipment goes to a storeroom or may be given to another employee.

Comment: SYMMETRIC RELATIONSHIP.

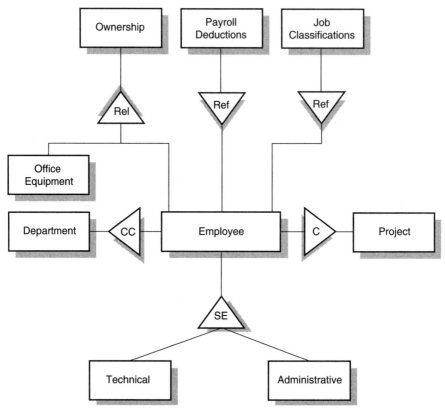

Figure 6.5. Reasonably Complete Specification

Look at Figure 6.5. It is a specification of the enterprise discussed in this section. In other words, this representation of some part of a business conveys a lot of interesting information. This information was uncovered by our question-and-answer sessions. Most of this information is captured by the associations.

Don't be misled by the small size of the picture. Each little triangle with a name in it represents a generic association type with lots of well-defined properties. These properties include the invariant for the association and the rules for CRUD operations. These are the fundamental business rules of the enterprise. Formal parameters used in the generic association library are replaced with application-specific parameters used in the enterprise.

A possible refinement.

Now the SMEs review this picture. They even understand it and start to ask questions; for instance, "Where is the department manager? How does the model show who manages a particular department?" The first answer is:

"You **can** allow for that if *job title* is a property of the *employee.*" (We can imagine another question about employees who are more than six feet tall if height is a property of interest of the employee. This question is answered in the same way. Through this question, we would have discovered an operation and a property (height); this property may or may not be important enough to create subtypes.) As a rule, important properties are a basis for SUBTYPING. Although whether something is important is subjective, "important" usually means that each subtype has its own association(s), in either this or some other area of interest.

Now a SME says: "OK, I agree. It's important to me, and therefore I want to be able to directly see it from the model."

19. *Q*   What do you want to see?

   A   That a department consists not just of employees, but rather has a manager and members; and also that there cannot be more than one manager.

   Comment: It can be easily done. Use SUBTYPING and COMPOSITION; the department is composed of a manager and members (we have a suspicion that here the default cardinality will not hold for the manager, and therefore we need to ask whether a manager always exists, and whether there is only one manager).

A possible improvement.

Any good modeler would note that the reasoning and general construct illustrated in Figure 6.6 probably applies to projects. A project may be composed of a project leader and project members, which are subtypes of employees. Therefore, the "department manager," "department member," "project leader," and "project member" are sub-types (possibly overlapping) of employees, and we must determine whether there is more than one subtype hierarchy: most probably, the project-related hierarchy will be orthogonal to the job-title-related one.

Any really good modeler would also realize that, first, it is quite possible

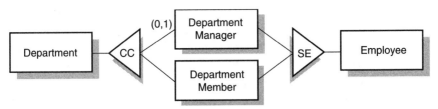

Figure 6.6.   Specifying that a Department Has a Manager

that in modeling the project hierarchy we should reuse the department hierarchy, and, second, there may be other similar hierarchies.

There probably are some other hierarchies . . .

20. *Q*   Now we have modeled the department hierarchy. If we replaced "department" with "project," "department manager" with "project leader," and "department member" with "project member," would it be a correct model for the project hierarchy?

   A   Almost. Except that, as we both noticed earlier, there are some employees who have no projects assigned; and some employees are assigned to several projects, so an employee may be a member in one project and a leader in another.

Comment: Our experience (reuse) suggests this question.

If all employees participated in projects, and if each employee participated in exactly one project, then the department hierarchy specification could be reused for projects without any changes (other than renaming, of course). However, as we have noticed, only some employees are project participants, and, moreover, an employee may participate in more than one project. Therefore, the department hierarchy specification can still be reused, but some changes are necessary. First, the CONTAINMENT will be replaced with SUBORDINATION (a project may still exist without any employees, but a project leader or a project member might be associated with more than one project), and second, the exhaustive and (default) non-overlapping subtyping will be replaced with exhaustive and overlapping subtyping into project leaders, project members, and project non-participants!

21. *Q*   You are right. Let's redraw the picture to specify it correctly.
This model (i.e., this specification) states that employees need not be either project leaders or project members; however, if an employee is either a project leader or a project member, then a corresponding project should exist. In other words, an employee cannot be a leader or a member of a nonexistent project. The model also states that an employee may be assigned to a project only as either a project leader or project member (because the subtyping is exhaustive, so that a subtype like "project observer" does not exist).

   A   Yes, that sounds correct.

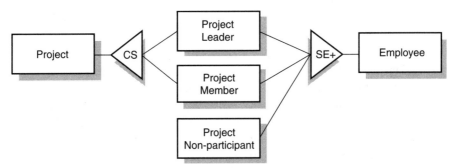

Figure 6.7. Corrected Association between Employees and Projects

*Comment: OK, if this hierarchy is representative, then a hierarchy does not need to include all employees. An employee belongs to one of the two subtypes—project leader and project member—**if the employee participates in a project**. If there were other constraints, for example, that the employee must have five years of service to be assigned to this project, then a REFERENCE association between employee and project would be called for.*

Some of the hierarchies are more important than others (e.g., the project and the management ones), so the business (the SME) chose to show them explicitly (see Figure 6.7). (Don't forget that each hierarchy has its own properties.) There may be some other hierarchies that may be shown later.

Some reasoning that led us to these hierarchies has been reused from the reasoning about the recursive association (see Section 5.3.1). However, we have not considered yet the possibility of several levels (e.g., a project leader reporting to the leader of a superproject). In this case, we may want to include, in addition, the organization hierarchy—an association between organization participants showing who reports to whom.

22. *Q* Consider a general hierarchy between employees belonging to an organization. In each organization, we have a hierarchy: supervisors and supervisees. Is an employee always either a supervisor or a supervisee?

A No. First, the same employee may be a manager and also report to a higher-level manager. Also, the same employee may be a manager of a group or a department, a member of a project, and a chair of the savings bond drive, to name a few.

Comment: There are several organization hierarchies—the SME mentioned the project one, the management one, and the savings bond drive one, and there may be others. We "feel" that these hierarchies have the same properties (we have, in fact, discovered this from considering the job-title-related and project-related hierarchies). We'll try to take a representative hierarchy and generalize its properties. If we succeed, we'll create an abstract hierarchy with certain known properties. We'll start with stating that an employee is subtyped into a supervisor and supervisee.

23. *Q* Are there employees that both supervise people and are supervised themselves?

A Yes; for example, department and project managers.

24. *Q* Is it important for you to know who supervises whom?

A Yes.

Comment: This points to overlapping subtypes. We shall call them supervisor and supervisee. We have also determined that supervisors and supervisees have an association of interest to the business. We decide to model the association as a SYMMETRIC RELATIONSHIP because it does not qualify as a COMPOSITION (e.g., no property of the supervisor depends on properties of the supervisees.) Figure 6.8 represents this construct, which is, of course, a reuse of a higher-level molecule—recursive association—presented in Section 5.3.1.

25. *Q* Are you interested in other ways of grouping employees?

A Not now.

Comment: This molecule can be subtyped into hierarchies for bond driving, project management, and so on; the model here is abstract and may be refined, if needed, by the customer and the modeler. The customer should decide whether this refinement is of interest. Of course, the customer should also decide whether, in each particular hierarchy, a COMPOSITION and a corresponding composite object (like project or department) is of interest. Now, when we have created this abstract molecule, the refinement is straightforward.

General comments.

Most of the pictures show only fragments of the system. Indeed, separation of concerns urges us to concentrate only on the part of the system that is currently of interest. However, the fragments (molecules, building

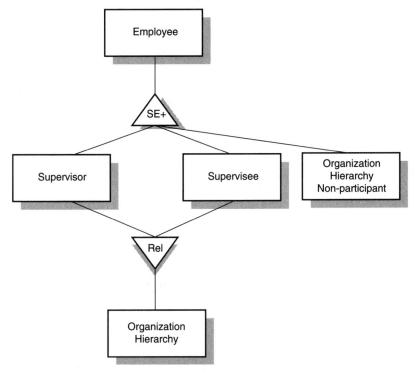

Figure 6.8.   Specification of an Organization Hierarchy

blocks) are not isolated: they participate in associations themselves. These associations can be understood better if their fragments (lower-level building blocks) are understood: fairly often, the components of a fragment have to be visible to understand a higher-level association. The very first picture in this chapter is a simple example: to understand how the two primitive associations (COMPOSITIONS) interrelate, we have to look into their components.

Some of the answers provided by the SMEs were simplified. To create the first cut of the model, we abstracted away "irrelevant details" [ODP 2]. For instance, in Question 1 we replaced the answer with "Yes" for the time being. After creating the first cut of the model, a modeler will reconsider those answers for which the irrelevant details were suppressed.

Up to this point, we have said almost nothing **explicitly** about CRUD operations, nor about pre- and postconditions. The questions and answers dealt mostly with the invariants to discover the types of associations between the objects of our little enterprise. The modeler can generate pre- and postconditions for CRUD operations from the understanding gained so far by reusing the generic CRUD behaviors specified in detail in the association library. In doing so, other questions will arise. Often a series of questions—of which the answers to the preceding define the formulation of the following—is equivalent to one "composite" question.

Further analysis may uncover more business rules. Some of these may be application-specific; some others may be expressible using the existing generic library. To take a simple example, it may be discovered that an employee may be assigned to several departments only if the employee is a "specialist." This rule may seem application-specific; however, this is SUB-TYPING, and should be modeled as such (if these properties are of interest, of course [Cusack 91]). Not all rules are that simple.

6.1.2. Why Is This a Specification?

The model produced so far is a reasonably complete specification. It's complete as far as we intended it to be. We consciously ignored the structural properties of each object; we did not need them to understand the important business rules of our enterprise.

We did not bother to produce a linear equivalent of the model, which has been represented graphically. This would be straightforward because of this equivalence.

The model tells us about the invariants of the enterprise. If the customer agrees that the model is complete, then contract specifications for application-specific operations of interest to the customer are implied by this model. These contracts will be implemented by some application, probably by writing application code.

Let's imagine that the customer requires a contract for hiring an employee. What information should be input by the customer, and what information should be output by the "system" (i.e., what is the signature of this operation)? From the model, it follows that the following should be input:

- The identity of the *employee* (required by the invariant of an entity)
- The identity of the *department* where the *employee* will work (required by the invariant for CONTAINMENT)
- The type of the *employee* in the subtyping hierarchy, distinguishing between technical and administrative (required by the invariant for EXHAUSTIVE SUBTYPING)
- The type of the *employee* in the subtyping hierarchy for projects (required by the invariant for EXHAUSTIVE SUBTYPING)

- Appropriate structural properties of the *employee* to satisfy the invariants of the REFERENCE associations between the *employee* and *payroll deductions* and between the *employee* and *job classifications*

This is the complete signature: the system will output nothing, except a possible error message, if the precondition is not satisfied.[6]

What is the precondition of the operation? We have almost formulated it already:

- The *employee* instance should not exist in the system.
- A *department* instance for that *employee* instance has to exist.
- The *employee* instance has to be of either the technical or administrative type.
- The *employee* instance has to be of some type in the *department*-oriented hierarchy.
- The *employee* instance has to be of some type in the *project*-related hierarchy.

In the latter rule, it is reasonable to make a business decision not to provide a project for a just-hired employee; another operation for assigning an employee to a project may be more useful (and also reusable, because an employee will usually participate in many projects during his or her career). Therefore, the project-related type of employee in this operation will be "non-participant."

What is the postcondition of the operation? Again, we have almost formulated it already:

- The *employee* instance exists.
- The *employee* instance is a member of the *department* referred to above.
- The *employee* instance does not participate in any *project*.
- The *employee* instance is either a department manager or a department member.
- The *employee* instance has either a technical or administrative type.

---

[6]This has nothing to do with defining the contract: if the precondition is not satisfied, anything can happen; on the other hand, in reality we want to inform the customer about this, and it is quite possible to define, for any contract, an "envelope" contract with the precondition TRUE and the postcondition:
"original precondition satisfied" implies "original postcondition satisfied" AND
"original precondition not satisfied" implies "an error message is output."

As we noted above, we'll also need some other contracts. In particular, we'll need a contract for creating a project leader or member (i.e., attaching a subtype). Again, it follows immediately from the invariants stated in the model (i.e., in the specification)! In this contract, we'll need to provide information about the identity of the employee, about a particular subtype in the project-related hierarchy, and also about the particular project (thanks to the SUBORDINATION invariant).

Finally, let's consider a contract for creating an instance of the organization hierarchy. Here, thanks to the invariant for a SYMMETRIC RELATIONSHIP, instances of a *supervisor* and *supervisee* (for a particular organization hierarchy) will need to exist as a precondition. If, however, the customer wishes to use a slightly different business rule—that is, attaching a *supervisor* or a *supervisee* type should be only possible simultaneously with creating an instance of the *organization hierarchy*—then the *supervisor* or the *supervisee* (or both) should have mandatory participation in this SYMMETRIC RELATIONSHIP (for a particular organization). Such an invariant immediately implies appropriate preconditions for a contract specification; for instance, to attach a *supervisee* type to a particular *employee*, if the *supervisee* has mandatory participation in this SYMMETRIC RELATIONSHIP, it is necessary to provide information about the *organization hierarchy* instance and also, thanks to the SYMMETRIC RELATIONSHIP invariant, about the corresponding *supervisor* instance. The specification of other contracts is also rather straightforward.

In other words, our model is a reasonably complete specification of the enterprise: there is no need for the customer or developer to consult any number of other documents to find out what's really going on.

6.1.3. On Finding Objects

Because of the comparatively trivial nature of this enterprise, the modelers had no trouble in discovering the objects—the SMEs knew what things were to be modeled (i.e., what objects were of interest to the enterprise). This example did not stress how to find the objects. In a more complex enterprise that deals with, for example, a telecommunications switching application, the modeler is not likely to know the subject matter and therefore cannot rely on common sense to find the objects. This forces both parties to explicitly formulate their criteria for finding objects. In these more complicated enterprises, finding the objects takes a lot of discussion between modelers and SMEs and a lot of time, although the SMEs may be sure they understand the objects. In a simpler enterprise, the modeler and the SME usually think that they share the same subject matter knowledge and may not be as careful about explicitly formulating everything they know.

An object is usually introduced by a SME; that is, it should have a valid business reason for its existence. An object should not be introduced to satisfy a particular methodology or technology. This does not mean that a SME is the only source of objects or associations. The modeler can introduce an object overlooked by a SME, and this object may be very important. However, such

> *There is 'no one right way' to do modelling; some choices will be better for some aspects of the problem, other choices better for other aspects, but probably no choice will be best for all aspects. [OO–Z], p. 5*

objects should have very good reasons for being introduced, and they should be discussed with SMEs. Even if the SMEs have discovered and named all the objects of the enterprise, they might overlook the existence of some important associations, especially if these associations have been hidden in attributes.

6.1.4. Answers That Were Not Needed

There was no discussion on relational normal forms, foreign keys, names, and so on. There was also no discussion on lengths of fields, fixed decimals, and so on. All these have nothing to do with analysis and will not be included in the information model. They represent a possible implementation. Also, such implementation concerns as lengths, fixed decimals, and so on may impose additional and very dangerous restrictions (i.e., change the invariants and preconditions for operations by, e.g., making some facts unacceptable although they are perfectly acceptable from the SME viewpoint, or, worse, keep facts acceptable and distort them "silently" within the computer system). The developers should not attach implementation-oriented restrictions to the information model. ("It's much cheaper to have 220,000,000 people write their last names first than to program a computer to read them the other way around. Why can't people just learn to do things the way that's easiest for us to program?" [Gilb 77].) For these reasons, the modeling sessions should not discuss implementation concerns, and if the SME introduces them, the modelers should explain why these concerns do not belong to information modeling and steer the discussion away from them.

Although we did not emphasize cardinalities, they belong to information modeling and may be included later; they are usually of less importance (see Chapter 4). In most cases, they are equal to the default ones and therefore need not be stated explicitly.

6.2.   Walkthroughs: The Essential Environment for Modeling

The business of the modeler is to uncover and explicitly define the model of the enterprise that is "there," though tacitly. Modelers ask questions that refer to this model of the enterprise. Even if there is an explicit model (and especially if there is none), there's another—not necessarily consistent—implicit model often hidden in lots of application programs, viewgraphs, folklore, heads of SMEs, heads of programmers, and so on. An implicit model always exists if the application exists (things have to run somehow). An application is not necessarily an enterprise: different applications may have different views of the enterprise, and these views may be inconsistent. This should be exposed, and modeling is the only way to understand it and make things explicit.

6.2.1. Why

To understand which things exist and are associated, you need a **walkthrough**. Even—and especially—when things are "evident," a walkthrough often puts on the table aspects of the model that have always been hidden under the rug, or those questions about the model that the SMEs don't want or don't have time to think about. It makes many aspects of the enterprise explicit and often suggests reasonable ways to develop the application(s) in the future.

For any nontrivial application, a walkthrough of the model is the only way to understand. The walkthrough may use a set of slides or an existing requirements document. The walkthrough is given to an audience of people who know nothing—or pretend to know nothing—about the subject matter. The walkthrough is presented by a SME, and a SME needs to explain to a modeler (and possibly, but not necessarily, to a programmer) in terms understandable to the president of the company. Only by a walkthrough can the modeler understand which objects exist and how they are associated.

In some cases, the only document provided to the customer and the developer is a collection of slides or a prototype (a collection of examples). Needless to say, these are not satisfactory specifications. They might be a good place to start. However, experienced modelers, after asking a substantial number of questions, will create an abstract, precise, and complete specification. They will "extract" the missing information from the SMEs and suppress the irrelevant details that may be encountered in the slides. They may also find and resolve inconsistencies, both within the application and between applications. They will also expose "default," "obvious" information that the SMEs never bothered to state explicitly, but which may be the basis of the business enterprise. Naturally, this activity is possible only in close cooperation with SMEs.

Sometimes a walkthrough exposes quite unpleasant facts; for instance, that the meaning of a term (even the meaning of an object that is encountered many times in the SME documentation) is not clear, or that the same term has substantially different meanings when explained (and used) by different members of the SME group.

A programmer often understands the business rules when a SME does not: if the programmer is a SME, you all too often won't find an explicit specification! The programmer often has to ask (implicit) questions that the original SME did not think about, because the programmer's job is to formulate precise and complete implementations of the corresponding computer system, without the need for continuous human intervention. The programmers either find answers to these questions from the original SMEs, or else use their judgement and invent these answers. Quite a few systems behave the way they do just because their behavioral rules were (partially) invented by their implementors rather than by the original SMEs. Naturally, the users may or may not like such behaviors. The answers provided by the SMEs to the programmers or invented by the programmers are often visible only in the application code, which is too complex to be understood. If the programmer is a SME, then the walkthrough becomes both easier and more difficult: the programmer can very quickly understand the goal of the modeler (after all, the programmer had already done this!), but on the other hand, the programmer may be unhappy with the interference of the modeler in a job that has been successfully completed. Good programmers, however, will be pleased when the results of the walkthrough support their modeling choices and even when these results—as results of any program review—show that improvements and other approaches are indeed possible.

There is a very serious danger if a modeler or programmer plays the role of a SME in a walkthrough. In this case, all too often, instead of discussing the business and its rules, the participants (led by the presenter) discuss an existing or planned computer implementation. Such an approach may lead to the loss or misinterpretation of business rules and to the introduction of new rules that have nothing to do with the business. As a result, the customers will be confronted with statements like "Our computer cannot do that," or "Sorry, computer error." One of the goals of modeling and walkthroughs is to avoid this.

6.2.2. How

How do you conduct a walkthrough (or call it a model review, or a modeling session)?

The SME presents the enterprise, and the other participants listen and ask questions. The modelers should ask questions both during and after the presentation. Usually, there will be many questions. In formulating questions, the participants should bear in mind that the goal of the walkthrough is not to criticize, but to make things clear and explicit! There should be at least one—and preferably several—participants that do not know the enterprise. Ideally, these participants should be the most experienced modelers or abstractors; their questions will make the presentation much more complete and consistent by exposing "evident" things. As a result, everything should be formulated explicitly: vague things become clear, and inconsistencies become exposed. Even if the modelers know the enterprise, they should ask about everything and pretend they do not know anything about the subject area. In this manner, quite interesting information may appear that was neglected by all the insiders and therefore missed.

At the beginning, the modeler's questions may be considered trivial and even stupid by the SME. Later, as the understanding of both progresses, the modeler will formulate questions for which the SME does not have immediate answers. This stage is a breakthrough—modeling proceeds very successfully after that! The trace of the difficult questions may need to be included in the specification (e.g., as comments) because it helps to justify the decisions made.

It is absolutely essential to have a scribe who will, at the very least, document all questions and answers. The scribe should carefully note the descriptions, especially object and association definitions that have been agreed upon during the modeling sessions. These definitions should be circulated among the walkthrough participants and agreed upon again explicitly, so as to avoid possible misunderstandings as well as the drudgery of trying the develop the definitions again afterwards, when some modeling decisions (and their justifications!) may have been forgotten.

Small modeling groups work best (more than five people or so will not work). The walkthroughs are very intensive intellectual exercises, and each of them usually cannot take more than three or four hours. It is not unusual for the participants of a good walkthrough to be exhausted earlier than that.

Understanding the business often takes a long time: not all businesses are like the little enterprise shown in our example! It is not uncommon to have modeling—prolonged walkthrough—sessions that take several months (e.g., one session per week). This should be explicitly recognized, because often there seems to be no "visible" progress in modeling. Often, as a result of preliminary walkthroughs, SMEs have to reconsider their approaches and present the walkthrough of the same (part of the) application again. This happens especially when the modeler asks hard questions, that is, questions for which the SME does not have an immediate definite answer. These questions uncover some business rules that may never have been explicitly stated. This approach is extremely useful for both modelers and SMEs because it substantially improves understanding and leads to creating an explicit and correct model of the enterprise. To quote [Potter 91], "the painfully acquired intimate knowledge of the product, which may be the practitioner's real value to his or her employer, is now to be made generally available." Of course, this intimate knowledge had never been made explicit earlier!

If, however, the business is well understood by the modeler or has been modeled before by others in an explicit and acceptable manner, then the existing—application-specific!—library may be reused, and therefore, modeling time will be much shorter. Examples of this approach are well known: consider any "vertical application" (e.g., mutual funds, personnel, etc.).

6.2.3. When to Stop Modeling?

An ideal model is not possible, and compromises are inevitable. However, having precise and explicit definitions of objects (entities) is essential. It is not always easy to understand that these definitions don't exist or that the meaning of these definitions is misunderstood. It is also essential to have contracts: if at least CRUD contracts have not been defined, then the model does not exist. The structure that exists in this case is not a model yet: it does not deal adequately with behavior. Common examples are unclear associations ("well, x and y are related, this is shown by a line between them . . . ")— a model does not exist yet for these associations. In particular, it may mean that there is no invariant that defines the association. Another characteristic of an unfinished model: when the question "does a property change of x mean that x becomes a new object instance?" does not have a definite answer. These observations and empirical rules may be considered as manifestations of the approach by Micheál Mac an Airchinnigh quoted at the beginning of this chapter.

6.3. *Exploring the Generic Library*

What did we learn by modeling? Applying object-oriented reasoning to ER modeling implies reusing the—precisely defined!—generic association library described in Chapter 5.[7] As we have seen throughout this book, this

---

[7]In an assembly language, it is possible to use low-level constructs (ifs and gotos) to write a "stupid" loop that is impossible to even formulate using higher-level constructs typical for Algol, Pascal, or PL/I; similarly, the usage of the generic object class library in information modeling makes it impossible to write stupid model fragments and therefore makes it more likely to get the whole model right. The emphasis is on higher-level semantics, if higher-level constructs are used; and on details of low-level syntax and semantics, if low-level constructs are used. This is known to every programmer and may be not so well known to every analyst.

library differs from most libraries used in "traditional" object-oriented programming: it consists of generic associations between classes rather than of generic classes. The "unit of work" in dealing with this library, the elementary molecule, is usually an association rather than an isolated object. This association is defined by its invariant and available operations (i.e., contracts). Although an elementary unit may be an object (and contracts will then apply to an isolated object, e.g., "name change"), information modeling is more concerned with associations. "Behavior of an object" is a part of the specification, but "behavior in which an object participates" is essential for understanding and specifying the enterprise. Application-specific behaviors (e.g., *hire an employee*) may be built upon these generic behaviors (e.g., *create an employee*, *add an employee to a department*, and *update department's budget*).

It is possible to distinguish between associations at the first level of the generic association library by appropriate invariants. For example, to distinguish between a COMPOSITION and a DEPENDENCY, it is often sufficient to ask whether there exists a property of the composite that depends upon (changes of) its components. If yes, then it's indeed a COMPOSITION; if not, then it's a DEPENDENCY. Of course, this presumes that in the eventual COMPOSITION, for a component to exist, its composite has to exist—or else the COMPOSITION-DEPENDENCY dichotomy would not arise in the first place. In other words, the association is a particular subtype of a general COMPOSITION, for example, a CONTAINMENT. CONTAINMENT is distinguished from its supertype—COMPOSITION—by its invariant. No CRUD rules for operations need be considered.

It is possible to distinguish between subtypes of associations at the first level of the generic association library by either refining the first-level invariants or defining the association in terms of CRUD rules. Refining the invariants, that is, stating whether the participation of an object in an association is optional or mandatory, is equivalent to defining CRUD rules that distinguish objects with mandatory participation from objects with optional participation in an association. For example, if a dependent has mandatory participation, then the first instance of this dependent can be created only together with (in the same business process as) the instance of its parent. Therefore, if a dependent instance may have only one parent instance—this is stated in the invariant—then separate creation of only the parent instance will be impossible because the precondition for this operation will be FALSE! From the viewpoint of refining the DEPENDENCY invariant, DEPENDENCY with mandatory existence means that the generic invariant for the DEPENDENCY (i.e., the existence of a dependent instance implies the existence of its parent instance) will be conjoined with the "subtype" invariant (i.e., the existence of a parent instance implies the existence of its dependent instance).

As we mentioned earlier, a dependent entity is not "intrinsically" dependent, but is dependent only as an element of a DEPENDENCY association, and outside of this association it is not dependent. By the same token, an entity is composite only because it is an element of a COMPOSITION association, and outside of this association it is not composite. In other words, an entity (e.g., an employee) is a subclass of a generic class only within a corresponding generic association. Of course, when an entity belongs to more than one association, the appropriate (association) invariants are conjoined.[8] If the resulting invariant is FALSE, then the construct cannot exist and therefore is modeled incorrectly. If, as a result, the construct is modeled correctly, but the precondition for a certain operation is FALSE, then such an operation cannot be executed. But this is only natural: it happens all the time at a slightly lower level when "isolated" entities share operations because they are associated. In the latter case, for instance, an operation "Create dependent" cannot be executed for the first instance of a dependent with mandatory participation and with one parent. This "atomic" operation will have to be replaced with a "molecular" operation, "Create a parent and a dependent." Generally, when molecules are created, their components cannot behave as isolated anymore, and therefore the preconditions for "trivial" operations will have to be changed; these operations may become inaccessible components of atomic higher-level operations!

6.4.   Extending the Generic Library

A modeler may trigger extensions to the generic association library. Although the extension of this library is uncommon, and each extension should be carefully justified, the library is by no means frozen. Our modeling experience suggests that it covers a substantial subset of real-life situations. Nevertheless, we do not pretend that the library presented in Chapter 5 is exhaustive.

For example, the most recent addition to the generic association library is the REFERENCE FOR CREATE. This concept has been added at the request of modelers who noted that quite a few modeling situations have not been cov-

---

[8]As [Zave 92] noted, "the semantics of a composition of a set of partial specifications is the conjunction of their assertions, and a set of partial specifications is consistent if and only if the conjunction of their assertions is satisfiable."

ered by any concept from the generic library. Although it was obvious that the original concept of a REFERENCE association was close, it was not sufficient. The modeling situations required the properties of the maintained entity instance to be frozen after its creation rather than updated to correspond to the updated properties of its reference entity (see the example of a notification in Chapter 5). To support this, a new supertype of REFERENCE association was created and subtyped into an ORDINARY REFERENCE (the original concept) and a REFERENCE FOR CREATE. A simple example of this construct is shown in Figure 6.9.

We want the generic library to be reused, and to be reused it must be understood. Therefore, it must consist of a small number of well-defined associations (molecules) that are encountered in most applications and are easily recallable. Therefore, too, not every new application situation deserves to become a part of the generic library. In most cases, this new application situation may be expressed in terms of existing, perhaps nonelementary, molecules (see Chapter 5). Adding an elementary molecule to the generic library should be done with extreme caution. Even for a nonelementary molecule, caution is needed. Just as a programming language should be simple and include, for example, a very limited number of ways to write a loop, the generic association library should be simple and include, for example, a very limited number of ways to express a composition.

To be recallable, these molecules should be simple and well defined. For any concept to be understood and reused, its formal definition is essential. Although a formal definition of properties of a molecule (e.g., of a COMPOSI-

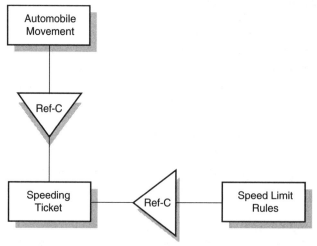

Figure 6.9. The REFERENCE FOR CREATE Association

TION) may be quite complicated (see Appendix A), its use is quite simple. Naturally, writing a nontrivial specification is more complicated than reading it and much more complicated than using it! Again, a comparison with traditional programming helps: a complicated program (if you wish, algorithm) is rather nontrivial to invent, especially if it is generic enough; its usage is almost trivial (e.g., quicksort required the genius of Hoare, but how many of its users need this genius to use it?).

The need for a molecule to be simple does not mean that it may be defined using only atoms. To define a nonelementary molecule, other molecules—both elementary and nonelementary—may be used. Again, this is done in the same manner in which procedures in a programming language are defined, or theorems in mathematics. Not all theorems are based on axioms: most are based on other theorems.

6.5.   *Beyond Elementary Associations: Combining Molecules*

Seldom are all the facts about an application completely captured by molecules from the generic library. For instance, you may be able to use only an isolated COMPOSITION to understand a simple part of the application. However, this COMPOSITION may not be isolated: its elements (atoms) may also belong to other molecules. A component of one COMPOSITION may also be a component of another COMPOSITION (as in our example above). In this manner, some application-specific properties appear that do not correspond to a single component of the generic library. Application-specific business rules often deal with building blocks larger (on a higher level) than generic rules. A typical example is "Hiring an employee," which refers to elements of several generic associations. This operation may be refined into CRUD operations on these generic associations. These CRUD operations should be combined into the same business process; otherwise, the semantics of the application (in fact, the invariant of the higher-level association) will be violated. Although we present a few common higher-level associations, we try to present a much more complete set of primitive ones. The general rules for declarative specification of all associations are the same (refinement, conjunction of invariants for associations of associations, conjunction of assertions for operations on "intersections," i.e., entities in common, etc.).

Can an application-specific operation be expressed only using CRUD operations? Some application-specific operations can be decomposed into a series of CRUD ones; however, selections (i.e., **if**s) and iterations (i.e., **while**s) may often be required in these series. In other words, CRUDs are not computationally complete. This can be compared with the use of SQL in relational DBMSs—SQL is not computationally complete. Of course, it does not mean that SQL should not be used in the relational world; nor does it mean that CRUD-based generic objects should not be used in the information modeling world. Both are extremely useful, although they do not provide all solutions.

How do the molecules (peer contracts) interact? Where does the "transitive closure" of these interactions stop? No object in an information model is an island—objects are interconnected. Therefore, theoretically the whole model should be considered when an operation is applied to an object. This would make understanding of an operation too difficult, almost impossible. However, in real life this process of expanding an operation stops rather quickly. For instance, a typical expansion of this nature will be necessary if an association has mandatory existence, and this does not happen too often. Of course, this is an empirical observation rather than a law.

To be more precise, when an object is one of the operation parameters, this operation is considered within the context of an association to which the object belongs (e.g., within a COMPOSITION for a composite object, etc.). Most objects belong to more than one association, and so the pre- and postconditions for the operation become much more complicated, because feature interactions have to be considered. If the postcondition of the operation includes changes in other objects, then these other objects need, of course, to be considered in the context of those eventually changeable associations to which these objects belong. On the other hand, if the precondition for a certain operation requires the existence of another object, then it may happen that this latter object will have to be created in the same business process as the operation; naturally, the same reasoning applies to the creation (it is also an operation!). Finally, we get the transitive closure (i.e., we have to consider the whole model). As Figure 6.10 shows, however, most models are not that complicated, because more often than not the feature interactions are simple.

In this example, creation of an instance of z (a component) may be easy if the DEPENDENCY does not have mandatory existence and may be more difficult if the DEPENDENCY does have mandatory existence. On the other hand, even in the latter case, this will not present any problems if the component z may exist independent of its composite a. More generally, invariants define associations to which an object belongs. All these associations will be defined by the conjunction of all these invariants, and an operation has to preserve the invariants. Most models are "simple," that is, an elementary operation will not need expansion to ensure that the invariants are not violated.

Naturally, when the DEPENDENCY and COMPOSITION generic specifications

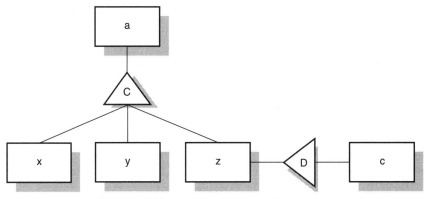

Figure 6.10.   A Simple Feature Interaction

in our example are instantiated and merged, the corresponding invariants are conjoined. The operation specifications are also merged. As noted above, there may appear some problems during this merging of operation specifications (and these problems seem to be independent of the way the specification is presented). Namely, if more than one operation has the same object type as a parameter, then only those of them that will not violate the conjoined invariant may be executed separately. For example, creating an instance of an Employee (z, see above) (without dependents) is possible, irrespective of whether the COMPOSITION is or is not a CONTAINMENT, because it will not violate the DEPENDENCY invariant conjoined with the COMPOSITION invariant. Our modeling experience suggests that this situation is a rule, and situations in which it is necessary to create specific "intersection" operations because each of the separately specified ones will violate the invariants are rare. As an example of such a rare situation, let us imagine that the object a has two different COMPOSITIONS—one COMPOSITION into x, y, and z, and the other into u and v—and the business rule states that only one of these COMPOSITIONS at a time is possible. In this case, object a can be subtyped (disjointly) into a1 and a2, depending upon the kind of COMPOSITION that is applicable to object a. This construct is a higher-level molecule (see Section 5.3); a Create, Delete, or Update operation is applied to the whole molecule rather than to its isolated lower-level fragment.

A library of application-specific molecules may be created, extended, and reused in the same manner as the generic association library described in Chapter 5. The only difference is between the scope of likely applications. The generic library is usable by all applications. For instance, the operation "create a component" is encountered in most applications. The situation (two molecules) shown in Figure 6.10 is likely to be encountered in quite a few applications. An abstractor (creator of a class library) may want to name and reuse these larger molecules. More realistic examples of these reusable higher-level molecules are discussed in Chapter 5 (e.g., "recursive COMPOSI-TIONS," "XORs," "notifications," etc.).

6.6. Patterns of Reasoning

To make information modeling a discipline, we must expose some patterns of reasoning that apply to information modeling. According to Dijkstra, such exposure is essential for moving from craft to a more disciplined

> ... The purpose of thinking is to reduce the detailed reasoning needed to a doable amount, and a separation of concerns is the way in which we hope to achieve this reduction.
> The crucial choice is, of course, what aspects to study "in isolation," how to disentangle the original amorphous knot of obligations, constraints, and goals into a set of "concerns" that admit a reasonable effective separation. To arrive at a successful separation of concerns for a new, difficult problem area will nearly always take a long time of hard work; it seems unrealistic to expect it to be otherwise ...
> As remarked above, the purpose of thinking is to reduce the detailed reasoning needed to a doable amount. The burning question is: can "thinking" in this sense be taught? If I answer "No" to this question, one may well ask why I have written this book in the first place; if I answer "Yes" to this question, I would make a fool of myself, and the only answer left to me is "Up to a point ...".
> ... But insofar as people try to understand (at first subconsciously), strive after clarity, and attempt to avoid un-mastered complexity, I believe in the possibility of assisting them significantly by making them aware of the human inability "to talk of many things" (at any one moment, at least), by making them alert to how complexity is introduced. To the extent that a professor of music at a conservatoire can assist his students in becoming familiar with the patterns of harmony and rhythm, and with how they combine, it must be possible to assist students in becoming sensitive to patterns of reasoning and to how they combine. The analogy is not far-fetched at all: a clear argument can make one catch one's breath, like a Mozart adagio can. [Dijkstra 76]

approach. What follows are some of the important patterns we have recognized. Most of them are directly applicable, even to our small example. We invite the reader to add new patterns.

A. Choose the right level of abstraction.   Choosing and using the right level of abstraction is essential for understanding and modeling the enterprise. This pattern occurs very often. The number of objects "in a picture" (i.e., simultaneously considered) should not be more than 15 to 20 (see [Dijkstra 72]). Clustering (usually COMPOSITION or SUBTYPING) should be used to manage complexity (like procedures in programming). If a pictorial representation is accepted, then multiple simple diagrams should be used instead of one complicated diagram. They may be considered as different viewpoints, perhaps, in different contexts. This also corresponds to a linear text: if a specification takes more than about one page, then it should be decomposed into smaller and simpler subspecifications.

Information modeling itself promotes understanding of the business without regard to a computer-based implementation. In particular, such concepts as keys, attributes, normal forms, and so on do not belong to information modeling. How to get out of the DBMS mindset? To understand the business rather than its implementation, try to ask: "What if there were no computers, just pencil and paper? How would your application (your enterprise) work then?"

Even within information modeling itself (i.e., when we don't deal with implementation), there usually exist several levels of abstraction. Lower levels are used to refine higher levels. This is necessary to understand a complicated business. Not knowing everything is acceptable. For example, the existence of an object is much more important than the knowledge of all its structural properties. Using supertypes instead of subtypes, as well as using composites instead of their components, are other examples. This is how a huge model may be decomposed into understandable pieces. The existence of a REFERENCE association does not say anything about the algorithm used for maintaining the property values of a maintained entity, and we accept that at a certain stage of modeling.

B. Ask questions.   The modelers should formulate questions to understand the business. Therefore, the SMEs present the business, and the modelers (at the walkthroughs) ask questions. The modelers should formulate questions in terms of available building blocks (try to fit in existing patterns). These building blocks may be either generic associations (see Chapter 5), higher-level molecules like "recursive" associations, or even still higher-level molecules which may be more application-specific. Be sure to keep the building blocks (molecules) understandable.

Using the generic association library as the basis for formulating questions leads to clear understanding of all business rules (i.e., to explicit and complete contracts). Modelers' questions are usually formulated in terms of invariants for elementary associations. A particular elementary association type (e.g., a COMPOSITION, a DEPENDENCY, etc.) implies particular pre- and postconditions for CRUD operations. Therefore, CRUD operations—as an alternative to invariants—can be used to uncover associations. Modelers' questions may include assertions for these operations, especially if the SMEs are more accustomed to thinking in these terms. Such operational questions are usually more detailed and therefore more complicated.

C. Think in terms of contracts.   Having an explicit and complete contract is essential. To formulate a contract, the modeler often has to ask hard questions to which the SME does not have immediate definite answers.

For instance, let's imagine a very simple contract: a consumer buys a dining room set at a discount. Naturally, the contract states that the consumer will pay, and the furniture store will deliver the set. Details of payment and delivery may also be stated. But is this a complete contract? What if, for example, the customer wants to return only one of the pieces of furniture and get a refund for it? How is this operation modeled? One approach, not always used, is to proportionally adjust the "money back"; however, the original discounts may not be proportional and may not even be explicitly stated. They probably should be. This is a good example of a hard question to which the SME may not immediately know the answer. This question is not usually even asked. But a good modeler who knows the concept of a COMPOSITION will ask it and insist on a clear answer: the question follows from the definition of a COMPOSITION. This is how a modeler helps a SME discover business rules that were missing.

Thinking in terms of contracts forces the modeler to think declaratively. Instead of such anthropomorphic metaphors as "objects decide," "objects are responsible for ... ," "an object receives a message," and so on, the modeler provides more careful definitions of behavior—preconditions, postconditions, and invariants. This kind of careful definition represents only observable behavior (compare [Zave 92]).

D. Treat cardinality as a less important detail.   Cardinality should be explicitly stated only for those associations where the SME requests it (i.e., where it is important). Most often and most probably, the SME will request information only about mandatory/optional participation (although perhaps not in these terms—see Chapter 4). Otherwise, cardinalities are default. If the SME is satisfied with default cardinalities, then the modeler is more than satisfied. Of course, it presumes that the SME understands the default cardinalities. As a rule, cardinalities enter the reasoning only after the associations are found.

Later, additional questions may be asked. These questions are less important, as the semantics of the (modeled part of the) enterprise does not change as a result of any answer to these questions. They are of the type: Are there limits to the number of projects assigned to a department? To the number of employees assigned to a department? These questions deal with "maximum cardinality" and are usually overemphasized by "traditional" modeling approaches. Abstraction suggests that they may be suppressed at the first, most decisive, stages of modeling. They also represent the more volatile aspects of the enterprise, and in many cases there are no corresponding restrictions in the business rules of the enterprise. Quite often, pressing for answers to questions about maximal cardinality will create unneeded business rules on the fly.

E. Question symmetric relationships: expect asymmetry.   Using a SYMMETRIC RELATIONSHIP for describing any association often does not tell the whole story: important components of semantics are left out. Too often, an association is considered to be a SYMMETRIC RELATIONSHIP because the modeler for some reason decided not to go too deep into the semantics of the association. In this case, SYMMETRIC RELATIONSHIPS are a way of hiding asymmetry between participating entities. Quite often, the asymmetry may be exposed in the English definitions of the objects or of the association ("X is an aggregation of Ys" may be a part of the definition of a SYMMETRIC RELATIONSHIP between X and Y; therefore, this "SYMMETRIC RELATIONSHIP" is really a COMPOSITION).

Consider the so called "1:N" relationships, for example, the famous "supplier-part-shipment" construct. Traditionally, they meant that one instance of one entity was "related to" several instances of another entity (e.g., one *supplier* ships many *parts*). However, most businesses manage information about shipments in terms of *line items* on a *shipping order*. Each *line item* associates the *supplier* with one or more instances of a particular *part*. The *shipping order* consists of several *line items*. The traditional representation, by not distinguishing between the two, misses essential business rules. The correct specification should be as shown in Figure 6.11.[9]

---

[9]If the business decides to distinguish between a *shipping order* and an *actual shipment,* then a reference association between these objects will solve the problem.

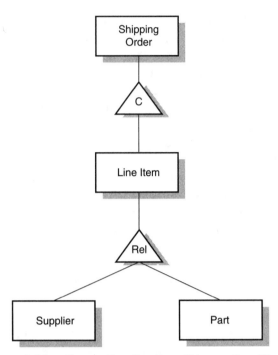

Figure 6.11. Correct *Supplier-Part-Shipment* Specification

If a modeler does not question symmetric relationships, then the composition between a *shipping order* and its *line item* (specified in Figure 6.11) may be incorrectly specified as shown in Figure 6.12.

This specification is incorrect because it does not show that a *shipping order* has properties dependent upon its *line items* (i.e., these two entities are not symmetric) and also because there are really two—and not three—business objects. Therefore, thinking of relationships in the manner suggested in this book and, in particular, distinguishing between a relationship object and a relationship association will discourage the modeler from errors of this kind. In a graphical representation, the use of a triangle instead of a diamond helps to avoid this error, because a triangle represents an association, not a business object.

Figure 6.12. Incorrect *Shipping Order/Line Item* Specification

F. Split parts of recursive associations.   We often need to model situations in which the same instance of an object directly or indirectly participates in different instances of the same association. For example, the same instance can be both a composite and a component in different instances of a COMPOSITION. This "recursive" association is a higher-level building block (molecule), the properties of which should be precisely specified and reused in modeling (some of them are presented in Chapter 5). You saw a typical example of this construct when we considered the association between a supervisor and supervisee above. Although the association in this example happened to be a SYMMETRIC RELATIONSHIP, any other kind of association may appear. For another example, consider the typical parts explosion situation where the association is a COMPOSITION (see Figure 6.13).

Why do we need to do that? Isn't Figure 6.14 better because it seems to be more succinct?

First of all, *SubA* and *SubB* are subtypes of the supertype *Super*, and they indeed have different properties. At a minimum, the predicate "is a *SubA*" is such a distinguishing property. There may be other distinguishing properties as well, including different associations: a supervisor may be entitled to taking courses a supervisee cannot take; the operation "get subordinates" is not applicable to a supervisee; and so on. This is important for the specification and needs to be shown. The same object instance (of type *Super*) may, in different instances of the association ASSN, belong to either subtype *SubA* or *SubB* (overlapping subtypes).

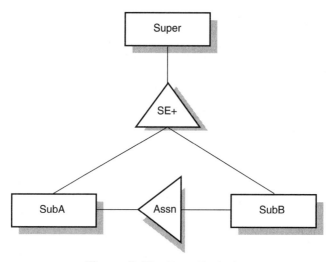

Figure 6.13.   Parts Explosion

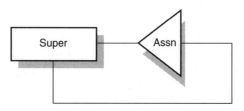

Figure 6.14.

Let's look at the linear specifications corresponding to the pictures. Then the situation is clarified immediately. The first one will be:

       A1: Association (SubA, SubB)

and the second, supposedly succinct, one will be:

       B1: Association (Super, Super)

In the first case, the formal parameters are distinct (in Figure 6.13, the boxes are different); in the second case, the formal parameters are not distinguishable[10] (in Figure 6.14, the box is the same). However, for the second case, we can't substitute different actual parameters for the same formal one. Of course, the parameters may be positional, but then they will be different ("first" and "second"), and you will have to explicitly distinguish the parameters (name the lines in the picture if a graphical notation is used). If you do that, then the result is the same: the parameters are distinct.

In some cases, the very first and very last levels could be modeled as separate subtypes because they have (slightly) different behavior. For instance, some parts (lowest level) are not assemblies, and some assemblies (highest level) are not components of any other assembly (see Figure 6.15).

This is certainly a refinement of the association discussed above; it should be used if it is "of interest." The SUBTYPING of the *Part* into *The Biggest Part*, the *Middle*, and *The Smallest Part* is non-overlapping because, should a *Part* have no components, we would consider it to be *The Biggest Part*. This SUBTYPING is different from the SUBTYPING of the *Part* into *Molecule* and *Atom* because a *Molecule* may participate in different instances of the COMPOSITION between *Molecule* and *Atom* (as either a composite or a component), whereas *The Biggest Part* is always a composite, and *The Smallest Part* is always a component. We have not shown that a

---

[10]Compare with the "self-evident" requirement [Bauer 82]: "all object declarations within a certain segment must introduce objects with different designations."

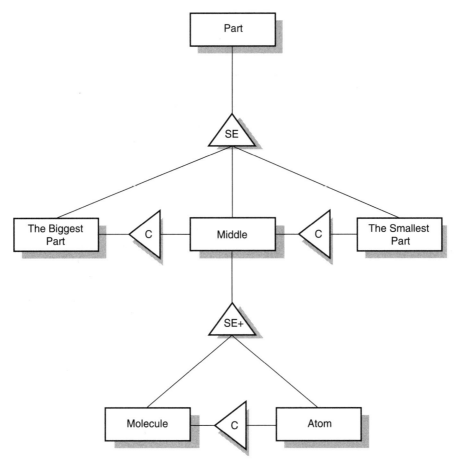

Figure 6.15. A More Detailed Parts Explosion

Molecule and *The Biggest Part* have common properties (i.e., that they have a common supertype); nor have we shown that an *Atom* and *The Smallest Part* have a common supertype. This would make the very complicated picture above even more complicated and therefore unacceptable.

This way of modeling is not the only possible one. The relative complexity and incompleteness of this pictorial specification are due to the intrinsic difficulties of subtyping [Wegner 88], and also due to a graphical representation being inadequate for all constructs. Although we must be careful to reduce the complexity by modeling only what is of interest, we must also be careful to include in the model all relevant business rules, even if a graphical representation for them is inadequate.

G. Determine the amount of flattening.   If subtypes of the same super-type do not have associations with each other, how many of them do you want to specify? Of course, if such associations exist, then these subtypes need to be distinguished. But what if they don't? If a company has 25 job titles for its employees, do we really want to show 25 subtypes? The specification—at least, at the higher levels—will be very cluttered and therefore complicated.

It is reasonable to use SUBTYPING if the number of subtypes is small, the business rules (behavior) of subtype instances are substantially different, and the volatility is low (i.e., the predicates that define subtypes do not change very often). Otherwise, REFERENCE associations are preferable because the model should not be overloaded with details (see Figure 6.16).

Model changes in the specification are not shown if reference entities are used: such a change amounts to a change in reference entity instances (e.g., in creating a new such instance). On the other hand, a change in subtype amounts to changing the model. Is such a change needed? This is subjective and should be done, to use the conceptual schema terminology, if it is "of in-terest." As Elspeth Cusack remarked [Cusack 91], it cannot be precisely specified when differences in predicates become important enough to be "recognized" as differences in types. Probably, the behavioral rules for choosing subtypes should be "substantially" different.[11] As the modelers' ob-jective is understanding, they should use subtypes if subtypes help them to understand business rules.

When a model changes, a change in subtypes will be shown on the model (and reflected in the schema), whereas a change in the instances of the

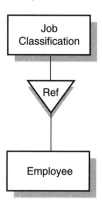

Figure 6.16.

---

[11]If the only difference between subtypes is, for example, in permissible attribute values then reference entities are good candidates.

reference entity will not be shown on the model. This is similar to the well-known dichotomy between compile-time and run-time in programming, or between explicitly specified and table-driven. Consider, for example, books in a library as subtypes of book titles (a correct, but stupid approach) vs. books published by a small publishing house (two to three titles per year) where SUBTYPING through book titles makes perfect sense.

A compromise may be the best solution—only subtypes of a certain level may be explicitly shown on the model. For instance, instead of showing 25 job titles, it is quite possible to show "groupings" (i.e., "technical staff," "professional staff," "managers," etc.). By using this approach, the subtype hierarchy will be much more understandable.

H. Show ties to other applications.   The scope of an application is delineated by the set of its contracts. If a model of the application is only a part of the bigger picture and refers to something outside of itself ("out-of-scope entities"), it is essential to build a firewall around the rest of the world, especially if this "rest of the world" has not yet been properly modeled. The simplest way is to create an extremely oversimplified model of this environment (i.e., of the out-of-scope things) with as few interactions with them as possible. This interface with the environment should be thin and visible (Dijkstra). If such a simple interface cannot be achieved, then some of the out-of-scope entities may belong to the scope of the model. These out-of-scope entities participate only in REFERENCE associations with objects within the scope. Therefore, contracts that create, update, or delete these out-of-scope entities do not belong to the application. These entities should always be explicitly included if there is a need to use them. The out-of-scope entities belong to the glue that hold applications together.

In a corporation of any significant size and complexity, the applications (i.e., sets of contracts demanded by the customer) will be modeled separately. Different sets of contracts may refer to the same things. Moreover, the same contracts may be used by different applications. However, each contract should be defined in exactly one application. Recall that to model an association between objects means to specify all contracts that define this association. Therefore, all contracts that define an association should be specified in exactly one application. However, the situation may be more complicated than that. Consider one application that models an association between X and Y, and another application that models a completely different association between X and Z. A contract for creating an instance of X, perfectly valid from the viewpoints of each of these applications, may lead to serious problems. If the creation of an instance of X will have to refer to instances of both Y and Z, this would be a surprise to both applications: the first one did not know about Z, nor the second one about Y. Therefore, a contract that was valid within the context of one application (i.e., did not violate the corresponding invariant) becomes invalid within another, "broader" context (i.e., will violate its invariant).

If the sets of contracts defined by different applications refer to properties of the same objects, then there is the problem of managing consistency across applications. To do that, higher-level non-decomposable contracts are needed. A contract exposed to the user of either application may have to become hidden from the user of the combination of these applications. This problem has also been mentioned, for example, in [Zave 91]: "an ineffective operation may be legal in itself, but cannot be carried out because a companion operation is not legal." This companion operation would have to be carried out because of the need to satisfy the invariant for the appropriate "companion" association after carrying out the original ("legal in itself") operation.[12] For this reason, the COMPOSITION of all these companion operations, together with the original one, constitutes a new operation that should have formal semantics equivalent to that of an atomic operation. Section 5.3, "Beyond Elementary Associations," describes some of these higher-level generic reusable associations.

Because applications are not isolated, each application will have to deal with things maintained by other applications. Each application should model only those features of things needed for the contracts that define it. Applications are held together by things that participate in more than one of these sets of contracts. (That's how different applications are integrated.) Most often, these things are seen as REFERENCE entities; that is, one of the applications only reads information maintained by another. Scaling considerations suggest that often an out-of-scope entity is, from the point of view of its application, a cluster. In the example at the beginning of this chapter, *Payroll Deductions* is such a cluster: at the very least, there may be federal, state, and city deductions, as well as FICA ones, IRA, and so on.

A model of an application may be considered as a view of the bigger corporate model which includes "all" applications. Why are views created? Because of the need for simplicity, because of our inability to understand large

---

[12]In our example, an attempt to add an *employee* (*department member*) to a *department*, perfectly legal in itself, may be illegal if the companion operation cannot be accomplished (e.g., if there is no *project* to be assigned to this *employee* [if, of course, the composition "*employee - project*" is a subordination one— see Chapter 5]). In this case, the atomic operation will have to add an *employee* to both a *department* and a *project*.

complex things without breaking them into understandable pieces. How are views created? By using operations on the bigger model. The bigger model itself is created when we understand how applications interact. Evidently, the view includes only a part of the bigger picture, but the objects and associations of interest to (and presented in) the view may be quite different from objects and associations in the bigger model. There may even be several layers of views (and they may appear within the same model if it is complex enough). In most cases, objects of interest to the view are composites or supertypes (i.e., abstractions from) objects in more detailed models. It is also possible that a view includes entire models ("large COMPOSITIONS") as reference entities. There should probably exist contracts for creating COMPOSITIONS that constitute a view (e.g., taking bits and pieces of the bigger model; in fact, these cannot be taken arbitrarily). It is not sufficient to state that there exists a "mapping" from the big model to a view: the mapping should have well-defined semantics (e.g., supertype or composite), and creating this "view entity" is an operation defined by an appropriate contract. In the implementation, it may mean that entities from the big model will become properties of the view, but this happens in COMPOSITIONS within one model as well.

I. Don't use "code": use domains.   Codes don't belong to information modeling. Therefore, replace everything that contains "code" or its synonyms in its name with something that doesn't. This is not a mechanical action! The existence of "code" is a symptom of a more serious problem: instead of considering the business enterprise, the modelers consider its computer-based implementation—a quite distinct activity (compare [Gilb 77, Kent 79]). If the model should reflect the existing, not always ideal, state of affairs, then at the very least business aspects of the enterprise model should be very clearly separated from computer-systems aspects. Usually, the existence of "codes" means that there is a REFERENCE association between the "code" and some "real" business entity (which, quite possibly, is a composite). Properties of the "real" entity have been manually encoded for some reason, and therefore the "code," if it has to be considered as an entity, will be a maintained one in the REFERENCE association between the "code" entity and the "real" entity.

From the viewpoint of a travel agency, airlines are, and airline codes are not, a part of the enterprise model. If the travel agency or its customers are interested in properties of an airline (safety records, delays, service records, etc.), then an airline becomes an entity (specifically a REFERENCE entity, because its properties are not changeable by the travel agency). Airline name is among the properties of this entity. It is defined on a domain of airline names. This domain enumerates the names of all airlines, and for each name there may be an associated airline code (or different kinds of codes, if needed). These different kinds of airline code are aliases of the airline name, of course. They may be used for interoperability with existing systems (that use only particular codes), for handling names in different natural languages, and so on.

J. Don't treat like properties as entities: use domains.   Different entities may have the same kind of properties (e.g., creation date, delivery date, completion date, etc.). These properties should be abstracted as a domain. As the concept of a domain is less well known than it deserves to be and usually does not show up in pictures, there is a tendency to express this commonality via creating an object for the common property (e.g., date), subtyping it, and drawing associations to its subtypes. This brings clutter to the information model. To avoid this tendency, use domains.

In some cases, domains are not sufficient. When a thing does not have any additional properties of interest (e.g., date), it tends to be a domain. A property of an object may in fact rely on several properties of another object. This is not a domain.

K. Supertype associations.   If the same association is valid for several similar sets of objects, it should be modeled as a single association rather than as several distinguishable associations. Sometimes an entity supertype may be created for this purpose only, and the entity subtypes will inherit this association. This should be done to get rid of clutter of complexity (i.e., to improve understanding). This is the same kind of reasoning that traditional programmers use when they introduce procedures. (As noted earlier, if a pattern recurs, it could be defined only once and reused later.)

Figure 6.17 is a simplified example of replacing a cluttered representation (at the left) with an equivalent, less cluttered one (at the right). Similarly, in traditional programming, introducing a procedure does not change the semantics of a program. The COMPOSITION between BBB and AAA (the same pattern) is shown only once and reused, that is, inherited by all subtypes of AAA (i.e., by xxx, yyy, and zzz). The entity AAA may, of course, not have existed in the left representation (but it still would have been more cluttered than the right one!). The COMPOSITION may, of course, be replaced by any other association.

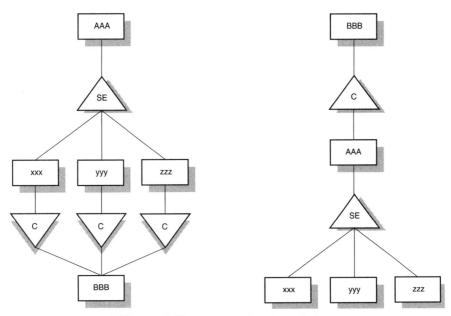

Figure 6.17.   Supertyping Associations

6.7.   What about Existing Models?

Very often, a modeling project will start with a failed model. Although the original modelers may have thought that they had successfully completed it, the model may never have been used, or it may be understandable only to the original team. However, it is this model that will be brought to a walk-through. But who is unhappy with the old model? It may be the original team if they had to explain the model to others or expand the model; it may be the developer team, who may have had to create their own model; it may be management, who want to finally understand what's going on in the application; or it may be top management, who want to understand what's happening with the data in the corporation and to integrate systems by sharing information between applications. There may also be a need to reengineer the business because the existing behavior of the business is imposed by the old model, which reflects the restrictions imposed by the old implementation. This existing behavior of the business may be inadequate because it has been imposed by the information systems department rather than by the business people or because the business rules have changed. When a bank is telling its customer that obtaining its credit card requires opening an account, then the unhappy customer becomes a victim of business rules dictated by an implementation.

As noted earlier, many existing models are implementation-based and reflect many things other than the business rules of the enterprise. For example, a construct is or is not considered to be a subtype, depending on whether it is implemented as one or three relational tables. This implementation has nothing to do with business rules. For another example, the subtype construct is not used at all because the underlying CASE tool does not support it. Codes created for the need to fit some value into three characters and considered to be entities are another example. Many existing models—often reverse-engineered—tend to contain these types of constructs. It is important to know how to deal with such models because most models never start from scratch and reflect at least some concerns of their implementation. While we want to develop a model independent of these concerns, we don't want to start from scratch, either. Therefore, we want to use as many facts—but not necessarily constructs!—from the existing models as possible. However, discovery of these facts is often difficult: a modeler will have to weed out extraneous information and harvest the facts, often with the help of SMEs. The harvest is even more difficult because the model is often incomplete: bits and pieces of business rules are not shown by the existing model, but reside only in application programs.

An analyst should clearly distinguish between two world views:[13] one capturing the business and its rules, and the other capturing the DBMS concerns. The latter is a refinement of the former. However, there may be more than one such refinement (see Appendix B); moreover, for the modeler, business analyst, and SME the refinement is of no interest. In the world of conceptual schemas, these approaches are distinguished as "enterprise" and "data" modeling. It is impossible to determine and interpret meanings directly from data [ACMF 92] as, for example, each of the generic associations described in Chapter 5 may be represented using the same relational concept of referential integrity.

Some existing models are based on object-oriented ideas. This does not necessarily mean that such models are good "by construction." Fairly often, they do not make explicit many associations between modeled objects. This happens because certain modeling methodologies recognize only some associations (e.g., subtypes) and do not deal with others (e.g., nonhierarchical COMPOSITIONS). As all kinds of associations exist in real-life enterprises, the

---

[13]*Weltanschauung*; they define "the point at which we resolve the ambiguities, imprecisions, and contradictions of our specification" [Swatman 92].

modeler will again need to harvest the facts, often with the help of SMEs. Often, these facts will exist only in implementation terms: certain attributes of objects will point to other objects. Fortunately, these shortcomings have been recently recognized and rectified by several prestigious national and international standardization communities (e.g., the General Relationship Model for ISO OSI Systems Management [GRM 93]; see also Chapter 7).

6.8. Tools of the Trade

"Which tool should I use?" is often asked. This question makes an unstated assumption that one such tool exists. A better question would be, "Is there a tool that might help?" An analyst may use tools that help in different aspects of modeling (e.g., graphics, specification language syntax checkers, model browsers, etc.).

Where do and don't tools help? First of all, a tool is a "word processor" (and a DBMS!) for the analyst. It is necessary to store and retrieve information using some criteria. This is, of course, not a replacement of thinking. Also, dealing with a library of components is easier when a tool exists. Also, there is a lot of textual information there, and browsing through this information may help a lot. (Probably, the most important help a tool can and should provide is browsing through the model, i.e., through the class library. Of course, names are not the only, and often not even the main, criteria for such a browsing; often the criteria are almost created on-the-fly by the browsing user.) Tools should be extensible: if a tool deals only with a rigidly fixed class library, it forces the modeler to use only its restricted set of concepts and is therefore of little help. Often, such a tool in fact hinders modeling (one can easily find many successful examples of using an extensible library by means of, e.g., object-oriented drawing tool for a personal computer instead of an expensive and restrictive CASE tool, etc.).

The understanding and elegance of an information model is improved when we don't have to deal with too many details. Therefore, the details should be hidden in the building blocks of the model. The benefits of this approach are especially apparent when compared with models that are developed using a restricted set of concepts (i.e., "relationships only" or even "restricted relationships only," the concepts supported by popular CASE tools). Understanding is improved, and more information is included in the same amount of square inches, because the library components (building blocks, molecules) used for modeling are of a higher level. (This can be compared with "lines of code" in programming: the same number of lines of code in Assembly language, in C, and in Smalltalk convey rather different information.)

Ideally, a graphical notation and a textual notation should be two alternative representations of the same language [BETA 91]. However, another view (from the same source) says that a graphical notation may not be able to represent everything: "it is not obvious that it is useful to have a graphical syntax for all language constructs." If a graphical notation becomes too complex, then perhaps it is better to stop using it for representing this complex part of the model and use textual notation instead. Needless to say, the textual notation should not be confined to natural language and "comments" to a picture (as some CASE tools still require); on the contrary, it should provide a precise and unambiguous specification. After all, the amount of graphics used becomes a user interface problem: some users like and some others hate pictures. (As Bertrand Meyer noted [Meyer 89], "A picture is worth a thousand words, but try to find seven errors in a picture.") In particular, when a picture becomes too cluttered (many crossed lines, etc.) and therefore too complex, it should be simplified. We can either decompose it into several simpler pictures or omit some details and confine them to the linear (textual) specification. In some cases, this is not even needed: as subtypes inherit associations from their supertypes, it may be possible to replace dozens of explicitly shown associations with only one. The same approach is used in such formal notations as Z and Object Z: redundant predicates may be included if they clarify the intent of an operation.

For reasonably big models, as for reasonably big programs, modularization is essential. This applies to both the linear representation (one of the reasons for using Object Z as a specification notation!) and the graphical representation. Therefore, a tool will help very much if it can support graphical modules (clustering) and associations between them, as well as different (user-specified) levels of detail. This is exactly the approach used by experienced modelers who start with the best possible tool: pencil and paper.

If the same model is shown using a graphical tool on many different diagrams from many different viewpoints (e.g., levels), then some (many?) objects will have more than one coordinate pair. In other words, the notion of "where the object is on the graphical representation" is very imprecise: it depends upon the viewpoint! This affects how the diagrams are represented in the tool's information encyclopedia.

If a model is presented using a formal notation (e.g., Z or Object Z), then a tool may be useful not just for storing and browsing through the information, but also for type checking. In other words, a tool should help the modeler get rid of trivial errors.

Standards

"The standardization of languages and interfaces in hardware and in software is a vital precondition for free competition and for propagation of technical advances to large numbers of satisfied customers." [Hoare 89]

The previous chapters of this book describe in detail why and how information modeling refers to the essential and precisely defined properties of objects and their associations rather than to properties of their computer-based implementations. This chapter will describe, in substantially less detail, the U.S. and international standardization activities that use the same approach. It will be shown that the concepts described earlier have influenced, and have been influenced by, these standardization activities. Most often, a proper conceptual framework follows from programming methodology considerations, and this approach to information management is stressed in such different national and international standardization documents as [ODP 2, ODP 4, ODP F, OODBTG 91, GRM 93, ACMF 92, API 92]. These documents, considered in more detail below, standardize or lead to the standardization of reference models. They do not try to standardize half-baked products, methodologies, or notations; rather, they deal with more fundamental (and vendor-neutral) issues of a common approach to information management.

The reference models considered by these standardization activities are independent of application specifics, methodologies, tools, or implementa-

183

tion. Therefore, these reference models are abstract and need to be instantiated for a particular application. They are usually very short (not more than several dozen pages). Indeed, to manage complexity these documents have to be as simple and general as possible.

The standardization activities discussed here are general-purpose rather than application-specific. Although the names of the committees responsible for these documents may sound specific to a particular area (databases or distributed processing, for example), the documents recognize and clearly outline a sound conceptual framework common to all or most information management systems, independent of their application area. These generic concepts will be discussed here. We hope that you will encounter nothing radically new: the previous chapters of this book have described such a conceptual framework.

The standardization activities described below use essentially the same approach. They emphasize concepts and semantics rather than syntactical considerations and do not promote—or even discuss—a particular methodology, notation, or tool. This corresponds to the conclusion of the Joint Standardization Meeting on the convergence of open systems interconnection and data management standards [OSI—Data Management 90]: separation of concerns between concepts, methodologies and tools, and representation languages is crucial not only for standardization efforts! The meeting participants also noted that a standardization document should deal with concepts, avoid methodologies, and use representation languages as notations for expressing concepts (excellent examples of the latter are provided in [ODP 4, ODP F]—see below). In this manner, activities that claim to be object-oriented can be evaluated with respect to such standardization documents. Pretty often, the results of such evaluation will show that these claims are premature.

One of these standardization activities was completed in 1991. It resulted in the Object Data Management (**ODM**) Reference Model[1] [OODBTG 91]. This work will be presented below in somewhat greater detail than the rest. It led to the creation of a new Technical Committee X3H7 on Object Information Management,[2] with the goal of harmonizing different standardization approaches in this area. The other standardization activities

---

[1]Developed by the Object-Oriented Database Task Group (OODBTG) of the Accredited Standards Committee X3 (Information Processing Systems) operating under the procedures of the American National Standards Institute (ANSI).

[2]Of the Accredited Standards Committee X3 (Information Processing Systems) operating under the procedures of the ANSI.

that we will discuss here are continuing; this discussion reflects the March 1993 status of their documents. Some of these documents are working documents of these standards committees used by members of the committees and other interested parties to assist in developing the actual standards.

Another important international standardization activity in progress deals with Open Distributed Processing. It produced the series of (draft) standards for the Reference Model for Open Distributed Processing (**RM-ODP**).[3] The ODM and the RM-ODP family of standards describe a single conceptual framework for all aspects of object information management. RM-ODP provides much more detail, with a slightly different emphasis than ODM. Essential aspects of a common framework (Descriptive Model) for RM-ODP are described in [ODP 2, ODP 4, ODP F] and used to express both viewpoints based on business rules (enterprise and information) and viewpoints based on computer implementation (computational, technology, and engineering). These particular viewpoints (Prescriptive Model) are described in more detail in [ODP 3]. Naturally, different viewpoints have a nonempty intersection (the system is not only modeled, but also implemented!), but they deal with rather different properties of the system.

In ODP terms, we may say that this book is about the information viewpoint. Naturally, any reasonable description of the information viewpoint would be impossible without a common conceptual framework. (Unfortunately, unreasonable descriptions are attempted and even promoted by some.) This book—as well as the standardization activities described in this chapter—stresses the need to explicitly formulate and reuse conceptual similarities between different viewpoints.

Another international standardization activity—the General Relationship Model[4] (**GRM**)—arose from the need to explicitly, formally, and uniformly represent relationships between managed objects. The GRM clearly separates the concerns of specifying relationships and of realizing or representing them. Therefore, it encourages the definition of generic, reusable relationship classes applicable to multiple applications. Annex D of the GRM presents examples of such generic classes, and they are sufficiently close to the ones presented in our generic association library.

Standardization documents described here emphasize the importance

---

[3]Developed by International Standards Organization / International Electrotechnical Commission Joint Technical Committee 1 / Special Committee 21 (ISO/IEC JTC1 SC21) Working Group 7 [ODP 2, ODP 3, ODP 4, ODP F].

[4]It belongs to the series of (draft) standards for Open Systems Interconnection Systems Management developed by ISO/IEC JTC1 SC21 Working Group 4. It is a part of a suite of standards for modeling object classes in the OSI systems management framework.

and role of abstraction for understanding a system. In particular, abstraction is defined as one of the first and most important concepts in [ODP 2]. This document also stresses that "specifications and their refinements typically do not coexist in the same system description" [ODP 2, 9.6]—a concept too often neglected in some existing information management systems. Consider the definition of business rules in terms of computer-based implementation (like foreign keys or attributes) or, alternatively, consider a system description consisting of several hundred pages of unstructured material. These descriptions are not understandable to their users, be they developers or SMEs, just because they are too long and usually unstructured. Therefore, such specifications are often scrapped, although they contain a lot of valuable material.

What happens when an inadequate specification is scrapped? A programmer cannot understand this inadequate specification and therefore creates a new and substantially better specification, often implicitly, himself or herself. Such a specification is usually unambiguous, precise, and structured, but there is—again, usually—no incentive for explicitly documenting it. Therefore, it exists in the mind of the programmer or in the collective mind of the programming team, but is not available outside of this team. Naturally, the viewpoint of the programmer includes not only business rules, but also implementation considerations, so that even if a precise specification is extracted from an application ("reverse engineering"), it will include more than the business rules, and therefore will be difficult for the SMEs to deal with. This is not the fault of the concept of specification: rather, this is the fault of an analyst who was, in creating the original specification, not abstract or precise enough for this specification to be evidently usable to the SME or developer. (Naturally, the developer of a complex system will create specifications for the implementation levels of the system: just as an analyst creates a specification for a business enterprise, a DBMS developer will create a specification for the DBMS to be developed.) The information modeling approach described in this book and the standardization activities described here try to solve exactly this problem.

Behavioral semantics has been explicitly referred to in all standardization efforts discussed here. Certain other standardization activities state that, although semantics is of importance, it is either not explicitly discussed or represented by an unstructured natural language. The dangers of such approaches are well known. To understand behavioral semantics and therefore be able to discuss it with both customers and developers, it has to be specified precisely [API 92]. If semantics is not specified or is described using a natural language, comments, and so on, then the problem of information interchange (interoperability) between humans and computer systems becomes hidden. It is relatively easy to exchange the operation signatures, and even prove that this interchange has been correct! It is substantially more difficult to exchange operation semantics and reason about the correctness of this interchange. To do that, semantics should be specified precisely (i.e., formally). Standardization activities described here recognize this.

A standardization—or any other—activity pretending that interoperability can be achieved only by means of signature interchange is inadequate because it is incomplete. Such activities will not be described here. Of course, an object reference model (and there exist quite a few of them—see, e.g., [Recommendations 91]) that does not precisely describe semantics is also incomplete: it does not deal with some fundamental issues of the object approach to information management. Therefore, it becomes quite difficult to compare some "legacy" object models with the ones that define semantics: their intersection may not be of substantial value because the underlying concepts of one model (semantics) are not covered by the other (signatures only[5]). This problem is very important in harmonizing different object standardization activities—another reason to stress the importance of these pioneering standardization activities that describe semantics.

Let us describe in slightly greater detail the ODM Reference Model, the only standardization activity discussed above that exists in its final form.

7.1.   The Object Data Management Reference Model—A Short Overview

Common object concepts cross the domains of object models used for DBMSs, programming languages, network management, repositories, operating system services, user interfaces, design methodologies, and so on—this is the most important observation of the ODM Reference Model. The object approach to information management is of utmost importance here because an object model supports encapsulation, which clearly separates between the external interface of an object and its internal implementation (ODM Glossary). Therefore, there is no need to assume object implementations (e.g., object-oriented DBMSs) to support the object approach to system development (recall that a disciplined approach to programming is possible

---

[5]Of course, some semantical properties exist in the description of a signature: having a particular type (i.e., satisfying this type's predicate) is certainly a semantical property. However, there exist other semantical properties without which understanding of an operation (or of a stable state of the system) becomes impossible.

even when "traditional" languages like Fortran are used [Gries 81]). By the same token, object orientation is not equivalent to using an object-oriented programming language, especially if the latter violates some of the general characteristics of object models.

The ODM Reference Model describes the general characteristics of object models. These characteristics are application- and implementation-neutral: they are valid across application domains and across "software development life-cycle" stages. Among these characteristics are: objects and operations (including both the classical (messaging) and generalized object models), encapsulation, object identity, types and classes, inheritance and delegation, noteworthy objects (including relationships, attributes, composites, and aggregates), extensibility, and integrity (including pre- and postconditions and invariants). These are the concepts that should be supported by methodologies and tools and implemented using representation languages. They provide a common ground (i.e., a framework) for understanding the common properties of different systems. The generalized object model is abstract and therefore not implementable; however, it may be instantiated providing for various concrete object models that are implementable. Such an approach corresponds very well to the one described in this book.

Taking into account that traditional boundaries between applications and DBMSs have shifted (see, e.g., Recommendations for Standards in Object Information Management), there exists a need for the standardization activities to adopt to this evolution. Therefore, a more abstract approach to object information management that concentrates on conceptual commonalities rather than differences between application domains will lead to interoperability between concrete object models developed for these domains.

The same approach is used in information modeling; the library in Chapters 4 and 5 and the concepts in Chapters 2 and 3 of this book are based on such conceptual commonalities. The other standardization activities referred to above also emphasize these commonalities, especially in their specification of behavior.

7.2. Behavior Specification

Let's consider some of these commonalities, in particular, the specifications of behavior by these standardization activities. Most important, behavior has to be precisely and completely specified in an implementation-independent and notation-independent manner. These specifications are declarative and are based on abstraction and precision (see the rest of this book).

Generally, behavior can be considered as a set of all sequences of operations that can occur from the initial state based on legal state transitions determined by the preconditions and postconditions of the operations [ODP 4]. As mentioned in Chapter 2 and elsewhere, this approach corresponds very well to the one used in traditional programming. Indeed, all operations are executed in a context specified by an invariant—an operation-independent condition that should be TRUE outside of any operation. The precondition for each operation defines exactly under which circumstances the operation is possible. The postcondition of an operation specifies what should be true immediately after the operation has been executed [ODP 2, OODBTG 91, GRM 93]. Naturally, an operation may change the state of the system, and the postcondition defines the new (desired) state. Then this new state will determine which operations are possible: the preconditions of these operations will have to satisfy the new state. (In terms of [ODP 2, 12.1.1], for each adjacent pair of actions, occurrence of the first action makes possible occurrence of the second action.) In addition, a contract is defined [ODP 2, 10.2.2] as an agreement between a set of objects governing part of their collective behavior. These definitions are traditional and correspond to the approach presented in this book and used in traditional programming. The previous chapters of this book show how they are used in information modeling in general and in specifying the contents of the generic association library in particular. They also show why these definitions are essential and how they are used to understand the enterprise to be modeled.

Not all standardization activities describe behavior in the same manner. However, the standardization activities presented here treat behavior essentially within the framework described above. Therefore, the manner of describing behavior in these documents is slightly different, but essentially converging. We will not discuss the details of these approaches here (see [Kilov 93-1]). All of them emphasize the need for declarative implementation-independent specifications of semantics and propose formal constructs (invariants and pre- and postconditions) for doing so. The same ideas have been elaborated in more detail and promoted in the modeling recommendations of an important international consortium—OSI/Network Management Forum for OSI managed objects [OSI/NM Forum 91]; these recommendations were often based on the approach in [Meyer 88]. The previous chapters of this book describe this approach in detail.

Evidently, with these characteristics in mind, a modeling approach that separates "data modeling" and "process modeling" cannot be considered object-oriented. Such an approach is inadequate, not because it lacks this label, but because it forces the modeler—and the SME—to make a distinction based on properties of certain computer-based implementations.

7.3. Formalization of Semantics

The need to clearly distinguish between operation signature and semantics is evidently stressed in all standardization efforts described here. These more recent standardization activities emphasize semantics and its formalization to a substantially greater extent than earlier ones. In addition to RM-ODP, ODM, and GRM mentioned above, let us also emphasize the activities of the OSI Systems Management on Formal Description Techniques,[6] Object Information Management Technical Committee,[7] and the ISO/IEC JTC1/SC21 Special Working Group on Modeling Facilities. Consider the U.S. position on the latter: it stresses that "the conceptual schema modeling facility should be written in a formal notation . . . [that] should be translatable into a representation suitable for subject matter experts; in case of doubt, however, the formal notation takes precedence" [ACMF 92]. This is exactly the approach taken to understanding and specifying the generic association library described in Chapters 4 and 5. A good example of such a formal notation is provided by Z and Object Z (see Appendix A). However, it appears that first-order logic is not always sufficient; for example, when we want to specify that some resultant property of a composite entity exists, we need to use second-order logic because we have to quantify over operations [Kilov 93].

All standardization activities described here discuss, to some extent, the need to precisely (i.e., formally), define operation semantics. This aspect of information management is considered very important by several international standardization committees and groups—for instance, a recent work item for several international standardization groups [API 92] specifically considers the need to clearly formulate semantics of a programmatic interface rather than specify its syntax and then rely on "common sense" or default considerations for specifying semantics. It stresses that natural-language comments "can provide some of the required information for simple interfaces, but are insufficiently rigorous for complex interfaces with stringent conformance requirements." This problem and some aspects of its solution have been mentioned quite a few times in the previous chapters of this book.

No particular mechanisms or notations are recommended by the standardization documents for the specification of behavioral semantics. This is as it should be: the semantics of a reference model should be independent of a notation used to represent this model. (Compare with the separation of con-

---

[6]Presented, e.g., in [US–Z 92].

[7]ASC X3H7.

cerns in a good programming text: concepts are presented independent of a particular notation (programming language) used for expressing these concepts [Dijkstra 76, Abelson 85, Gries 81].) Several formal notations may be appropriate to express behavioral semantics. Two standardization documents—[ODP 4 and ODP F]—describe how different formal notations (LOTOS, SDL, Z, Object Z) may be used to express the architectural semantics of the most important aspects of the descriptive model for Open Distributed Processing. To accomplish this goal, invariants, preconditions, and postconditions are used in these documents to specify the semantics of the essential concepts from [ODP 2] in Z and Object Z. Quite a few of these concepts and their formally specified semantics are sufficiently close to the ones described in this book.

As the introduction to [ODP 4] stresses, the formal specification of ODP's modeling concepts has, "through the process of iterative development and feedback," improved the consistency of their definitions in the base document (i.e., [ODP 2]). But this is evident because only a formal specification shows that the concept is understood in a precise and unambiguous manner. For quite a few readers of [ODP 2], the formal specification of its concepts in [ODP 4 and ODP F] provided the best way to understand them. Of course, even a partial formal specification helps a lot: as [ODP 4] notes, only the most basic concepts of the base document are considered there. Again, this corresponds very well to the approach taken in application-specific models [Zave 91] where a partial formal specification helped to understand the problem and led to exposing quite a few errors in an existing (specified and implemented) system.

7.4. Object Models: Message-Oriented and Generalized

In information modeling, an object usually is not independent and cannot "respond autonomously to messages directed to it" (a typical expression for the messaging model). If the messaging paradigm is used in information modeling, then there appears a semantically essential need to impose something like an ER model on top of such an object model. This happens because of the need to somehow describe relationships between objects in a specification. As you have seen earlier, quite a few properties are jointly owned by several objects and cannot be reduced to properties of these isolated objects. Moreover, the message-oriented paradigm leads to making unneeded choices in specifying an operation ("who will be the message recipient?"). Although it is possible to use multiple dispatching to implement a jointly owned operation (e.g., in Smalltalk), this approach need not be prescribed by an object model. Also, finally, the messaging paradigm makes very attractive the rather dangerous notion of a side effect of an operation— this is what may happen with "other" objects that do not explicitly receive the message.

Associations can and should be an integral part of a standardized object model. This has been done in [GRM 93] (in fact, this has been the goal of developing the general relationship model for OSI managed objects in the first place). The existence of collections of objects defined by their jointly owned behavior has been referred to in [ODP 2, ODP 4] and also in [OODBTG 91], where both the classical and generalized object models have been described. In particular, [OODBTG 91] stresses that classical and generalized object models are founded on different metaphors. "Generalized object models do not distinguish a recipient from other request parameters. In generalized models, a request is defined as an event which identifies an operation and optional parameters.... Classical or messaging object models do distinguish a recipient. In classical models, a request is defined as an event which identifies an operation, a recipient, and optional parameters." In a generalized object model, unlike in a classical object model, all parameters are equal. Moreover, in classical models, the interface is defined for an "isolated" object—the recipient of the corresponding operations. On the other hand, in generalized models, an interface usually does not belong to one object: an operation is usually jointly owned by several objects, none of which is singled out.

In this manner, relationships between objects become explicit and implementation-independent. They can be described by substantially the same paradigms used for describing isolated objects. There is no need to reason about relationships based on their implementation by means of, for example, attributes of interrelated objects.[8] A property of a collection of objects does not have to be artificially ascribed to one of these objects. This approach is very successfully used, for example, for specifying the general relationship model for managed objects in [GRM 93].

Some standardization activities explicitly recognize that an object association—in the same manner as an object—is not isolated. An object usually participates in more than one elementary association (see the rest of this book), and therefore, to specify the behavior in which a particular object par-

---

[8]In fact, attribute-oriented operations should not be available by default; this access to the implementation (e.g., for attributes that implement relationships) violates abstraction and makes understanding difficult. It may also lead to semantic integrity violation.

ticipates, all the "primitive" invariants for the object existing due to its participation in these elementary associations are conjoined. The resulting invariant—the conjunction of all these primitive invariants—defines the complete behavior in which the object may participate (compare [Zave 92]). In other words, "an object may be in a number of contexts simultaneously, in which case the behavior is constrained to the intersection of the behavior of each individually" [ODP 2, 12.2.3].

Formalization of the "informal" ER model therefore permits, in the context of OSI managed objects, the consideration of the formalized ER model as a natural constituent of the object information model rather than, as often happens, as an alien body used only to improve understanding of examples. A careful specification of association-related concepts will make precise and explicit the large and often implicit body of knowledge assumed "evident" to the reader of such informal ER specifications. These assumptions often lead to misunderstanding because they have been never specified precisely and explicitly: too many "extended ER models" differ in seemingly subtle but essential aspects. These differences may be easily recognized only when the models are clearly (i.e., formally) defined. Several standardization activities (e.g., [GRM 93, OODBTG 91, ODP 2, ODP 4, ODP F]) explicitly recognize this need.

A good example of a formal approach to a real-life generic application is provided by the first component standard to be developed under the RM-ODP, the ODP Trader [Trader 92]. It is described using Z, Object Z, and "structured" English, and these specifications are synchronized (in fact, the Z specification has been translated from Object Z). Detailed English comments in these Z and Object Z specifications, as well as their usage of rather simple notational tools, make them easy to follow.

7.5.   Harmonization of Standardization Activities

The different standardization activities described here, as well as many other ones, consider various approaches to object modeling. Naturally, there exists a clear need to understand and harmonize them because in many cases the models only look different, but are in fact similar. It is also very desirable to reuse good ideas and concepts described in a particular object model by modelers having different backgrounds. This harmonization is one of the most important goals of the recently created ASC X3H7 Object Information Management Technical Committee.

The activities of X3H7 will include both tangible deliverables (e.g., the base document) and intangible deliverables (e.g., influencing other standardization activities through liaisons and informal communications). The main goal is to understand the underlying semantics of different models in a notation-independent and implementation-independent way in order to ensure interoperability. One of the important results of these activities—currently being worked on—is the features matrix, in which different object models are compared on the basis of several very general criteria [Features Matrix 93, Dialogue 93]. Among the most interesting of these criteria are the specification of behavioral semantics (in addition to signatures) and the specification of properties of groups of objects (including shared behavior and shared state).

The difference and possible reconciliation between classical (messaging) and generalized object models (described, in particular, in Section 4) have been among the most interesting topics at the X3H7 meetings. It was noted that there may exist workarounds for mapping from generalized to classical object models. However, these workarounds do not lose information, unlike the workarounds from object models to many existing CASE tools and vice versa, which do. The concept of multiple ownership of an operation has been stressed as being crucial for information management. It was noted that a distinguished recipient of an operation is often not reasonable in information management: for most operations, the choice of a recipient is artificial and unneeded. The Committee will consider how relationships between objects are dealt with in various object models. This is in very good agreement with our approach to information modeling.

One of the most important characteristics of harmonizing different object models is the explicit differentiation between the modeling of business rules and that of their "database implementations." This has been clearly recognized in the different viewpoints described in the ODP documents. The same, or a sufficiently close approach is referred to in the official U.S. position on modeling facilities [ACMF 92]. It states, in particular, that the work scope of the SWG/MF should clearly distinguish between syntax, semantics, and methodologies. It clearly distinguishes between conceptual schema and data modeling facilities, stating that "the purpose of conceptual models and schemas is to describe and satisfy the requirements, meanings, intentions, purposes, and interpretations associated with (a) information elements of an enterprise, and (b) the interrelationships of these information elements." It further states that enterprise modeling should not be concerned with implementation and technology issues. It refers to the impossibility of determining semantics from a data model, that is, from an implementation and technology-based model, alone.[9] Note how close this U.S. position is to the approach taken by X3H7 and other standardization groups, especially ODP, and also note that it corresponds very well with the information modeling approach described in this book. Although ODP does not use these terms, the explanations presented by SWG-MF are consistent with the understanding of RM-ODP and do not conflict with terms used in ODP. Indeed, ODP has no requirement for a data modeling facility: data models are viewed by ODP as being inherently representational and implementation-oriented. ODP's requirement for a conceptual schema modeling facility is expressed in the enterprise and information viewpoints, as well as in terms of concepts common to all viewpoints [ODP 2, ODP 3].

The information modeling approach described in this book clearly corresponds to the conceptual modeling of [ACMF 92], describes the same information elements of an enterprise and their interrelationships referred to above, and does it in a rigorous manner supported by a formal specification (see Appendix A). As you have seen from this book, information modeling also clearly separates the business rules of an enterprise from their possible representations in data models.

X3H7 recognized that understanding is essential for harmonization. Therefore, the precise specification of behavioral semantics—rather than only its syntax—has been among the activities of substantial interest and importance to this committee. The Mission Statement of this committee includes, as one of its goals, providing "a common conceptual framework for understanding of basic concepts (e.g., behavior) and (semantic) interoperability between various object models both at the same and at different frames of reference" [Mission 92]. The need to distinguish between object-oriented systems and an object model was considered by X3H7 to be essential. Restrictions imposed by certain existing systems should not be imposed on an object model. As a consequence, X3H7 has stressed the need to consider the shared behavior of objects and the need to specify behavior declaratively, although certain existing object-oriented systems do not support these approaches. Some systems assume that the complexity of a real-world situation can or must always be carved up into discrete self-contained objects and provide minimal mechanisms for specifying the underlying behavior in any form other than procedural code implemented in a particular programming language. Naturally, these restrictions are artificial and therefore un-

---

[9]Such activities are very difficult, indeed, because different concepts may have the same representation: referential integrity represents all kinds of semantically quite different associations between objects; "cascade delete" represents certain deletion rules for these different associations; and so on.

necessary. Lifting of these restrictions corresponds very well with the material presented in this book and to the approach used by several standardization activities described here.

Conflicting terminology represents another problem in understanding and harmonizing different approaches to object information management. This problem, however, is not that severe. The object community "at large" already has a sort of common understanding: thousands of participants from both industry and academia at important object orientation conferences essentially speak the same language, at least some of the time. There is no need to (re)define the basic concepts at the beginning of each conference: the participants understand each other reasonably well. Of course, there may exist "skewed" views, but they are recognized as such and usually mapped onto the "generic" view. Therefore, a better characterization of an abstract object model seems to be the most important result of X3H7 activities of harmonization: standardization activities have to reach the same kind of understanding. Adopting a common object model need not mean that there will be no other models: the common model is generic and will certainly be instantiated and extended by the interested parties. Therefore, the common model should not be, for example, language-specific or application-specific (i.e., should not be confined within a "traditional" boundary); a model based on a particular popular language or a model dealing mainly with databases is indeed liable to be controversial and may be skewed itself. The same model should be applicable to all abstraction levels—in traditional terms, to analysis, design, and development. A model should not rely on the syntax of a particular language or on a worldview where information integrity could be easily violated. It should be as simple and elegant as possible, and to do this, more abstraction is needed! Good examples of a sufficient level of abstraction have been described above: the OODBTG Reference Model (in fact, its first part) and also appropriate passages from the ODP and GRM models. Presumably, a common object model should be based on the same approaches.

Mapping between different object models means much more than syntactic mapping. Operations with the same signature may have very different—and often incompatible—semantics. This has been stressed by [API 92], which served as a basis for a very important new work item in international standardization activities. The standardization community has recognized that interoperability based on syntax considerations alone does not lead to preserving integrity in information exchange, and is therefore woefully inadequate. Naturally, syntactic mapping is also difficult (e.g., due to the differences between classical and generalized models, different kinds of inheritance, different base types, etc.), but even more important is preserving the meaning of the information when the appropriate mappings are accomplished. To do that, understanding of information semantics is essential, both for the static state of information (invariants) and for available operations (specified by their pre- and postconditions). This problem is well recognized by the standardization activities described above. Choosing a particular existing object-oriented modeling language may lead to the same problems, because many of them are not extensible, are restricted by the methodologies and tools used by their vendors, and, most important, usually do not represent information semantics in a complete manner. To deal with these problems, concepts should be considered first. Therefore, the harmonization of different object models should be as specified in [Recommendations 91]—to reexamine traditional boundaries, to promote harmony across these boundaries, to promote families of mutually consistent standards with *object model concepts and terminology* that should be *defined and implemented the same throughout all standards*, and to provide a unified object model that will cross the boundaries and be instantiable and extensible.

Such harmonization of different object models is not easy! It should lead to a conceptual framework of core common concepts—eventually a standard—invariant across different frames of reference, that is, common to programming languages, databases, specifications ("enterprise modeling"), design, user interfaces, and so on. The specification of these common concepts should be notation-neutral and emphasize semantics rather than signatures [Mission 92]. These concepts should be able to describe the semantics of base class libraries for different frames of reference (e.g., programming languages, generic analysis, etc.). This program of work is very challenging, but quite a few already existing standardization activities (see above) provide a good basis for accomplishing its goals.

A More Formal Specification

"A major aspect of all intellectual activity is the selection or creation of the appropriate "language" to talk and reason about the topics at hand. The transition from "natural language" to "formal language" can be viewed as a reduction of the bandwidth and constitutes a major simplification." [Dijkstra 91]

Formal notations force specifiers to precisely and explicitly formulate their understanding of existing or future systems and make it possible to decide unambiguously whether a system does or does not conform to its specifications. In particular, "natural language" specifications of the generic association library (and also of other systems—from PBX [Zave 92] and CICS [Potter 92] to the Descriptive Model of Open Distributed Processing [ODP 2]) have been understood much better, and inconsistencies and discrepancies in these specifications have been found and resolved only after the formal specifications (in Z) have been produced.

The use of formal methods makes a system specification explicit and understandable. However, "a specification written directly in some logic is an unstructured collection of formulae from which it is difficult to extract its meaning" [Fiadeiro 92]. It is therefore also necessary to provide some structuring facilities for specifications of nontrivial size. The Z and Object Z notations provide such convenient structuring mechanisms. The Z specification, although very clear and convenient, does not support information hiding, operation grouping, and inheritance. This need for a better use of abstraction is (partially) satisfied by Object Z [Duke 91, Rose 92]. It makes it possible to specify generic associations directly, as generic class schemas (and reuse them by parameter substitution), combine all facts about a generic association in one place, and provide encapsulation at the same time. In particular, all operations available to the user of the association are listed in the visibility list.

The particular choice of a notation is not the most important aspect of this appendix. Any notation that supports formal and disciplined specifications is acceptable. We also agree with the "liberal" rather than the "strict" approach to formalism [Nicholls 92]: "the important idea is to use mathematics to model systems and to employ as much formality as turns out to be useful." We do not consider formal proof techniques as a "touchstone for entry into the formal methods club": rather, we want to use formal methods to better understand what we are doing.

In what follows, a more formal specification of two generic associations in extended Object Z will be presented and commented upon. Other generic associations may be specified in the same manner, although some difficulties may also appear (see [Kilov 93]). Suffice it to say that we understood the generic object class library (see Chapter 4) much better when its important fragments had been specified more formally because a formal specification is the only one that guarantees understanding.

A generic association class is defined in the same manner as any other object class—by defining its invariant and the set of available operations (e.g., making them visible to the user by means of "visibility lists" [Duke 91, Rose 92]).

A.1. Dependency

Dependency is a generic association between the generic type "Parent" and the generic type "Dependent," described in detail in Chapter 4. It is represented in our specification as a class schema which uses a relation parentOf: Dependent ↔ Parent. This class schema encapsulates its state schema and operation schemas. This approach clearly distinguishes between the conceivable instances of the Dependent type and actual instances of this type, and therefore permits some reasoning about the creation and deletion of instances of this type. Namely, actual instances of the Dependent type belong to the domain of the relation parentOf. Of course, not all conceivable instances of this type are actualized. Moreover, our specification clearly shows that the existence of an instance of the relation parentOf (corresponding to the DEPENDENCY association) is equivalent to the existence of an actual instance of a Dependent and a corresponding actual instance of a Parent. Only one operation has been shown here; other operations can be specified in the same manner. It is also possible to specify operations like "Parent Exists?" ("Dependent Exists?"), with a parameter of type Parent (with a parameter of type Dependent) and a Boolean result: it returns TRUE if a conceivable instance of the type Parent belongs to the range of parentOf (if a conceivable instance of type Dependent belongs to the domain of parentOf).

Naturally, both the Parent and Dependent types may participate in other generic associations. In this case, operations, for example, for creation of these instances will have preconditions that are obtained by conjoining preconditions for their creation formulated for all of their generic associations. In other words, these preconditions may only be strengthened and not weakened. Therefore, for example, the existence of an instance of the Parent type will always be essential for creating an instance of the Dependent type, even if either or both of these types will participate in other associations as well. As there are no restrictions imposed by the generic class DEPENDENCY on creating an instance of a Parent, this operation is not specified here.

In what follows, the formal elements of the definition will be presented in this type, and informal comments *in italics*.

A.1.1. Definition

Dependency [Parent,Dependent]

↾ (createDependent, . . .)

This is a visibility list: only features enumerated in the visibility list are available to the user of Dependency.

Parent, Dependent: Entity

Entity is a generic type defined elsewhere (see text below).

dependentInstances: **P** Dependent
parentInstances: **P** Parent
parentOf: Dependent ↔ Parent
dom parentOf = dependentInstances
ran parentOf ⊆ parentInstances

This relation represents all instances of Dependency available to its user. The only way to access this relation is through operations enumerated in the visibility list of Dependency; the relation itself is not included in this visibility list.

It is a relation because generally, a dependent instance may have more than one parent instance. However, if the number of parent instances related to a dependent instance is exactly one, then the relation becomes a partial function: each conceivable instance of a dependent can relate to at most one conceivable instance of a parent. Of course, each actual instance of a dependent will relate to exactly one actual instance of a parent. A partial function will be represented by replacing the arrow ↔ in the definition of the relation with the arrow →

All dependent instances belong to the domain of the relation parentOf: for a dependent instance to exist, it has to have a parent instance. A parent instance can exist without having any dependent instances, and so the set of parent instances is a superset of the range of parentOf. This is as it should be: the Dependency association is asymmetric.

This concludes the state schema. What follows are the operation schemas.

---

createDependent
Δ (parentOf, dependentInstances, parentInstances)

This Δ-list includes all variables that are changed. In Object Z, by convention, variables not in this list are unchanged. However, an application-specific object usually participates simultaneously in several generic associations. In this case, the corresponding invariants are conjoined. The operation schemas are also merged, leading to the change of variables not in this Δ-list.

d?:Dependent
p?:Parent

These are the input variables; by convention, their identifiers end with a question mark.

---

d? ∉ dependentInstances

This is the only precondition: the dependent instance to be created does not exist.

The parent instance may already exist.

dependentInstances' = dependentInstances ∪ {d?}
parentInstances' = parentInstances ∪ {p?}
parentOf'=parentOf ⊕ {d? ↦ p?}

A new instance of the relation parentOf is a maplet (pair) consisting of the new dependent instance and a new or already existing parent instance.

This instance will be added to the existing set of instances of this relation. The state of a variable after the execution of an operation is primed. Of course, the last line implies the first two lines of this fragment (if we also consider the state schema, i.e., the definitions of domain and range of parentOf). It is possible to use redundancy in Z and Object Z; such an approach is recommended if it improves understandability.

. . .

A.1.2. Use

To use DEPENDENCY, it should be instantiated, that is, its formal (generic) parameters should be replaced with actual object classes:

```
| edd: Dependency [EMPLOYEE, CHILD]
```

Here the particular instance of DEPENDENCY is given a name (edd), and actual parameters EMPLOYEE and CHILD replace formal parameters PARENT and DEPENDENT.

To (re)use an operation from the visibility list of DEPENDENCY, its name should be qualified by the name of a particular instantiation of DEPENDENCY:

```
| . . . edd.createDependent . . .
```

(The dot notation is in accordance with [Duke 91, Rose 92].) Although input and output parameters for the operation are not included in the operation header, in accordance with the approach of Z and Object Z, it may be very desirable to do so in order to make the specification clearer. This approach is suggested by [Duke 91].

As mentioned earlier (and noted in the comments in the specification above), DEPENDENCY (as well as other generic associations) may have subtypes that are still generic. One of these subtyping hierarchies may be defined by whether a Dependent instance can have more than one Parent instance. Another, orthogonal, subtyping hierarchy may be defined by whether a DEPENDENCY association has mandatory existence (i.e., by whether an instance of a Parent can exist independently of an instance of Dependent; see Chapter 4). Object Z provides a very simple mechanism for doing that. By using these subtypes, the specifier decides to be more detailed. This may not be necessary, and Object Z (in the same manner as Z) provides the possibility for the specification to be as abstract or refined as the specifier desires.

A.2. Symmetric Relationship

The generic associations between information modeling object classes are often more complicated than DEPENDENCY. In particular, they may associate more than two object types, and this may lead to some technical problems in their specification in Object Z along the same lines as the generic DEPENDENCY.

Consider, for instance, the Chen-like SYMMETRIC RELATIONSHIP described in Chapter 4. Its invariant states that, when instantiated with application-specific object classes, an instance of a symmetricRelationship corresponds to exactly one instance of each participating (regular) Entity. In this manner, a symmetricRelationship type associates a set of (named) participating Entity types. Therefore, it is necessary to introduce explicitly both the set of regular Entity types and the set of their instances. Otherwise, the approach here is the same as that used for specifying the DEPENDENCY association: actual instances of the symmetricRelationship type belong to the domain of the relation entitiesOf. Of course, not all conceivable instances of this type are actualized. Moreover, our specification clearly shows that the existence of an instance of the relation entitiesOf (corresponding to the SYMMETRIC RELATIONSHIP association) is equivalent to the existence of an actual instance of a Symmetric Relationship object and a corresponding set of actual typed instances of Entities.

Comments that follow refer only to the new material; they do not repeat ideas from comments in the DEPENDENCY specification.

---

symmetricRelationship [R, Ts, Es] ───────────────────────

↾ (createsymmetricRelationship, ...)

> *Again, only one operation is shown here (and in the visibility list).*

E, R: Entity
T: Type

Es: $\mathbb{F}$ E
Ts: $\mathbb{F}$ T

> *Es and Ts are finite sets of entities and their types, correspondingly, that are associated in the symmetric relationship R.*

symmetricRelationshipInstances: $\mathbb{P}$ R
entitiesOf: R $\twoheadrightarrow$ (T $\twoheadrightarrow$ E)

This is a relation (partial function) the instance of which associates an instance of the symmetric relationship R with a set of partial functions from a type to an instance of a regular entity. The first "partial function" means that a (conceivable) instance of the symmetric relationship corresponds to at most one instance of the set of typed regular entities. An actual instance of the symmetric relationship corresponds to exactly one instance of this set of regular entities. The second "partial function" means that there will exist at most one conceivable instance of a regular entity for each type in an instance of entitiesOf.

#(ran entitiesOf) $\geq$ 2

There should be at least two typed entities in this set.

symmetricRelationshipInstances = dom entitiesOf
$\forall$r: symmetricRelationshipInstances $\bullet$ dom (entitiesOf r) = Ts

All declared entity types participate in the symmetric relationship association for each instance of the symmetric relationship type.

---

createsymmetricRelationship
Δ (entitiesOf, symmetricRelationshipInstances)

entities?: $\mathbf{P}$ (T $\times$ E)
symmetricRelationship?:R

This defines only the signature (syntax) of the operation. The semantics is below the line.

The entities (to be) participating in the symmetric relationship may or may not exist beforehand.

dom entities? = Ts

All entity types (and instances) defined in the parameters for this symmetric relationship should participate in creating a symmetric relationship instance.

symmetricRelationship? $\notin$ symmetricRelationshipInstances
symmetricRelationship?.create

An instance of the symmetric relationship object should be created. This is done by referring to the create operation defined in the entity class schema.

entitiesOf'=entitiesOf ⊕ {symmetricRelationship? ↦ entities?}

This is analogous to adding a maplet to the parentOf in the specification of Dependency. However, entities? is an instance of a set.

. . .

From the technical viewpoint, this specification is written in extended Object Z; not all generic parameters are base types. Some of them have a very definite structure.

This specification, like the previous one, is not the only one possible. Both Z and Object Z provide and encourage several ways to write specifications. In the same manner as it is difficult and often undesirable to reason about the best way to write a program in a programming language, it is difficult and often undesirable to reason about the best way to write a specification in a specification notation. However, some guidelines for programming languages exist, and certain programming-language idioms are suggested for reuse. It seems to be a bit too early to provide such a library of idioms for Object Z.

A.3.   On Infrastructure

A complete Object Z specification of an application will include instantiations of the appropriate generic associations. However, there is a need to specify other properties of the entities as well. In particular, structural properties of an isolated entity should be specified. This is rather straightforward and may use some infrastructure provided by the abstractor who specifies the generic association library. Evidently, entity types belong to the set of these structural properties represented, for example, in a mapping from an entity instance to a set of its types. This mapping (a total function) will look like:

$$\text{ENTITY} \rightarrow \mathbb{F}\ \text{TYPE}$$

This mapping shows, in particular, that every entity can have several types. This is evident: as noted earlier, even from the viewpoint of generic associations, the same entity may be simultaneously a dependent in one association, a composite in another, a parent in still another, and so on. Of course, some of these types will be application-specific.

This mapping will be needed for specifying and reasoning about other generic associations. In particular, it will be needed to specify irreflexivity of a COMPOSITION association; to do that, a transitive closure of a relation like componentOf (in the COMPOSITION schema) will have to be used. Irreflexivity here means that a composite and its (direct or indirect) component may not have exactly the same set of types. This mapping from an entity to a set of its types may also be used to better specify various fragments of the invariants for COMPOSITION, SYMMETRIC RELATIONSHIP, and so on; and, naturally, it is indispensable in reasoning about subtyping! These aspects, however, are relatively straightforward.

A.4.　On Reading and Writing Formal Specifications

One of the most important problems in using formal specifications deals with the complexity of notation. This problem is cited for any formal specification technique. Notations used in these techniques are based on (very simple concepts of) predicate calculus and therefore may not be familiar to the SME. However, the usage of a class library of concepts formulated by means of such a precise notation does not demand that all users of this library completely understand all the formal specifications of its components. Specifications may and should be provided to their users on different levels of formality and different levels of detail.

Using (*reading*) a specification component is not equivalent to being able to create (*write*) one, and in most cases specification authors and users refer to already existing specification components. However, in any case these components should ultimately be defined in a precise and formal manner, to have an "ultimate reference point" that should take precedence in case of any doubts or misunderstandings. These definitions need not be exposed to all users: a formal specification may be (almost straightforwardly) translated into a "structured" English one. This is not too difficult; just try to read it aloud. Naturally, translating a specification from a natural language into a formal notation is highly nontrivial and requires the work of a specialist, who will probably ask many questions (see Chapter 6). This happens because of the inherent ambiguity of natural languages. However, writing a formal specification happens much more seldom than reading such a specification; and it is substantially easier to read a good specification than to write one.

The most important merit of a formal specification is its explicitness: the modelers have to specify exactly what they (and the SMEs) want—no more and no less—instead of handwaving to describe sort of what they think they have in mind, more or less.

Refinement

This appendix will show how a generic association precisely defined by its business rules can be refined into a computer-based implementation. There is no one way, and there is usually no "best" way of refining an association. Let's consider a simple association (what could be simpler than a DEPENDENCY?) and refine it using a relational implementation (what could be conceptually simpler than a relational DBMS?).

A DEPENDENCY association is a collection of two object types—a Parent and a Dependent. The invariant of this association refers to both (see Chapter 5). In the same manner, operations applicable to this association are jointly owned by both (see Chapter 5 and Appendix D).

There exist several ways to refine this association using a relational DBMS. This refinement will, first and foremost, be a refinement of the state; we'll need to replace object types and their association with relational tables and use foreign keys for this purpose. After this is done, operations will be refined in a straightforward manner. Some of these operations will lead to writing a small application program, unless the supporting DBMS provides some mechanisms (like referential integrity) for supporting certain semantic rules.

How many relational tables will there be? There are three possibilities; for each of them, the refinement will be correct as it will provide an implementation that conforms to the model (i.e., to the specification).

Three tables. One table for the Parent, one table for the Dependent, and one table for the DEPENDENCY association. The latter will consist only of foreign keys. The first two tables will not contain any foreign keys. There are no semantic restrictions imposed by this implementation.

Two tables. One table for the Parent and one table for the Dependent. One (or both) of these tables will contain foreign keys referring to the tuples of the other table. Usually, the foreign keys are put in the Dependent table because there is usually exactly one Parent instance for a given Dependent instance. However, an important caveat is in order: "usual" does not mean "always." This restriction of having exactly one Parent instance for each Dependent instance should **never** be imposed by the implementation! (In other words, the Database Administrator should not dictate business rules.)

One table. This table will contain all the information and will not be "fully normalized" (usually, the Parent instance information will be repeated). No foreign keys are needed here.

Obviously, the relational tables also represent objects (e.g., we may consider them as compositions of tuples). Implementation-independent operations on these objects are defined in [Codd 70].

A tuple in a relational table does not necessarily correspond to an object defined in the information model: for three tables, for instance, the table with foreign keys consists of clearly identifiable tuples (objects with, if you wish, object identifiers) that do not correspond to any single information object.

Which refinement is the best?

First of all, this is not a problem for the SME or modeler to solve. Business rules have nothing to do with the solution of this problem. The database administrator has the right expertise to solve this very important problem. For instance, if the underlying DBMS is rather slow and does not provide reasonable performance for joins (e.g., on a microcomputer) the "one table" refinement may be preferable. Moreover, if the number of dependents for each parent is "small" (e.g., not more than one), then, again, the "one table" solution may be acceptable. How many tables can remain open at the same time may also be a valid consideration. Of course, transaction performance may also influence the refinement choice.

If we choose three tables, then each table corresponding to an object will not have any foreign keys, and an SQL statement like SELECT * FROM PARENT will yield no extraneous data. This may or may not be a blessing: the user may want to get the "extraneous" data about the dependent(s) of the parent as a result of executing this SQL statement. However, to do that, it will be necessary to include foreign keys of all dependents into a parent tuple. This is possible, but not desirable in the case of multiple dependents. Naturally, this problem does usually not appear in SELECT * FROM DEPENDENT: as a rule, there is only one Parent instance for a given Dependent instance. Nevertheless, the "three-table" solution is the most general: it will work for whatever invariants (and therefore cardinalities) are defined by business rules!

As you have seen, even in such a simple case there are many, possibly related, considerations in choosing the best (or even an acceptable) refinement. This book is not about database administration or database design; there exist excellent books that already deal with these issues. It is clear that separation of concerns (separating business rules from DBMS considerations) leads to clean and correct implementations, without restricting business rules by peculiarities of a particular database administration policy.

Naturally, the problem of multi-attribute keys may also be encountered. If, for instance, the key of a Parent is spread across several attributes, then most probably an artificial surrogate key will have to be created for appropriate references. However, there is nothing new here; this idea corresponds very well to that of a unique object identifier.

A good relational DBMS will provide means to support referential integrity constraints that follow from business rules. For instance, it will not permit the creation of a Dependent instance for a nonexistent Parent instance, whatever the number of tables chosen. Sometimes, only partial support is provided by the DBMS. For "three tables," it will most probably be necessary to write a small program or a trigger that checks the existence of a Parent instance before attempting to create its Dependent instance. Evidently, there is no need to write this program again and again. In the same manner as a library of generic associations (see Chapter 5) can be reused, a library of their possible refinements can also be written and reused. In this case, a database programmer, together with the database administrator, will just have to pick and choose the refinement most suitable for their needs.

Finally, even within the same data model (e.g., relational), there exist different implementations with varying support of referential integrity and other semantic rules, so the choice of a particular refinement from the library may often be product-specific. Of course, relational DBMSs are not the only ones possible, and other refinement libraries will be needed for other (e.g., hierarchical or object-oriented) DBMSs. Needless to say, some object-oriented DBMSs support certain associations and their business rules directly, and so help to solve the refinement problem in the easiest possible way.

Other associations are usually more complicated than DEPENDENCY. However, it is always possible—and rather straightforward—to provide some correct refinement (be careful to support all business rules!). It may be more difficult, although also possible, to provide a "better" refinement. This book does not present a refinement library.

To conclude this appendix, let us very briefly examine SUBTYPING. It may be preferable to create a separate relational table for each subtype of a given supertype, and a separate one for the supertype itself. In this manner, an instance of a particular object will be represented in a relational implementation as more than one tuple! From the business-rule viewpoint, it is irrelevant how many tuples represent one object instance, and different tuples may well represent the same object instance.

The Enterprise-Wide Information Model

" ('That's exactly the method,' the Bellman bold
In a hasty parenthesis cried,
'That's exactly the way I have been always told
That the capture of Snarks should be tried!')

'But oh beamish nephew, beware of the day,
If your Snark be a Boojum! For then
You will softly and suddenly vanish away,
And never be met with again!' "

Lewis Carroll, "The Hunting of the Snark"

The problems discussed in this appendix have traditionally been on the borderline between information systems development and "business planning." To introduce discipline into enterprise-wide information modeling, we need to use the same concepts discussed throughout the book. However, this is not easy, and precise specifications of enterprise goals and business plans in the manner presented here are not very usual. We will try to provide some basic ideas and concepts that may help you to understand enterprise goals and business plans better. We will also show that changes in these goals and plans lead to changes in information models, applications, and systems.

Everything we have said about the use of information models to promote understanding at the analysis level applies to the planning level. The understanding in this case is at a higher level, and the building blocks used are precisely specified applications ("higher-level" associated objects and their operations), whether existing or planned. The resulting model may be thought of as an enterprise-wide information model.

C.1.   Integration

In a big enterprise, the problem of cross-application support for common business rules appears; that is, the need may arise for integration of applications to support existing or new operations in the enterprise. Integration leads to the need for an enterprise-wide information model that defines business rules consistently across components of the enterprise. A component of the enterprise may support one or more applications (i.e., one or more sets of contracts for operations). Information models, including the enterprise-wide information model, are not primarily for aiding the design of databases; information models are used to understand business rules and systems. By the same token, the goal of an application is not to write code or even to develop a computer-based system. The goal is to solve a business problem, and this problem should be precisely specified. Of course, this solution should not destroy the existing business rules—it should not violate the enterprise invariants expressed in other information systems of the enterprise. An enterprise-wide information model is a basis for understanding and defining cross-application responsibilities for managing the information resources of the enterprise.

Why did different applications (and different components of the enterprise) appear in the first place? Consider a very small enterprise (e.g., a doctor, a nurse, and a receptionist). It probably has clearly defined contracts for adding a patient, treating a patient (refined into, e.g., making an appointment, diagnosing, issuing a prescription, billing, etc.), collecting a payment, and so on. However, integration problems described in this appendix would hardly ever arise for such an enterprise. These problems arise because understanding the business rules of a big enterprise is difficult; to do that, we need to separate our concerns (see Chapter 2) and treat different components of this enterprise in isolation. Understanding the business rules of a small or simple enterprise is substantially easier and might not require separate treatment of different components of such an enterprise. Therefore, the problem of redundant and inconsistent information so typical for big enterprises is quite seldom encountered in small or simple ones.

Of course, simplicity is the most important issue for the enterprise to be understandable (i.e., for its information model to be usable). It is achieved by considering only business rules and abstracting (possible) implementation(s) away, as described elsewhere in this book. However, the business rules may also be complicated enough; therefore to understand the enterprise we may need to use abstraction. We will have to suppress irrelevant details; either we will consider the "top-level" view, without going into too many details, or we may be more detailed, but consider only a particular, reasonably coherent and reasonably isolated, component of the enterprise, or we may consider only that part of applications impacted by a new business strategy.

Applications supporting higher-level operations are building blocks, into which a specification of the (planned) operation is decomposed. An application is understood as a building block by understanding the operations it supports externally: its contractual interfaces. The high-level information model should not be too detailed; understanding is otherwise impossible (abstraction at work again—we do not need to know about any internal, lower-level operations used to support the external, higher-level ones). Developing requirements for supporting a higher-level business activity should take into account existing operations supported by applications (reuse). Difficulty in such reuse appears when the existing operations supported by applications are not well understood, and, as a result, existing objects are redesigned and redeveloped by information models created for a new application, leading to possible inconsistencies.

A component of the enterprise has to have a "thin and visible interface" (Dijkstra) with the world outside. To create an enterprise-wide information model, you will have to rely on both these components and the top-level view. Success is possible only if the intercomponent interfaces are clearly defined (using contracts) and if the same object or association between objects is not modeled by each of the different components of the enterprise (or, worse, by different applications referring to the same component of the enterprise). The information modeling approach presented in this book provides a framework for creating simple models with clear interfaces and therefore for successful enterprise-wide information models.

Different applications often refer to the same information, and inconsistently applied operations will lead to "bad-quality data." This slang expression refers to violating the enterprise-wide invariants by operations applied in a particular component of that enterprise. This happens because the enterprise-wide invariants are unknown or have never been formulated. Also, the enterprise-wide information model is a combination of invariants of interest across applications. (Operations exposed to the customer come and go, but the invariants are preserved.) Preserving "data quality" means maintaining the invariants, and this requires substantial effort in legacy systems.

Many enterprises are nearing, or have reached, maximum benefit from building large, stand-alone systems (to implement applications). These systems provide mechanized support for the various work centers or departments of the business. Many enterprises need to share the information resources of their business across multiple existing systems. Ideally, all applications, and therefore systems, of an enterprise would have been developed from a common information model, ensuring the compatibility of definition and minimizing information management problems such as incorrect and inconsistent data. These problems may appear only as a result of incorrect or inconsistent refinement(s) of the common information model.

C.2.   On Legacy Systems

Most enterprises are faced with legacy systems, each with its own vertical view ("model") of information (in some cases, even an explicit model). The same information may be repeated many times, and of course, the "copies" may not be kept consistent. Each legacy system maintains handcrafted interfaces to other applications. Additionally, legacy systems often hold information "captive": an application cannot openly gain access to the information of the legacy system, particularly for update operations, through any means other than a component of the legacy system.

When the existing information resource of an enterprise is not adequately specified, it is not understood, and therefore we find information captive in applications. Many existing interfaces, even those intended to be "open," may require substantial system engineering and development before they can be used by another application for access to corporate information. This is a result of developing interfaces without explicit contracts or with contracts that are too detailed and implementation-specific, and therefore not reusable. In many cases, it is not clearly stated who checks the preconditions, the customer or the "system," and the application cannot guarantee the integrity of its information without a trusted invoker who is thoroughly familiar with the development details of the application. The end result is that the information is made available, but only as batch, read-only files. The information may be read, but it is still captive to the application because the meaning of the information is often expressed in implementation-specific, rather than business-specific, terms. One is therefore forced to upgrade the application directly to support new business activities; the application may grow large and unwieldy. Of course, different applications dealing with the same information make these problems more complicated; one of them may easily violate the other's invariant (or the invariant of the enterprise).

The adverse business consequences stemming from redundant and inconsistent information and the lack of open and efficient access to information are well documented. Implementation of new software solutions is slow and expensive, and the cost of operating existing software systems is enormous. Also, of course, inconsistent information may lead to costly errors in conducting the business (see lots of examples in *ACM Software Engineering Notes*).

An enterprise-wide information model is part of an approach to information systems planning and development that directly supports information sharing and open systems. Open sharing of the information resources of an enterprise, enabling information to be reused by multiple systems, leads to the more rapid and less costly introduction of systems that provide the best, correct solution to business problems, no matter from what supplier the solution comes. Additionally, reducing inconsistent information reduces costly errors in conducting the business and the enormous operational cost of information management.

C.3.   Uses of an Enterprise-Wide Information Model

An enterprise-wide information model provides an overall context (invariant) for planning and developing information systems that reduce operational difficulties and reduce the need for duplicate information, increase efficiency by speeding deployment of open contract interfaces between a company's systems, and manage information according to the business rules of the corporation.

An enterprise-wide information model is a common framework (set of high-level invariants) that should be supported by each (existing or future) application. If it is developed "bottom-up" based on existing models of enterprise components, then, for a complicated enterprise, it is absolutely essential to abstract away the details—to "compose" objects and associations out of existing lower-level ones. Understanding of the enterprise, as usual, is possible only by suppressing irrelevant details, even though these details have been important for the business rules for the lower-level models. The bottom-up approach leads to the discovery of invariants of the enterprise-wide information model based only on existing models. On the other hand, a "top-down" approach is also useful because it should provide a starting point for creating new, and possibly changing old, models. In fact, we will probably use a combination of both approaches.

Precise specification of business rules (using invariants and contracts) is the key concept that makes business strategies understandable. Understanding the business rules for a business activity treats the business activity as an operation, as it should be. As we have seen in Chapter 2, the business activity of assigning an employee to a project can be understood in an implementation-independent manner, by using pre- and postconditions (a programmer understands how to program an insertion into a relational table in the same manner). Therefore, planning and reengineering the business may reuse this well-understood, disciplined approach.

C.4.   Planning: Change Management

Nearly everything said in this book about analysis applies to planning. **Planning is changing or creating business rules**—and where these rules are understood explicitly, they are easier to implement (i.e., put into effect). Strategies are effective only if the behavior of the enterprise changes, which of course means that the behavior of the people and information systems of the enterprise change.

Information systems planning, insofar as it supports strategic planning (and it had better), means understanding the business strategy and expected change in behavior and getting the information systems of the enterprise to support that behavior.

Can strategy be understood using assertions? Of course! Let's take an example.

When a planner decides on a new business strategy, for example, on hiring and retaining consultants as employees who are not assigned to existing projects or departments (this is what the company's president will say), a new concept of a general pool of employees is introduced. This new strategy can be refined into a business rule, for example, *when they are not assigned to a project, employees should be assigned to a general pool rather than a department.* Therefore, **a new invariant will need to be formulated** and supported by all applications. Of course, new operations will need to be specified and implemented (e.g., *add an employee to a general pool).* These changes will need to be understood without writing a computer program and without referring to one. They can be understood by writing down the business rules:

> *Invariant:* Every employee is either a member of a department or of the general pool.
> No member of the general pool has a project assignment.
>
> *Precondition for add an employee to a general pool:* an employee is not a member of the general pool and has no project assignments.
>
> *Postcondition for add an employee to a general pool:* the employee is added to the pool.

The strategy will cause changes in the applications and therefore infor-mation systems, which have to integrate the required changes.

Should integration requirements for information systems be understood as assertions? Let's take an example. When integration shows that an appli-cation has a stronger business rule than the enterprise rule, for example,

Application invariant: every employee is a member of a single department

Enterprise invariant: every employee is a member of a single department or of the general pool.

an existing application, perhaps a human resources organization responsible for placing employees within the company, may decide to add the new *add employee to general pool* operation to their existing operation *add employee to department.*

Additionally, the precondition of the *add employee to department* opera-tion must change to check whether the employee is assigned to a project. Pre-sumably, the operation *is assigned to project (employee id)* is also available.

Within this employee placement application, logic such as the following may be created to support assignment of employees under the new business rule:

```
IF    NOT add employee to department succeeded
         (employee id, department id)
      ;; i.e., if the operation fails because its new
      ;; precondition is not met.
THEN  add employee to general pool (employee id)
FI
```

Naturally, the precondition could be checked directly as an entry clause in the logic of the module, and the existing *add employee to department* op-eration is unchanged:

```
IF    NOT is assigned to project (employee id)
      ;; check the new precondition
THEN  add employee to general pool (employee id)

ELSE  add employee to department (employee id,
         department id)
FI
```

These modules, of course, implement the OR of the invariant, and the postcondition of both is **the employee is a member of a single department or of the general pool.** (Note that the steps of these modules may be executed manually rather than by a computer system. Also note that no identifier of the general pool is needed.)

Graphically, the employee placement application model may be shown as in Figure C.1.

A second application, which is responsible for publishing the company organization charts, may elect to support the required invariant by changing an existing atomic operation *add employee to org-chart*. The new operation could have the following signature:

```
Add employee to org-chart
      (employee id, organization type [department | pool],
      organization id)
```

This shows that this application views the general pool and departments as kinds of organization, each to be treated differently. For example, the printout of the employee pool portion of the organization chart may have different information than the printout of the rest of the organization chart. Notice there is no assumption of the employee pool identity: it is treated, as the business rule implies, as a single, separate object. This appears to be consis-

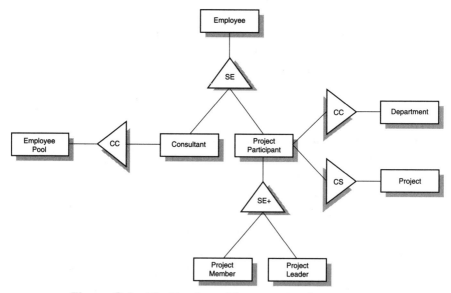

Figure C.1.   The Employee Placement Application Model

tent with the enterprise-wide rule and with the employee placement model given above.

Graphically, the organization chart application model may be shown as in Figure C.2.

A third application, which is responsible for accounting, may elect to support the required invariant using a workaround for the existing operation *add employee to department*. Here, a special identifier is set aside for the employee pool, and employees are added to the pool using the existing operation and treating the employee pool as a "special" department:

```
Add employee to department
        (employee id, department id, participation status)
```

Unless great care is taken, this application creates a future problem: when this application needs to interface with the employee placement application or the organization chart application, it will require rework, retraining, and redevelopment. In this application, the new business rule is not explicit; the application has in effect chosen to use a local, application-specific rule rather than the enterprise-wide rule. This may be a source of many severe business problems.

Graphically, the accounting application model is very primitive and may be shown as in Figure C.3.

In addition, other existing contracts may be affected: the postcondition for the operation *transfer employee*, which before guaranteed that the employee becomes a member of the new department, must now guarantee the preservation of the changed invariant, that is, that the employee becomes a

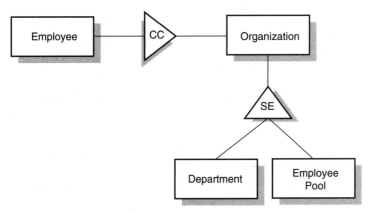

Figure C.2.   The Organization Chart Application Model

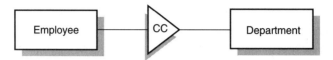

Figure C.3.   The Accounting Application Model

member of another department or of the general pool. As above, whether an application implements this change by modifying the existing *transfer employee* operation or by adding logic which reuses the existing operation, the behavior is the same.

As we have seen, during business planning, a new invariant is formulated. The easiest course of refinement would be to reuse existing systems and their operations. This is not always possible: new applications or more or less drastic changes to existing applications may be needed. During refinement, the enterprise-wide information model may change, of course. Inter-application, and therefore intercontract, dependencies are understood and dealt with, and the planner decides whether a new operation is required or existing ones may be enhanced.

Where an information model is explicitly shared across applications, the resulting operations will not contradict one another or the business rules expressed as invariants in the enterprise-wide information model. Contracts for these operations may **appear** different (i.e., may have quite different signatures). However, they preserve the same invariant and are therefore consistent with the enterprise-wide information model. The amount of detail used for representing the same object or collection of objects in different contracts may, of course, be quite different.

Naming.

Although we have not emphasized naming (but have mentioned it when discussing domains in Chapter 4), maintaining consistency of object and property names is essential for successful harmonization of different applications and their information systems. The problem of naming basically refers to different names for the same thing and the same name for different things (see, e.g., [Kent 83]). Although property names and definitions (e.g., base type, length, format) are an important part of understanding information across existing applications, understanding the semantics of information is critical for both the corporate information supplier, who must ensure the integrity of information, and the corporate information invoker, who needs to know the available operations.

The most visible problems addressed by naming in information systems are incompatibility of data fields and the existence and incompatibility of manual numeric codes for the same values. As Gilb and Weinberg mentioned in 1977, the latter should not be used in a modern information system [Gilb 77]. Although the customers indeed use abbreviations for naming, these abbreviations are not numbers. Such numeric codes are often used for object identification, causing incompatibility of object identifiers across applications. This is a major source of data management problems and their associated costs. It is caused by inconsistent or artificial (i.e., non-business-related) naming rules supported by the various applications.

C.5.   Cross-Application Rules

Enterprise-wide information modeling specifies the requirements for correctness of the information about the enterprise through documented contractual interfaces and explicitly specified invariants. Of course, contracts for business rules must be clearly distinguished from (and refined into) contracts for a computer-based implementation. This development approach is not "construction-centered," and it supports a consistent approach to the planning, analysis, design, and construction of corporate information systems. This approach promotes sharing common concepts from planning through construction, including the development and reuse of libraries in all phases of information system development.

Supporting a high-level operation may require the interplay of several applications, possibly of several components of the enterprise. The applications and their operations may be viewed as building blocks at the next level of decomposition, and a shared information model will be developed. Insofar as this shared view is understood and written down explicitly, there is (at least part of) an enterprise-wide information model. Naturally, having the appropriate building blocks at this level is as important as having them at lower levels.

To be consistent, applications acting independently have to at least maintain the consistency of property values (e.g., the value of an employee identifier). As mentioned in Chapter 6, maintaining the consistency of information across applications usually depends on each application's reference to the objects of another.

Let us consider an application that has references to "out-of-scope" objects that have to be modeled by another application. From the viewpoint of our application, these objects should be reused (almost) as is from the other application. However, life is more complicated than that; we may discover that:

- The other application does not model these objects at all.
- The other application models them using different names or identifiers.
- The other application models other objects (e.g., components) that may be used for modeling these entities.
- The other application models these objects partially, that is, does not include all of their properties relevant for our application.
- The other application does not exist yet.

All of these problems are serious obstacles to developing an enterprise-wide information model. The following rules may help:

- Insist on having all out-of-scope objects included in a particular information model.
- In an information model, explicitly use entities borrowed from other models (as out-of-scope).
- Attempt to go "one object outside" of each of the information models, (i.e., to show the envelopes of the information models).
- Assign appropriate stewardship.

C.6. Contracts in the Enterprise-Wide Information Model

The primary vehicle for achieving the benefits of shared information and open systems is the development of consistent, usable contractual interfaces for accessing (to both read and update) the information in a company's information systems. When the supplier and invoker of a contractual interface share a model of information—an enterprise-wide information model—the interoperability of information is greatly enhanced.

One of the most important problems in contract (re)use deals with the amount of information needed for this purpose. How are the contract specifications stored? How are they accessed? How is it possible to find a contract ("affinity browsing" [Pintado, Tsichritzis 88]; see also [Arapis, Kappel 88], [Kilov 90])? In the simplest case, how is it possible to find out which contracts refer to a particular entity? To a particular property? How to find a contract "related" to a particular contract? As contract specifications include much more than just "data" in the traditional sense, the problem of storing both signatures and assertions for contract operations is not trivial. It is not even clear that "structured" storage of these specifications (i.e., mechanical decomposition of specifications into more than character strings) is reasonable. What are the search criteria for a contract? (In other words, if contracts are stored in an "information encyclopedia" in the form of, say, tables, then what are the column names for these tables? Is it at all reasonable to store contracts in this manner?) As a very crude approximation, enumeration of entities and properties participating in a contract specification will help a lot and even permit querying these meta-data, although this kind of stored information about a contract is very far from being complete—it captures only the signature of the contract, not the semantics. Browsing the "schema" based on different associations between entities may also help, although this approach should be extended to application-specific associations.

CRUD contracts may easily be developed and included in an enterprise-wide information model (see Appendix D). These contracts define the generic operations for collections of objects in particular applications. It is only natural to include, in addition, contracts that are application-specific, that is, define higher-level operations for particular applications. This problem is not trivial, but it may and should be solved: objects cannot exist without contracts, and contracts cannot exist without objects. Note also that the enterprise-wide information model incorporates objects at the higher level of enterprise modeling, and therefore, it is only natural to include contracts for these objects as well, that is, to include contracts that define top-level requirements ("functional specifications"). In order to solve both of these problems, it is necessary to use the same enterprise model because the application-specific contracts as well as the top-level requirements refer to the same objects—but perhaps at different levels of refinement—that are also described in detail (refined) in low-level specifications found in the enterprise model. Moreover, these contracts deal with associations between these objects rather than with isolated entities, and these associations of various kinds are also already described in detail in the enterprise-wide information model.

In the same manner as an enterprise-wide information model is used for ensuring that information in different applications of the enterprise are consistent and not redundant, contracts in the model will be used to ensure that different applications treat this information in a disciplined way, that corporate information will not be distorted, accidentally or otherwise, by unconstrained operations, and that the operations used by these applications are consistent and not redundant. These operations may, if needed, be reused by different applications because contracts for these operations will be readily available. In this manner, shared corporate contracts will be achieved. This is exactly the approach to be used in object-oriented analysis and design. Note that implementation of these contracts is not specified and is left to the developers, therefore attaining interoperability.

Contracts for CRUD Operations

*"There was one who was famed for the number of things
He forgot when he entered the ship:
His umbrella, his watch, all his jewels and rings,
And the clothes he had bought for the trip.*

*He had forty-two boxes, all carefully packed,
With his name painted clearly on each:
But, since he omitted to mention the fact,
They were all left behind on the beach."*

Lewis Carroll, "The Hunting of the Snark"

This appendix describes some generic reusable contracts for the elementary associations described in Chapter 5. These contracts specify CRUD operations applied to the entities that belong to these associations. Usually, such an operation refers to more than one of those entities. The contract specifications are based on the invariant for the (subtype of) the corresponding association in Section 5.1. This invariant is repeated here.

To formulate a contract specification for an operation, you need to specify both the signature and the semantics of the operation. First and foremost, however, you need to know the invariant, because the operation specified by the contract should preserve the invariant. This is the most important consideration from which the pre- and postconditions for the contract specification often follow quite straightforwardly.

In what follows, we will specify generic contracts; an application-specific contract is a refinement of the appropriate generic one. Therefore, we will not include property information in our contract specifications. This

---

Joseph Morabito and Naidu Guttapalle contributed to the text of this appendix.

information is application-specific and can be provided by the application in a straightforward manner. For example, in the contract for creating an application-specific dependent instance—*performance history*, which is a dependent of *employee*—we will need to provide property types, the values of which characterize this instance. Naturally, additional application-specific pre- and postconditions referring to these property values will also be included in the contract specification. However, all contracts for creating a dependent instance have essential common characteristics, and they are more important: if they are specified incorrectly, their application-specific refinement will also be wrong. In specifying these generic characteristics, we cannot refer to particular property types or values: we can refer only to object existence and identity. Of course, the particular way of identifying an object is also application-specific.

A thorough understanding of these essential common characteristics—the semantics of generic associations—will enable an analyst to reuse them as building blocks in the specification of behavior for collections of application objects. In this manner, a very substantial part of the behavior of application-specific objects will be reused from this association library, rather than reinvented again and again for every application.

For each contract, we will specify the pre- and postconditions for the appropriate operation. Preconditions for most operations depend, **among other things,** upon optional or mandatory participation of an entity in an association. Since there are only a few possibilities for each generic association, we will summarize them below:

Optional participation

Optional participation or mandatory/not first instance

Mandatory participation

Mandatory participation/first instance

Mandatory participation/not first instance

Optional participation or mandatory/not last instance

Mandatory participation/last instance

Mandatory participation/not last instance

For every contract, we will not repeat the pre- and postconditions that follow from the invariant for the generic association (see Section 4.3.1). For example, for the create operation the postcondition of which asserts the existence of instances of associated source and target types, we will not assert the existence of an instance of the association between the source and target type instances. Moreover, we will not repeat the postconditions discussed in Section 4.3.2 related to the sets of associated entity instances for the creation and deletion of an entity instance.

We will present here only some contracts, for CRUD operations applied to some generic associations. We have chosen both simple contracts (for DEPENDENCY) and more complicated ones (for COMPOSITION and SUBTYPING). The latter are interesting because, in particular, some subtypes of COMPOSITION and SUBTYPING are exceptions referred to in the invariant for the generic association. Contracts for REFERENCE and SYMMETRIC RELATIONSHIP associations have not been included because formulating them is rather straightforward.

D.1.   Entity

The *invariant for an object* (i.e., an entity) in Section 4.2 states:

Each object instance is unique and can be identified independent of its behavior or state. An object is not isolated: there exists at least one association of this object with some other object.

The specification of a contract for an entity will be inherited by any of its subtypes (e.g., by a composite entity). The existence of an association between an entity type and another entity type referred to in the invariant does not imply the existence of an association instance between an entity instance and another entity instance. Therefore, this clause of the invariant is not reflected in the CRUD contract specifications below. The particular association(s) is a refinement of this clause of the invariant.

CREATE
Create an entity instance

Signature.	The type and identity of the entity instance to be created.
Precondition.	The given entity instance does not exist.
Postcondition.	The given entity instance exists.
Important note.	Any object has an identity that is independent of its structural and behavioral properties. The object is identified by a logical identifier which is

implementation-independent. The logical identifier is implemented as an object identifier. Object identifiers are usually system-generated (from the viewpoint of the user) and associated with an object when it is created. An object identifier uniquely identifies an entity instance and can never be changed. It may or may not be visible to the user.

DELETE
Delete an entity instance

Signature.	The type and identity of the entity instance to be deleted.
Precondition.	The given entity instance exists.
Postcondition.	The given entity instance does not exist.

UPDATE
Update a structural property in an entity instance

Signature.	The type and identity of the entity instance to be updated; the structural property type(s).
Precondition.	The given entity instance exists.
Postcondition.	The given entity instance with the same identity and new values of the structural properties exists.

READ
Read an entity instance

Signature.	The type and identity of the entity instance to be read.

Precondition.   The given entity instance exists.

Postcondition. The given entity instance is successfully read, and its property (types and their) values are available.

If an operation for an entity did not succeed because the precondition was not satisfied or the postcondition could not be satisfied, then the operation for its subtype (i.e., for a particular generic object class—e.g., a Dependent, Composite, etc.) will not succeed. An error message should be produced in this case. For example, if an instance of a generic object class is to be created, then the precondition for such a Create will include the precondition for *Create an Entity Instance*. Therefore, if the entity instance to be created already exists, then this instance of this generic object class cannot be created, and an error message should be produced.

D.2. Dependency

Generic invariant.

A parent type corresponds to one dependent type. The existence of a dependent instance implies the existence of at least one corresponding instance of its parent type.

Invariant for optional participation of a parent (default).
No changes.

Invariant for mandatory participation of a parent.

If a parent entity has mandatory participation in the DEPENDENCY association, then the existence of an instance of a parent entity implies the existence of at least one corresponding instance of its dependent entity.

Operations: the importance of the invariant

It is easy to see that the following contract specifications for the CRUD operations follow very straightforwardly from the invariants for the DEPENDENCY association. The signature and semantics (pre- and postcondition) for each operation are the only possible ones that satisfy the invariant. Consider, for example, the creation of a dependent instance. Naturally, from the invariant for the DEPENDENCY association it follows that at least one corresponding parent instance should exist. Therefore, the type and identity of a parent instance should be provided in the signature. Moreover, for this particular operation (which does not create the parent instance), this parent instance has to exist beforehand; hence, the first clause of its precondition. The second clause of its precondition immediately follows from the precondition for creating an entity instance (you can't create the same instance more than once). Finally, only the third clause—optional participation or mandatory/not first dependent—makes the operation possible; otherwise, the invariant for the DEPENDENCY association will be violated unless the dependent and corresponding parent instances are created in the same business process.

CREATE
Create an instance of one object (default)

Create a parent instance (default)

Signature.	The type and identity of the parent instance to be created.
Precondition.	Optional participation (follows from the invariant for optional).
Postcondition.	The parent instance exists.
Comment.	There exist no associated dependent entity instances (yet).

Create a dependent instance (default)

Signature.	The type and identity of the dependent instance to be created; the type and identity of the appropriate parent instance to be associated with this dependent instance.
Precondition.	A corresponding parent instance exists. The dependent instance does not exist. Optional participation or mandatory/not first dependent.
Postcondition.	The dependent instance exists.

Create a non-first parent instance

Signature.	The type and identity of the parent instance to be created; the type and identity of the appropriate

existing dependent instance to be associated with
this parent instance.

Precondition.   A corresponding dependent instance exists.
The parent instance does not exist.
Mandatory/not first parent.

Postcondition.   The parent instance exists.

Create instances of both objects

Create parent and the first corresponding dependent instance

Signature.   The type and identity of the parent instance to be
created; the type and identity of the dependent instance to be created and associated with this parent instance.

Precondition.   The parent and dependent entity instances do not
exist.
Mandatory/first dependent.

Postcondition.   The parent and dependent entity instances exist.

DELETE
Delete an instance of one object

Delete a parent instance only (a.k.a. "Delete restrict")

Signature.   The type and identity of the parent instance to be
deleted.

Precondition.   Corresponding dependent instances do not exist.
Optional participation.

Postcondition.   The parent instance does not exist.

Delete a dependent instance

Signature.   The type and identity of the dependent instance to be deleted.

Precondition.   The dependent instance exists.
Optional participation or mandatory/not last dependent.

Postcondition.   The dependent instance does not exist.

Delete a non-last parent instance

Signature.   The type and identity of the parent instance to be deleted.

Precondition.   The parent instance exists.
Mandatory/not last parent.

Postcondition.   The parent instance does not exist.

Comment.   The dependent instance still exists because it has at least one other parent instance.

Delete instances of both objects

Two variations exist, depending upon the signature: the input parameter may refer to the (type and) identity of a dependent instance or a parent instance. The former requires that the mandatory invariant be valid (Delete dependent with parent instances), while in the latter case, it does not matter whether the parent has an optional or mandatory associated dependent ("Delete cascade").

Delete dependent with parent instances

Signature.   The type and identity of the dependent instance to be deleted.

Precondition.   The parent and dependent instances exist.
Mandatory/last dependent.

Postcondition.   The parent and all its dependent instances do not exist.

Comment.   This operation essentially has the same semantics as the *Delete parent with dependent instances* (see below), as follows from the postcondition, but its signature is different: it need not include the identity of the parent.

Delete parent with dependent instances (default)

Signature.   The type and identity of the parent instance to be deleted.

Precondition.   The given parent instance exists.

Postcondition.   The parent and all its dependent instances do not exist.

Comment.   There is no specific precondition requiring a parent to have either an optional or mandatory dependent. This operation is applicable in either case. The identity of the dependent(s) need not be included in the signature.

D.3.   Composition

D.3.1. General

Generic invariant.   A composite type corresponds to one or more component types, and a composite instance corresponds to zero or more instances of each component type. There exists at least one resultant property of a composite instance dependent upon the properties of its component instances. There exists also at least one emergent property of a composite instance independent of the properties of its component instances. The sets of application-specific types for the composite and its components should not be equal.

The change of the actual composition (i.e., the set of component instances) of an instance of a composite entity does not in itself change the identity of this instance,[1] as long as the components belong to the "permitted" set of component types. In particular, an operation of adding/deleting a component does not necessarily change the identity of the composite entity. Identity change for a composite entity is a different operation, which may well include (as its implementation!) adding/deleting components.

We will not consider here contracts for subtypes of the generic COMPOSITION based on serializability, changeability, or hierarchy. They may be formulated in a straightforward manner. However, the subtyping based on linkage represents the most complicated—and most often encountered—classification of a Composition. Therefore, in what follows, only this classification will be treated in detail.

D.3.2. Linkage Contracts

Let's recall the **Invariants for Linkage subtypes.** For an ASSEMBLY, the existence of a composite instance implies the existence of at least one corresponding component instance. For a SUBORDINATION, the existence of a component instance implies the existence of at least one corresponding composite instance. For a LIST, the existence of a composite instance implies the existence of at least one corresponding component instance, and the existence of a component instance implies the existence of at least one corresponding composite instance. For all Linkage subtypes, except PACKAGE, the existence of an instance of the composition association is **equivalent to** the existence of instances of both the corresponding composite and component entities. It is very important to recall that for the PACKAGE—and only for the PACKAGE—operations *create an association instance* and *delete an association instance* are permitted, because of the exception referred to in the generic association invariant.

CREATE
Create an instance of one object

The four variations shown below follow from the invariant of the particular Linkage subtype of the COMPOSITION association and also, if appropri-

---

[1]So that "=" is an identity compare operation (see [OODBTG 91]).

ate, from the considerations about operating upon an isolated instance—
a (mandatory or optional) element of an association (Section 4.4.1).

Assembly—composite may not exist independently

Create a composite instance

Signature.	The type and identity of the composite instance to be created; the type and identity of the appropriate existing component instance(s) to be associated with this composite instance.
Precondition.	The component instance(s) exists. The composite instance does not exist.
Postcondition.	The composite instance exists.
Comment.	The corresponding component instances have been created independent of the composition and are now being associated with the composite instance that has been created.

Create a component instance

Signature.	The type and identity of the component instance to be created.
Precondition.	The component instance does not exist.
Postcondition.	The component instance exists.
Comment.	There exists no associated composite entity instance (yet).

Subordination—component may not exist independently

Create a composite instance[2]

Signature.	The type and identity of the composite instance to be created.

---

[2]Note the symmetry with creating a component instance for the ASSEMBLY.

Precondition.   The composite instance does not exist.

Postcondition.   The composite instance exists.

Comment.   There exists no associated component entity instance (yet).

Create a component instance[3]

Signature.   The type and identity of the component instance to be created; the type and identity of the appropriate existing composite instance to be associated with this component instance.

Precondition.   The composite instance(s) exists.
                      The component instance does not exist.

Postcondition.   The component instance exists.

Comment.   The corresponding composite instance has been created independent of the composition and is now being associated with the component instance that has been created.

Package—both composite and component may exist ndependently (default)

Create a composite instance

Signature.   The type and identity of the composite instance to be created.

Precondition.   The composite instance does not exist.

Postcondition.   The composite instance exists.

Comment.   There exists no associated component entity instance (yet).

---

[3]Note the symmetry with creating a composite instance for the ASSEMBLY.

Create a component instance

    Signature.   The type and identity of the component instance to be created.

    Precondition.   The component instance does not exist.

    Postcondition.   The component instance exists.

    Comment.   There exists no associated composite entity instance (yet).

Create a composition association between existing composite and component instances[4]

    Signature.   The type and identity of the existing component instance(s); the type and identity of the appropriate existing composite instance to be associated with these component instances.

    Precondition.   Composite and component instance(s) exist. Composition association does not exist.

    Postcondition.   Composition association exists.

List—composite and component may exist only within a composition

Create a non-first component instance

    Signature.   The type and identity of the component instance to be created; the type and identity of the appropriate existing composite instance to be associated with this component instance.

    Precondition.   A composite instance and some other component instance associated with this composite instance exist.

---

[4]This operation is unique: it is available only for COMPOSITION-PACKAGE and is not available for any other generic association.

The component instance does not exist.
Mandatory/not first component.

Postcondition.   The component instance exists.

Comment.   The component instance is included in the existing composition association.

Create instances of both objects

Create composite and corresponding component instances

Signature.   The type and identity of the component instance(s) to be created; the type and identity of the composite instance to be created and associated with these component instances.

Precondition.   Composite and component instance(s) do not exist.
Mandatory/first composite and component.

Postcondition.   Composite and component instance(s) exist.

Comment.   This postcondition implies a Mandatory/not first component predicate—the third clause of the precondition for the operation *Create a non-first component instance* (scc above).

DELETE
Delete an instance of one object

The four variations shown below follow from the invariant of the particular Linkage subtype of the COMPOSITION association and also, if appropriate, from the considerations about operating upon an isolated instance—a (mandatory or optional) element of an association (Section 4.4.1).

Assembly—composite may not exist independently

Delete a composite instance

Signature. The type and identity of the composite instance to be deleted.

Precondition. Composite instance exists.

Postcondition. Composite instance does not exist.
Component instance(s) exists.

Delete a component entity instance

Signature. The type and identity of the component instance to be deleted.

Precondition. The component instance exists and is not associated with any corresponding composite instance.

Postcondition. Component instance does not exist.

Comment. Once the composite instance has been deleted, the former "component" instance is no longer a component in this association (i.e., the precondition is satisfied).

Subordination—component may not exist independently

Delete a composite instance

Signature. The type and identity of the composite instance to be deleted.

Precondition. The composite instance exists and is not associated with any corresponding component instance.

Postcondition. Composite instance does not exist.

Comment.	Once all component instances associated with this composite instance have been deleted, the former "composite" instance is no longer a composite in this association (i.e., the precondition is satisfied).

Delete a component instance

Signature.	The type and identity of the component instance to be deleted.
Precondition.	Component instance exists.
Postcondition.	Component instance does not exist. Composite instance(s) exist.

Package—both composite and component may exist independently (default)

Delete the composition association between given composite and component entity instances (default)[5]

Signature.	The type and identity of the existing component instance(s); the type and identity of the appropriate existing composite instance associated with these component instances.
Precondition.	The composition association instance, the composite instance, and the component instance(s) exist.
Postcondition.	The composition association instance does not exist. Both the composite and component instances exist.
Comment.	After deletion of a composition association, both the "composite" and "component" instances are no longer associated in this composition associa-

---

[5]This operation is unique: it is available only for COMPOSITION-PACKAGE and is not available for any other generic association.

tion (i.e., the postcondition is satisfied). See the next two complementary contracts.

Delete a composite instance only (default)

Signature.   The type and identity of the composite instance to be deleted.

Precondition.   The composite instance exists and is not associated with any corresponding component instance.

Comment.   Once all composition association instances associated with this composite instance have been deleted, the former "composite" instance is no longer associated with any component instances in this association (i.e., the precondition is satisfied).

Delete a component instance only (default)

Signature.   The type and identity of the component instance to be deleted.

Precondition.   The component instance exists and is not associated with any corresponding composite instance.

Comment.   Once all composition association instances associated with this component instance have been deleted, the former "component" instance is no longer associated with any composite instances in this association (i.e., the precondition is satisfied).

Delete a composite instance together with the composition association(s)

Signature.   The type and identity of the composite instance to be deleted.

Precondition.   Composite instance exists.
Composition association instance(s) exists.

Postcondition.   Composite instance does not exist.
Composition association instance(s) does not exist.
Component instance(s) exists.

Comment.   This operation would be equivalent to the one for the ASSEMBLY if the invariants for the PACKAGE and ASSEMBLY were the same. These invariants are different.

Delete a component instance together with the composition association

Signature.   The type and identity of the component instance to be deleted.

Precondition.   Component instance exists.
Composition association instance(s) exists.

Postcondition.   Component instance does not exist.
Composition association instance(s) does not exist.
Composite instance(s) exists.

Comment.   This operation would be equivalent to the one for the SUBORDINATION if the invariants for the PACKAGE and SUBORDINATION were the same. These invariants are different.

List—composite and component may exist only within a composition

Delete a non-last component instance

Signature.   The type and identity of the component instance to be deleted.

Precondition. The component instance exists.
Mandatory/not last component.

Postcondition. The component instance does not exist.
Composite instance(s) exists.

Delete instances of both objects

List—composite and component may exist only within a composition

Delete the only component and the composite instances

Signature. The type and identity of the component instance to be deleted.

Precondition. The composite and the only (last) component exist.
Mandatory/last component.

Postcondition. The component instance and all composite instances associated with this component instance in this association do not exist.

Assembly, Subordination, Package, and List

Delete composite with component instances

Signature. The type and identity of the composite instance to be deleted.

Precondition. The composite instance exists.

Postcondition. The composite instance and all associated component instances do not exist.

Comment. This delete operation is applicable to all Linkage subtypes.

Delete component with composite instances.

Signature.	The type and identity of the component instance to be deleted.
Precondition.	The component instance exists.
Postcondition.	The component instance and all associated composite instances do not exist.
Comment.	This delete operation is applicable to all Linkage subtypes.

UPDATE
Update a property of a component (aka "update component cascade") (default)

Signature.	The type and identity of the component instance; its structural property type(s) and value(s).
Precondition.	The component and associated composite instances exist.
Postcondition.	A component instance has new value(s) of the structural property(ies); all corresponding composite instance(s) have new value(s) of their resultant property(ies).

D.4.　Subtyping

Generic invariant.　A supertype may participate in several SUBTYPING associations; a subtype may participate in several SUBTYPING associations. A supertype in a SUBTYPING association corresponds to one or more subtypes. The set of instances of a subtype is a subset of the set of instances of its static supertype. If an instance of a subtype belongs to its supertype, then the structural and behavioral properties of a subtype constitute a superset of the structural and behavioral properties of its supertype. (This is property inheritance. It is always true for a static supertype. If SUBTYPING is dynamic, then it is true only for those instances of a subtype that belong to its dynamic supertype.)

As follows from the invariant for the elementary association (see Section 4.3.1), the existence of an instance of the SUBTYPING association is equivalent to the existence of an instance of a supertype having the properties of one of its subtypes.

Invariant for exhaustive.   The union of sets of instances of all subtypes is equal to the set of supertype instances.

Invariant for overlapping.   There exist two different subtypes such that the intersection of the sets of instances of these subtypes may be not empty.

These invariants imply that it is possible to attach a subtype to, or to detach a subtype from, an instance of a supertype if and only if the SUBTYPING is overlapping or nonexhaustive. It is possible to attach a supertype to, or detach a supertype from, an instance of a subtype if and only if the SUB-TYPING is dynamic. The following contract specifications will satisfy these invariants.

For the SUBTYPING association, the set of instances of the target type is a subset of the set of instances of the source type. Therefore, operations for the SUBTYPING association will include acquiring[6] properties of a type and detaching properties of a type.

CREATE
Create properties of one type only

Static Overlapping, Static Nonexhaustive, or Dynamic Subtyping Hierarchies

Create a supertype instance only (for nonexhaustive subtypes only)

Signature.   The type and identity of the supertype instance to be created.

Precondition.   The subtyping hierarchy is nonexhaustive.
                    A supertype instance does not exist.

---

[6]The means of acquiring (and detaching) are to be provided by the implementation; they are not specified here.

Postcondition.   The supertype instance exists and does not have properties of any subtype.

Attach a subtype to a given instance (for static subtypes only)

Signature.   The type and identity of the existing supertype instance; the subtype to be attached.[7]

Precondition.   The subtyping hierarchy is static.
A supertype instance exists.
The conjunction of the predicate for the new subtype and the predicate that the existing (supertype) instance satisfies is not false.

Postcondition.   The supertype instance acquires the properties of the new subtype.

Comment.   For overlapping subtypes, the supertype instance had the properties of another corresponding subtype instance of a different type prior to this operation, acquired by means of the operation *Create an instance with properties of both a supertype and its subtype* (see below). For nonexhaustive subtypes, the supertype instance was created (using the operation *Create a supertype instance only (for nonexhaustive subtypes only))* without referring to any subtype.

Attach a supertype to a given instance (for dynamic subtypes only).

Signature.   The type and identity of the existing subtype instance; the supertype to be attached.[8]

---

[7]Together with its properties if their explicit specification is required for this subtype.

[8]Together with its properties if their explicit specification is required for this supertype.

Precondition.   The subtyping hierarchy is dynamic.
A subtype instance exists.
The conjunction of the predicate for the new supertype and the predicate that the existing (subtype) instance satisfies is not false.

Postcondition.   The subtype instance acquires the properties of the new supertype.

Comment.   The instance has been created earlier, as an instance of some other type(s).

Create an instance with properties of both a supertype and its subtype (default)

All Subtyping Classifications

Create an instance with properties of both a supertype and its subtype (default)

Signature.   The supertype, subtype and identity of the instance to be created.[9]

Precondition.   The instance does not exist and therefore does not have properties of the supertype or any of its subtypes.

Postcondition.   The instance exists and has properties of the supertype and one of its subtypes.

Comment.   With overlapping subtypes, there may be more than one subtype associated with a given supertype. Therefore, for the "non-first" subtypes, the operation *Attach a subtype to a given instance (for static subtypes only)* (see above) will have to be used.

---

[9]Together with its properties if their explicit specification is required for this supertype or this subtype.

DELETE
Delete properties of one type only

Static Overlapping, Static Nonexhaustive, or Dynamic Subtyping Hierarchies

Detach a subtype from an existing instance (static subtypes only)

Signature.	The supertype, subtype, and identity of the instance.
Precondition.	The subtyping is static. The instance exists and has properties of a given subtype and its supertype (i.e., satisfies the predicates for both the subtype and the supertype).
Postcondition.	The instance exists and does not have the properties of the given subtype (i.e., does not satisfy the predicate for the subtype).
Comment.	The instance continues to exist because it will correspond to another subtype in the same hierarchy, or because it will correspond to a subtype in another hierarchy, or because the classification hierarchy is nonexhaustive.

Detach a supertype from an existing instance (dynamic subtypes only)

Signature.	The supertype, subtype, and identity of the instance.
Precondition.	The subtyping is dynamic. The instance exists and has properties of a subtype and a supertype in the dynamic subtyping hierarchy (i.e., satisfies the predicates for both the subtype and the supertype).

Postcondition.   The instance exists and does not have the properties of the given supertype in this dynamic subtyp-
ing hierarchy (i.e., does not satisfy the predicate
for the supertype).

Comment.   The subtype instance continues to exist after the
operation because it corresponds to (i.e., satisfies
the predicate of) another, static, type.

Delete an instance together with the properties of all its subtypes

All Subtyping Classifications

Delete cascade (default)

Signature.   The supertype and identity of the instance.

Precondition.   A supertype instance exists.

Postcondition.   The supertype instance, together with its properties and the properties of all existing subtypes in
all static subtyping hierarchies and properties of
all existing supertypes in all dynamic subtyping
hierarchies, does not exist.

UPDATE
Change of type for an entity instance

Signature.   The supertype, old subtype, new subtype, and
identity of the instance.[10]

Precondition.   The old and new subtypes belong to the same subtyping hierarchy.
The entity instance exists and has properties of a
supertype and a subtype in this subtyping hierarchy (i.e., satisfies the predicates for both the supertype and this—old—subtype).

---

[10]Together with its properties if their explicit specification is required for this new subtype.

Postcondition.   The entity instance exists and has properties of a
supertype and another subtype in this subtyping
hierarchy (i.e., satisfies the predicates for both the
supertype and the new subtype).

References

[**Abelson 85**] H. ABELSON and G. J. SUSSMAN, *Structure and Interpretation of Computer Programs*. Cambridge, MA: MIT Press, 1985.

[**ACMF 92**] ISO/IEC JTC1/SC21, USA Contribution to the SC21 Special Working Group Meeting on Modeling Facilities, Dec. 7–11, 1992 in Namur, Belgium. ISO/IEC JTC1/SC21 N 7392, Oct. 15, 1992.

[**API 92**] ISO/IEC JTC1/SC21, Draft First Report on the New Work Area on Programmatic Interfaces. ISO/IEC JTC1/SC21 N 7425, Nov. 17, 1992.

[**Arapis 88**] C. ARAPIS and G. KAPPEL, Organizing Objects in an Object Software Base, in *Active Object Environments*, ed. D. Tsichritzis. University of Geneva, 1988, pp. 32–50.

[**Batory 91**] D. BATORY, On the Differences between Very Large Scale Reuse and Large Scale Reuse, in *Proceedings of the Fourth Annual Workshop on Software Reuse (Reston, VA, November 1991)*, ed. L. Latour, S. Philbrick, and C. BHAVSAR. IEEE Computer Society and the University of Maine, 1991.

[**Bauer 82**] F. BAUER and H. WÖSSNER, *Algorithmic Language and Program Development*. Berlin, Germany: Springer Verlag, 1982.

[**Bayer 72**] R. BAYER and E. McCREIGHT, Organization and Maintenance of Large Ordered Indexes, *Acta Informatica*, Vol. 1, No. 3 (Feb. 1972).

[**BETA 91**] B. KRISTENSEN, O. MADSEN, B. MØLLER–PEDERSEN and K. NYGAARD, *Object-Oriented Programming in the BETA Programming Language*, (draft). Sept. 22, 1991.

[**Booch 91**] G. BOOCH, *Object-Oriented Design with Applications*. Redwood City, CA: Benjamin/Cummings, 1991.

[**Carasik 90**] R. P. CARASIK, S. M. JOHNSON, D. A. PATTERSON, and G. A. VON GLAHN, Towards a Domain Description Grammar: An Application of Linguistic Semantics, *Software Engineering Notes*, Vol. 15, No. 5 (Oct. 1990), pp. 28–43.

[**Casais 90**] E. CASAIS, Managing Class Evolution in Object-Oriented Systems, in *Object Management*, ed. D. Tsichritzis. University of Geneva, 1990, pp. 133–195.

[**Chen 76**] P. P. CHEN, The Entity-Relationship Model: Toward a Unified View of Data, *Transactions on Database Systems*, Vol. 1, No. 1 (1976), pp. 9–36.

[**Codd 70**] E. F. CODD, A Relational Model of Data for Large Shared Data Banks, *Communications of the ACM*, Vol. 13, No. 6 (1970), pp. 377–387.

[Codd 79] E. F. CODD, Extending the Database Relational Model to Capture More Meaning, *Transactions on Database Systems*, Vol. 4, No.4 (1979), pp. 397–434.

[Codd 90] E. F. CODD, *The Relational Model for Database Management, Version 2*. Reading, MA: Addison-Wesley, 1990.

[Conrad 91] BRUCE A. CONRAD and A. LEWIS BASTIAN, Insecurities in Smalltalk Programming, in *Proceedings of TOOLS-91 (Technology of Object-Oriented Languages and Systems, 1991)*. Englewood Cliffs, NJ: Prentice Hall, pp. 195–201.

[Cunningham 89] W. CUNNINGHAM and K. BECK, Constructing Abstractions for Object-Oriented Applications, *Journal of Object-Oriented Programming*, Vol. 2, No. 2 (July–Aug., 1989), pp. 17–19.

[Cusack 91] E. CUSACK, Object-Oriented Modeling in Z for Open Distributed Processing, in *Proceedings of the First International Workshop on Open Distributed Processing (Berlin, Germany, 1991)*, ed. J. de Meer, V. Heymer, and R. Roth. Amsterdam: North Holland, 1992.

[Dahl 70] O.-J. DAHL, B. MYHRHAUG, and K. NYGAARD, *Simula 67, Common Base Language*. Norwegian Computing Center, 1970.

[Dahl 90] O.-J. DAHL, Object Orientation and Formal Techniques, in *VDM '90: VDM and Z—Formal Methods in Software Development*, ed. D. Bjørner, C. A. R. Hoare and H. Langmaack. Lecture Notes in Computer Science, Vol. 428, Berlin, Germany: Springer Verlag, 1990, pp. 1–11.

[Date 90] C. J. DATE, What is a Domain?, *Relational Database Writings 1985–1989*. Reading, MA: Addison-Wesley, 1990.

[Dialogue 93] HAIM KILOV and FRANK MANOLA, *Dialogue on the X3H7 Features Matrix*, ANSI X3H7/93–42, 1993.

[Dijkstra 68] E. W. DIJKSTRA, The Structure of the THE Multiprogramming System, *Communications of the ACM*, Vol. 11, No. 5 (1968).

[Dijkstra 72] E. W. DIJKSTRA, The Humble Programmer, *Communications of the ACM*, Vol. 15, No. 10 (1972), pp. 859–886.

[Dijkstra 76] E. W. DIJKSTRA, *A Discipline of Programming*. Englewood Cliffs, NJ: Prentice Hall, 1976.

[Dijkstra 76-1] E. W. DIJKSTRA, The Teaching of Programming, i.e., the Teaching of Thinking, in *Language Hierarchies and Interfaces*, ed. F. L. Bauer and K. Samelson. Lecture Notes in Computer Science, Vol. 46, Berlin, Germany: Springer Verlag, 1976, pp. 1–10.

[Dijkstra 82] E. W. DIJKSTRA, *Selected Writings on Computing: A Personal Perspective*. New York: Springer Verlag, 1982.

[Dijkstra 86] E. W. DIJKSTRA, *Management and Mathematics*. EWD 966. 14th June 1986.

[Dijkstra 86-1] E. W. DIJKSTRA, On a Cultural Gap, *The Mathematical Intelligencer*, Vol. 8, No. 1 (1986), p. 51.

[Dijkstra 89] E. W. DIJKSTRA, *Mathematical Methodology*. O. Preface. EWD 1059. 22 Sept. 1989.

[Dijkstra 90] *Formal Development of Programs and Proofs*, ed. E. W. Dijkstra. Reading, MA: Addison-Wesley, 1990.

[Dijkstra 91] E. W. DIJKSTRA, *A Manuscript for the Coahuila Student Chapter of the ACM*. EWD 1115, 29 November 1991.

[Dijkstra 92] E. W. DIJKSTRA, *On the Economy of Doing Mathematics.* EWD 1130, written for the 2nd International Conference on the Mathematics of Program Construction, 29th June–3rd July, 1992, Oxford.

[Dijkstra 93] E. W. DIKSTRA, Position Statement, *American Programmer*, January 1993, p. 5.

[Diller 90] A. DILLER, *Z: An Introduction to Formal Methods.* Chichester: Wiley, 1990.

[Duke 91] R. Duke, P. King, G. Rose and G. Smith, *The Object Z Specification Language, Version 1.* Technical Report 91–1. The University of Queensland, Queensland, Australia, January 1991.

[Embley 92] D. W. EMBLEY, B. D. KURTZ and S. N. WOODFIELD, *Object-Oriented Systems Analysis: A Model-Driven Approach.* Englewood Cliffs, NJ: Prentice Hall, 1992.

[Features Matrix 93] X3H7 Object Model Features Matrix. ANSI X3H7/93–007 V3 1 (September 8, 1993).

[Ferguson 92] E. S. FERGUSON, *Engineering and the Mind's Eye.* Cambridge, MA: The MIT Press, 1992.

[Fiadeiro 92] J. FIADEIRO and T. MAILBAUM, Temporal Theories as Modularization Units for Concurrent System Specification, *Formal Aspects of Computing*, Vol. 4, No. 3 (1992), pp. 239–272.

[Framework 92] *The Framework: A Disciplined Approach to Analysis.* Bellcore Science and Technology Series, ST-OPT-002008, May 1992.

[Garlan 91] D. GARLAN and D. NOTKIN, Formalizing Design Spaces: Implicit Invocation Mechanisms, in *VDM '91: Formal Software Development Methods*, ed. S. Prehn and W. J. Toetenel. Lecture Notes in Computer Science, Vol. 551, Berlin, Germany: Springer Verlag, 1991, pp. 31–44.

[van Gasteren 90] A. J. M. VAN GASTEREN, *On the Shape of Mathematical Arguments.* Lecture Notes in Computer Science, Vol. 445, Berlin, Germany: Springer Verlag, 1990.

[Gilb 77] T. GILB and G. WEINBERG. *Humanized Input.* Cambridge, MA: Winthrop Publ., 1977.

[Gotzhein 90] R. GOTZHEIN, Specifying Open Distributed Systems with Z, in *VDM '90: VDM and Z—Formal Methods in Software Development*, ed. D. Bjørner, C. A. R. Hoare, and H. Langmaack. Lecture Notes in Computer Science, Vol. 428, Berlin, Germany: Springer Verlag, 1990, pp. 319–39.

[Gries 81] D. GRIES, *The Science of Programming.* New York: Springer Verlag, 1981.

[GRM 93] ISO/IEC JTC1/SC21/WG4, Information Technology–Open Systems Interconnection–Management Information Services–Structure of Management Information–Part 7: General Relationship Model. CD ISO/IEC 10165-7.2. Aug. 6, 1993.

[Halasz 90] F. HALASZ and M. SCHWARTZ, The Dexter Hypertext Reference Model, in *Proceedings of the Hypertext Standardization Workshop (January 16–18, 1990)*, ed. J. Moline, D. Benigni, and J. Baronas. NIST Special Publication 500–178. Gaithersburg, MD: National Institute of Standards and Technology, March 1990, pp. 95–133.

[Halmos 60] P. HALMOS, *Naive Set Theory.* Princeton, NJ: D. Van Nostrand, 1960.

[Hayes 93] I. HAYES, *Specification Case Studies* (2nd ed.). Hemel Hempstead, UK: Prentice Hall, 1993.

[Hehner 84] E. C. R. HEHNER, *The Logic of Programming.* Hemel Hempstead, UK: Prentice Hall, 1984.

[Helm 90] R. HELM, I. HOLLAND and D. GANGOPADHYAY, Contracts: Specifying Behavioral Compositions in Object-oriented Systems, in *Proceedings of OOPSLA-90 (Conference on Object-Oriented Programming Systems, Languages, and Applications, Ottawa, Canada, October 1990),* ACM Press, 1990, pp.169–80.

[Hoare 89] *Essays in Computing Science,* ed. C. A. R. Hoare and C. B. Jones. Hemel Hempstead, UK: Prentice Hall, 1989.

[Horowitz 92] B. HOROWITZ, A Run-Time Execution Model for Referential Integrity Maintenance, in *Proceedings of the 8th International Conference on Data Engineering (Tempe, Arizona, 1992).* IEEE Computer Society Press, 1992, pp. 548–56.

[Ince 90] D. C. INCE, *An Introduction to Discrete Mathematics and Formal System Specification* (2nd ed.). Oxford: Oxford University Press, 1990.

[ISO ODP 91-3] ISO/IEC JTC1/SC21/WG7, Basic Reference Model for Open Distributed Processing. Use of Z for Information Viewpoint Models. US Position. (ISO/IEC JTC1/ SC21/WG7 N 362, March 15, 1991).

[ISO/IEC 91-1] ISO/IEC 10165–1, Information Technology–Open Systems Interconnection– Management Information Services–Structure of Management Information–Part 1: Management Information Model. (ISO/IEC JTC1/SC21 N 6351, June 1991).

[ISO/IEC 91-2] ISO/IEC 10165–2, Information Technology–Open Systems Interconnection– Management Information Services–Structure of Management Information–Part 2: Definition of Management Information. (ISO/IEC JTC1/SC21 N 6363, August 1991).

[Jacobson 91] I. JACOBSON, Industrial Development of Software with an Object-Oriented Technique, *Journal of Object-Oriented Programming,* Vol. 4, No. 1 (March/April 1991), pp. 30–41.

[Johnson 91] R. JOHNSON and R. WIRFS-BROCK, *OOPSLA-91 Tutorial Notes–T11: Object-Oriented Frameworks.* ACM, 1991.

[Kalman 91] K. KALMAN, Implementation and Critique of an Algorithm which Maps a Relational Database to a Conceptual Model, in *Advanced Information System Engineering,* ed. R. Andersen, J. A. Bubenko Jr. and A. Sølvberg. Lecture Notes in Computer Science, Vol. 498, Berlin, Germany: Springer Verlag, 1991, pp. 393–415.

[Kent 79] W. KENT, *Data and Reality.* Amsterdam: North-Holland, 1979.

[Kent 83] W. KENT, Fact-based Data Analysis and Design, in *Entity-Relationship Approach to Software Engineering,* ed. C. G. Davis, S. Jajodia, P. Ng, and R. Yeh. Amsterdam: North-Holland, 1983, pp. 3–53.

[Kilov 83] H. KILOV, An Approach to User Interface and Semantic Integrity for a Relational DBMS, *SIGMOD Record,* Vol. 13, No. 2 (1983), pp. 64–71.

[Kilov 84] H. KILOV, An Approach to Conceptual Schema Support in a Relational DBMS Environment, in *Proceedings of the IV Jerusalem Conference on Information Technology.* IEEE Computer Society Press, 1984, pp. 347–9.

[Kilov 89] H. KILOV, Domains and Semantic Integrity, *Computer Standards & Interfaces,* Vol. 9 (1989), pp. 143–147.

[Kilov 90] H. KILOV, From Semantic to Object-Oriented Data Modeling, in *Proceedings of the First International Conference on Systems Integration, (Morristown, NJ, April 1990).* IEEE Computer Society Press, 1990, pp. 385–93.

[Kilov 90-1] H. KILOV, Extending the Entity-Relationship Data Model to Capture More

Meaning: The Path to Object Data Management, in *Proceedings of SOOPPA-90 (Symposium on Object-Oriented Programming Emphasizing Practical Applications, Poughkeepsie, NY, 1990)*, pp. 26–34.

[Kilov 91] H. KILOV, Generic Information Modeling Concepts: A Reusable Component Library, in *Proceedings of TOOLS-91 (Fourth International Conference on Technology of Object-Oriented Languages and Systems, Paris, 1991)*. Englewood Cliffs, NJ: Prentice Hall, 1991, pp. 187–201.

[Kilov 91-1] H. KILOV, Conventional and Convenient in Entity-Relationship Modeling, *ACM Software Engineering Notes*, Vol. 16, No. 2 (April 1991), pp. 31–32.

[Kilov 91-2] H. KILOV, Reuse of Generic Concepts in Information Modeling, in *Proceedings of the Fourth Annual Workshop on Software Reuse (Reston, VA, November 1991)*, ed. L. Latour, S. Philbrick, and C. Bhavsar. IEEE Computer Society and the University of Maine, 1991.

[Kilov 91-3] H. KILOV, Contracts in OO Analysis: Precise Declarative Specifications of Behavior, in *OO Domain Analysis Workshop @ OOPSLA-91 (Phoenix, AZ, October 1991)*, ed. D. de Champeaux, J. Burnham, and R. Wirfs-Brock.

[Kilov 92] H. KILOV, From OSI Systems Management to an Interoperable Object Model: Behavioral Specification of (Generic) Relationships, in *Conference Record of TINA-92 (Third Telecommunications Information Networking Architecture Workshop, Narita, Japan, January 1992)*, pp. 23-3-1–23-3-8.

[Kilov 93] H. KILOV, Information Modeling and Object Z: Specifying Generic Reusable Associations, in *Proceedings of NGITS-93 (Next Generation Information Technology and Systems, Haifa, Israel, June 28–30, 1993)*, ed. O. Etzion and A. Segev, pp. 182–91.

[Kilov 93-1] H. KILOV and L. REDMANN, Specifying Joint Behavior of Objects: Formalization and Standardization, in *Proceedings of the Software Engineering Standards Symposium (Brighton, England, 1993)*. IEEE Computer Society, 1993, pp. 220–226.

[Lange 90] D. LANGE, A Formal Approach to Hypertext Using Post-Prototype Formal Specification, in *VDM '90: VDM and Z—Formal Methods in Software Development*, ed. D. Bjørner, C. A. R. Hoare, and H. Langmaack. Lecture Notes in Computer Science, Vol. 428, Berlin, Germany: Springer Verlag, 1990.

[Mac an Airchinnigh 91] MICHEÁL MAC AN AIRCHINNIGH, Tutorial Lecture Notes on the Irish School of the VDM, in *VDM '91: Formal Software Development Methods*. Lecture Notes in Computer Science, Vol. 552, Berlin, Germany: Springer Verlag, 1991, pp. 141–237.

[Manning 90] K. MANNING and D. SPENCER, Model Based Network Management, in *Proceedings of the Fourth RACE TMN Conference (Dublin, Nov. 14–16, 1990)*, pp. 233–43.

[Martin 92] J. MARTIN and J. ODELL, *Object-Oriented Analysis and Design*. Englewood Cliffs, NJ: Prentice Hall, 1992.

[Materials 92] *The Materials: The Generic Object Class Library For Analysis*. Bellcore Science and Technology Series, ST-OPT-002010, October 1992.

[Meyer 88] B. MEYER, *Object-Oriented Software Construction*. Hemel Hempstead, UK: Prentice Hall, 1988.

[Meyer 89] B. MEYER, From Structured Programming to Object-Oriented Design: The Road to Eiffel, *Structured Programming*, Vol. 1, No. 1 (1989), pp. 19–39.

[Meyer 92] B. MEYER, *Eiffel: The Language*. Hemel Hempstead, UK: Prentice Hall, 1992.

[Morgan 90] C. MORGAN, *Programming from Specifications.* Hemel Hempstead, UK: Prentice Hall, 1990.

[Morris 90] J. MORRIS, Piecewise Data Refinement, in *Formal Development of Programs and Proofs,* ed. E. W. Dijkstra. Reading, MA: Addison-Wesley, 1990, pp. 117–37.

[Nicholls 92] J. E. NICHOLLS, Domains of Application for Formal Methods, in *Z User Workshop (York 1991),* ed. J. E. Nicholls. Workshops in Computing, Berlin, Germany: Springer Verlag, 1992, pp. 145–56.

[ODP 2] ISO/IEC JTC1/SC21/WG7, Basic Reference Model for Open Distributed Processing–Part 2: Descriptive Model (CD 10746–2.3, June 1993).

[ODP 3] ISO/IEC JTC1/SC21/WG7, Basic Reference Model for Open Distributed Processing–Part 3: Prescriptive Model. (ISO/IEC JTC1/SC21/WG7 N 8125, June 15, 1993).

[ODP 4] ISO/IEC JTC1/SC21/WG7, Basic Reference Model for Open Distributed Processing–Part 4: Architectural Semantics. (ISO/IEC JTC1/SC21/WG7 N 752, Nov. 1992).

[ODP F] ISO/IEC JTC1/SC21/WG7, Basic Reference Model for Open Distributed Processing. Use of formal specification techniques for ODP. (ISO/IEC JTC1/SC21/WG7 N 753, Nov. 1992).

[OO-Z 92] *Object Orientation in Z,* ed. S. Stepney, R. Barden, and D. Cooper. Workshops in Computing Series, Berlin, Germany: Springer Verlag, 1992.

[OODBTG 91] *Object Data Management Reference Model.* (ANSI Accredited Standards Committee. X3, Information Processing Systems.) Document Number OODB 89–01R8. 17 September 1991. (Also in: *Computer Standards & Interfaces,* Vol. 15 (1993), pp. 124–142.)

[OSI—Data Management 90] The Convergence of Open Systems Interconnection and Data Management Standards, in *Proceedings of the Second Joint Meeting in Orlando, Florida, January 22–23, 1990,* ed. Elizabeth Fong. CBEMA, March 1990, (Distributed by ANSI X3 Secretariat), pp. 34–35.

[OSI/NM Forum 91] *Modeling Principles for Managed Objects.* Technical Report Forum TR102, Issue 1.0, January 1991. OSI/Network Management Forum, Bernardsville, NJ.

[Overcoming Barriers—91] *Overcoming Barriers to Open Systems Information Technology: First Official Report.* January 27, 1991. Distributed by User Alliance for Open Systems, McLean, VA.

[Petroski 85] H. PETROSKI, *To Engineer is Human: The Role of Failure in Successful Design.* New York: St. Martin's Press, 1985.

[Pintado 88] X. PINTADO and D. TSICHRITZIS, An Affinity Browser (Work in Progress), in *Active Object Environments,* ed. D. Tsichritzis. University of Geneva, 1988, pp. 51–60.

[Potter 91] B. POTTER, J. SINCLAIR and D. TILL, *An Introduction to Formal Specification and Z.* International Series in Computer Science, Hemel Hempstead, UK: Prentice Hall, 1991.

[Recommendations 91] ANSI X3/SPARC/DBSSG/OODBTG Recommendations for Standards in Object Information Management, (Revision 7). August 6, 1991.

[Reynolds 81] J. REYNOLDS, *The Craft of Programming.* London: Prentice Hall, 1981.

[Rose 92] G. A. ROSE, Object-Z, in *Object Orientation in Z,* ed. S. Stepney, R. Barden and D. Cooper. Workshops in Computing, Berlin, Germany: Springer Verlag, 1992, pp. 59–77.

[Rudkin 91] S. RUDKIN, Modeling Information Objects in Z, in *Proceedings of the First In-*

ternational Workshop on Open Distributed Processing (Berlin, Germany, 1991), ed. J. de Meer, V. Heymer, and R. Roth. Amsterdam: North Holland, 1992.

[Shelton 92] R. SHELTON, From the Editor, *Hotline on Object-Oriented Technology*, November 1992, p. 2.

[Simon 91] L. SIMON and L. MARSHALL, Using VDM to Specify OSI Managed Objects, in *Proceedings of the IFIP TC6/WG6.1 Fourth International Conference on Formal Description Techniques (FORTE '91)*. Amsterdam: Elsevier, 1991.

[Spivey 92] J. M. SPIVEY, *The Z Notation: A Reference Manual* (2nd ed.). Hemel Hempstead, UK: Prentice Hall, 1992.

[SR 91] *Information Modeling Concepts and Guidelines*. Bellcore Special Report, SR-OPT-001826, January 1991.

[Stocks 92] P. STOCKS, K. RAYMOND, D. CARRINGTON and A. LISTER, Modeling Open Distributed Systems in Z, *Computer Communications*, Vol. 15, No. 2 (March 1992), pp. 103–113.

[Swatman 92] P. SWATMAN, D. FOWLER and C. Y. MICHAEL GAN, Extending the Useful Application Domain for Formal Methods, in *Z User Workshop (York 1991)*, ed. J. E. Nicholls. Berlin, Germany: Springer Verlag, 1992, pp. 125–44.

[SWG-MF 93] ISO/IEC JTC1/SC21, The Inter-Relationships between a Conceptual Schema Modeling Facility (CSMF) and a Data Modeling Facility (DMF). ISO/IEC JTC1/SC21 N 7545. Feb. 2, 1993.

[ter Hofstede 92] A. H. M. TER HOFSTEDE and T. P. VAN DER WEIDE, Formalization of Techniques: Chopping Down the Methodology Jungle, *Information and Software Technology*, Vol. 34, No. 1 (January 1992).

[Trader 92] ISO/IEC JTC1/SC21/WG7, Working Document on Topic 9.1–ODP Trader. ISO/IEC JTC1/SC21/WG7 N 743. November 25, 1992.

[US - Z 92] ANSI X3T5.4, Use of Z to Describe the Management Information Model. Document No. X3T5.4/92–110. September 11, 1992.

[Wand 89] Y. WAND, A Proposal for a Formal Model of Objects, in *Object-Oriented Concepts, Databases, and Applications*, ed. Won Kim and Frederick H. Lochovsky. Reading, MA: Addison-Wesley, 1989, pp. 537–59.

[Wegner 88] P. WEGNER and S. ZDONIK, Inheritance as an Incremental Modification Mechanism or What Like Is and Isn't Like, in *Proceedings of the European Conference on Object-Oriented Programming (ECOOP '88)*, ed. S. Gjessing and K. Nygaard. Lecture Notes in Computer Science, Vol. 322, Berlin, Germany: Springer Verlag, 1988, pp. 55–77.

[Weinberg 71] G. WEINBERG, *The Psychology of Computer Programming*. New York: Van Nostrand Reinhold, New York, 1971.

[Wirfs-Brock 90] R. WIRFS-BROCK, B. WILKERSON and L. WIENER, *Designing Object-Oriented Software*. Englewood Cliffs, NJ: Prentice Hall, 1990.

[X3H7 92] ASC X3H7, Object Information Management: Mission Statement, Strawman Version 1.2 (July 1, 1992). Document Number X3H7/SD-0011.

[Zave 91] P. ZAVE and M. JACKSON. Techniques for Partial Specification and Specification of Switching Systems, in *VDM '91, Formal Software Development Methods*. Lecture Notes in Computer Science, Vol. 551, Berlin, Germany: Springer Verlag, 1991, pp. 511–25.

[Zave 92] P. ZAVE and M. JACKSON, Conjunction as Composition. AT&T Technical Report, 1992.

[Zeldovich 82] YA. B. ZELDOVICH and I. M. YAGLOM, *Calculus for Beginning Physicists and Engineers*. Moscow: Nauka Publishers, 1982.

[Zemanek 90] H. ZEMANEK, Two proofs for Pythagoras, in *Beauty is Our Business (A Birthday Salute to Edsger W. Dijkstra)*, ed. W. H. J. Feijen, A. J. M. van Gasteren, D. Gries, and J. Misra. New York: Springer Verlag, 1990, pp. 442–47.

Index

"Well, I must say one thing—"
"Did oo know, Mister Sir," Bruno thoughtfully remarked, "that Sylvie ca'n't count? Whenever she says 'I must say one thing,' I know quite well she'll say two things! And she always doos."

Lewis Carroll, "Sylvie and Bruno Concluded"

A

D

E

F

L

M

N

O

P

R

S

T

U

understanding (*see also* specifications), 1–13, 15–51

V

versions, 105–107, 109
views of an enterprise, 59, 156, 176, 177, 216

W

walkthroughs, 138, 139, 156–159, 167, 179
Weltanschauung, 180
what vs. how, 9, 17, 29, 30, 40, 63